SELECTED SOLUTIONS MANUAL

KAREN C. TIMBERLAKE
Los Angeles Valley College

GENERAL, ORGANIC, AND BIOLOGICAL
CHEMISTRY
Structures of Life

KAREN C. TIMBERLAKE

Third Edition

Prentice Hall

New York   Boston   San Francisco
London   Toronto   Sydney   Tokyo   Singapore   Madrid
Mexico City   Munich   Paris   Cape Town   Hong Kong   Montreal

Acquisitions Editor: Dawn Giovanniello
Assistant Editor: Jessica Neumann
Editor in Chief, Science: Nicole Folchetti
Marketing Manager: Elizabeth Averbeck
Managing Editor, Chemistry and Geosciences: Gina M. Cheselka
Project Manager, Science: Maureen Pancza
Operations Specialist: Amanda A. Smith
Supplement Cover Manager: Paul Gourhan
Supplement Cover Designer: Paul Gourhan
Cover Image: Food Collection/Getty Images, Inc.

The author and publisher of this book have used their best efforts in preparing this book. These efforts include the development, research, and testing of the theories and programs to determine their effectiveness. The author and publisher make no warranty of any kind, expressed or implied, with regard to these programs or the documentation contained in this book. The author and publisher shall not be liable in any event for incidental or consequential damages in connection with, or arising out of, the furnishing, performance, or use of these programs.

Printed in the United States of America

10 9 8 7 6 5 4 3 2 1

ISBN-13:   978-0-321-61663-0
ISBN-10:   0-321-61663-4

Prentice Hall
is an imprint of

www.pearsonhighered.com

Contents

P.1 Many chemicals are listed on a vitamin bottle, such as vitamin A, vitamin B_3, vitamin B_{12}, vitamin C, folic acid, etc.

P.3 No. All of these ingredients are chemicals.

P.5 One advantage of a pesticide is that it gets rid of insects that bite or damage crops. Two disadvantages are that a pesticide can destroy beneficial insects and a pesticide can be retained in a crop that is eventually eaten by animals or humans.

P.7 **a.** An observation (O) is a description or a measurement of a natural phenomenon.
   b. A hypothesis (H) proposes a possible explanation for a natural phenomenon.
   c. An experiment (E) is a procedure that tests the validity of a hypothesis.
   d. An observation (O) is a description or a measurement of a natural phenomenon.
   e. An observation (O) is a description or a measurement of a natural phenomenon.
   f. A theory (T) confirms a hypothesis of a possible explanation for a natural phenomenon.

P.9 **a.** Form a study group.
   c. Visit the professor during office hours.
   e. Become an active learner.

P.11 Yes. Sherlock's investigation includes observations (gathering data), formulating a hypothesis, testing the hypothesis, and modifying it until the hypothesis is validated.

P.13 If experimental results do not support your hypothesis, you should b. write another hypothesis, and c. do more experiments.

P.15 A hypothesis is an important part of the scientific method, because it is the initial generation of a proposed explanation that can be verified by experiment.

P.17 **a.** Determination of a melting point with a thermometer is an observation.
   b. Describing a reason for the extinction of dinosaurs is a hypothesis or theory.
   c. Measuring the completion time of a race is an observation.

P.19 **a.** An observation (O) is a description or a measurement of a natural phenomenon.
   b. A hypothesis (H) proposes a possible explanation for a natural phenomenon.
   c. An experiment (E) is a procedure that tests the validity of a hypothesis. Also, an observation (O) was made during the experiment.
   d. A hypothesis (H) proposes a possible explanation for a natural phenomenon.

1
Measurements

1.1 **a.** In the United States your mass would be measured in pounds (lbs) and in Mexico it would be measured in kilograms (kg).
   b. In the United States your height would be measured in feet (ft) and inches (in.) and in Mexico it would be measured in centimeters (cm).
   c. In the United States the amount of gasoline would be measured in gallons (gal.) and in Mexico it would be measured in liters (L).
   d. In the United States the temperature would be measured in degrees Fahrenheit (°F) and in Mexico it would be measured in degrees Celsius (°C).

1.3 **a.** The unit is a meter, which is a unit of length.
   b. The unit is a gram, which is a unit of mass.
   c. The unit is a liter, which is a unit of volume.
   d. The unit is a second, which is a unit of time.
   e. The unit is degrees Celsius, which is a unit of temperature.

1.5 **a.** Move the decimal point left four decimal places to give 5.5×10^4 m.
   b. Move the decimal point left two decimal places to give 4.8×10^2 g.
   c. Move the decimal point right six decimal places to give 5×10^{-6} cm.
   d. Move the decimal point right four decimal places to give 1.4×10^{-4} s.
   e. Move the decimal point right three decimal places to give 7.85×10^{-3} L.
   f. Move the decimal point left five decimal places to give 6.7×10^5 kg.

1.7 **a.** The value 7.2×10^3, which is also 72×10^2, is greater than 8.2×10^2.
   b. The value 3.2×10^{-2}, which is also 320×10^{-4}, is greater than 4.5×10^{-4}.
   c. The value 1×10^4 or 10 000 is greater than 1×10^{-4} or 0.0001.
   d. The value 6.8×10^{-2} or 0.068 is greater than 0.000 52.

1.9 **a.** The standard number is 1.2 times the power of 10^4 or 10 000, which gives 12 000.
   b. The standard number is 8.25 times the power of 10^{-2} or 0.01, which gives 0.0825.
   c. The standard number is 4 times the power of 10^6 or 1 000 000, which gives 4 000 000.
   d. The standard number is 5 times the power of 10^{-3} or 0.001, which gives 0.005.

1.11 Measured numbers are obtained using some kind of measuring tool. Exact numbers are numbers obtained by counting or from a definition in the metric or the U.S. measuring system.
   a. measured   **b.** exact   **c.** exact   **d.** measured

1.13 Measured numbers are obtained using some kind of measuring tool. Exact numbers are numbers obtained by counting or from a definition in the metric or the U.S. measuring system.
   a. 3 hamburgers is a counted/exact number, whereas the value 6 oz of meat is obtained by measurement.
   b. Neither are measured numbers; both 1 table and 4 chairs are counted/exact numbers.
   c. Both 0.75 lb and 350 g are obtained by measurements.
   d. Neither are measured numbers; the values in a definition are exact numbers.

1.15 **a.** Zeros preceding significant digits are *not significant*.
   b. Zeros between significant digits are *significant*.
   c. Zeros after significant digits in a decimal number are *significant*.
   d. Zeros in the coefficient of a number written in scientific notation are *significant*.
   e. Zeros in a number with no decimal point are considered as placeholders only and are *not significant*.

1.17   **a.** All five numbers are significant figures.
   b. Only the two nonzero numbers are significant; the preceding zeros are placeholders.
   c. Only the two nonzero numbers are significant; the zeros that follow are placeholders.
   d. All three numbers in the coefficient of a number written in scientific notation are significant.
   e. All four numbers to the right of the decimal point, including the last zero, in a decimal number are significant.
   f. All three numbers including the zeros that follow a nonzero digit in a decimal number are significant.

1.19   Both measurements in **c** have two significant figures, and both measurements in **d** have four significant figures.

1.21   **a.** 5000 is the same as 5×1000, which is written in scientific notation as 5.0×10^3 L with two significant figures.
   b. 30 000 is the same as $3 \times 10\,000$, which is written in scientific notation as 3.0×10^4 g with two significant figures.
   c. 100 000 is the same as $1 \times 100\,000$, which is written in scientific notation as 1.0×10^5 m with two significant figures.
   d. 0.000 25 is the same as $2.5 \times \dfrac{1}{10\,000}$, which is written in scientific notation as 2.5×10^{-4} cm.

1.23   Calculators carry out mathematical computations and display answers without any regard to significant figures. Our task is to round the calculator's answer to the number of significant figures allowed by the precision of the original data.

1.25   **a.** 1.85, the last digit is dropped since it is 4 or less.
   b. 184, since the fourth digit is 4 or less, the last four digits are dropped.
   c. 0.004 74, since the fourth significant digit (the first digit to be dropped) is 5 or greater, the last retained digit is increased by 1 when the last four digits are dropped.
   d. 8810, since the fourth significant digit (the first digit to be dropped) is 5 or greater, the last retained digit is increased by 1 when the last digit is dropped.
   e. 1.83×10^5, the last digit is dropped since it is 4 or less. The $\times 10^5$ is retained so that the magnitude of the answer is not changed.

1.27   **a.** $45.7 \times 0.034 = 1.6$ Two significant figures are allowed since 0.034 has 2 SF.
   b. $0.002\,78 \times 5 = 0.01$ One significant figure is allowed since 5 has 1 SF.
   c. $\dfrac{34.56}{1.25} = 27.6$ Three significant figures are allowed since 1.25 has 3 SF.
   d. $\dfrac{(0.2465)(25)}{1.78} = 3.5$ Two significant figures are allowed since 25 has 2 SF.

1.29   **a.** 45.48 cm $+ 8.057$ cm $= 53.54$ cm Two decimal places are allowed since 45.48 cm has two decimal places.
   b. 23.45 g $+ 104.1$ g $+ 0.025$ g $= 127.6$ g One decimal place is allowed since 104.1 g has one decimal place.
   c. 145.675 mL $- 24.2$ mL $= 121.5$ mL One decimal place is allowed since 24.2 mL has one decimal place.
   d. 1.08 L $- 0.585$ L $= 0.50$ L Two decimal places are allowed since 1.08 L has two decimal places.

1.31   The km/h markings indicate how many kilometers (how much distance) will be traversed in 1 hour's time if the speed is held constant. The mph markings indicate the same distance traversed *but measured in miles* during the 1 hour of travel.

1.33   Because the prefix *kilo* means one thousand times, a *kilo*gram is equal to 1000 grams.

1.35 **a.** mg **b.** dL **c.** km **d.** kg **e.** μL **f.** ng

1.37 **a.** 0.01 **b.** 1000 **c.** 0.001 (or 1×10^{-3})
  d. 0.1 **e.** 1 000 000 (or 1×10^{6}) **f.** 0.000 000 000 001 (or 1×10^{-12})

1.39 **a.** 1 m = 100 cm **b.** 1 km = 1000 m
  c. 1 mm = 0.001 m **d.** 1 L = 1000 mL

1.41 **a.** kilogram, since 10^3 g is greater than 10^{-3} g.
  b. milliliter, since 10^{-3} L is greater than 10^{-6} L.
  c. km, since 10^3 m is greater than 10^{-2} m.
  d. kL, since 10^3 L is greater than 10^{-1} L.
  e. nanometer, since 10^{-9} m is greater than 10^{-12} m.

1.43 Because a conversion factor is unchanged when inverted; $\dfrac{1 \text{ m}}{100 \text{ cm}}$ and $\dfrac{100 \text{ cm}}{1 \text{ m}}$

1.45 **a.** 100 cm = 1 m; $\dfrac{1 \text{ m}}{100 \text{ cm}}$ and $\dfrac{100 \text{ cm}}{1 \text{ m}}$

  b. 1000 mg = 1 g; $\dfrac{1 \text{ g}}{1000 \text{ mg}}$ and $\dfrac{1000 \text{ mg}}{1 \text{ g}}$

  c. 1 L = 1000 mL; $\dfrac{1000 \text{ mL}}{1 \text{ L}}$ and $\dfrac{1 \text{ L}}{1000 \text{ mL}}$

  d. 1 L = 10 dL and 1 L = 1000 mL so 10 dL = 1000 mL or 1 dL = 100 mL;
  $\dfrac{100 \text{ mL}}{1 \text{ dL}}$ and $\dfrac{1 \text{ dL}}{100 \text{ mL}}$

1.47 **a.** 1 yd = 3 ft; $\dfrac{1 \text{ yd}}{3 \text{ m}}$ and $\dfrac{3 \text{ ft}}{1 \text{ yd}}$

  b. 1 mi = 5280 ft; $\dfrac{1 \text{ mi}}{5280 \text{ ft}}$ and $\dfrac{5280 \text{ ft}}{1 \text{ mi}}$

  c. 1 min = 60 s; $\dfrac{1 \text{ min}}{60 \text{ s}}$ and $\dfrac{60 \text{ s}}{1 \text{ min}}$

  d. 1 gal = 27 mi; $\dfrac{1 \text{ gal}}{27 \text{ mi}}$ and $\dfrac{27 \text{ mi}}{1 \text{ gal}}$

  e. 100 g sterling = 93 g silver; $\dfrac{93 \text{ g silver}}{100 \text{ g sterling}}$ and $\dfrac{100 \text{ g sterling}}{93 \text{ g silver}}$

1.49 **a.** since 3.5 m = 1 s; $\dfrac{1 \text{ s}}{3.5 \text{ m}}$ and $\dfrac{3.5 \text{ m}}{1 \text{ s}}$

  b. since 3500 mg K = 1 day; $\dfrac{1 \text{ day}}{3500 \text{ mg K}}$ and $\dfrac{3500 \text{ mg K}}{1 \text{ day}}$

  c. since 46.0 km = 1.0 gal gasoline; $\dfrac{1.0 \text{ gal gasoline}}{46.0 \text{ km}}$ and $\dfrac{46.0 \text{ km}}{1.0 \text{ gal gasoline}}$

  d. since 50 mg Atenolol = 1 tablet; $\dfrac{1 \text{ tablet}}{50 \text{ mg Atenolol}}$ and $\dfrac{50 \text{ mg Atenolol}}{1 \text{ tablet}}$

  e. since 29 μg pesticide = 1 kg plum; $\dfrac{1 \text{ kg plum}}{29 \ \mu\text{g pesticide}}$ and $\dfrac{29 \ \mu\text{g pesticide}}{1 \text{ kg plum}}$

1.51 When using a conversion factor, you are trying to cancel existing units and arrive at a new (desired) unit. The conversion factor must be properly oriented so that unit cancellation (numerator to denominator) can be accomplished.

1.53 **a.** **Given:** 175 cm   **Need:** m

       Plan: cm $\rightarrow$ m

$$\frac{1\ m}{100\ cm}$$

       Set Up: $175\ \cancel{cm} \times \dfrac{1\ m}{100\ \cancel{cm}} = 1.75\ m\ (3SF)$

     b. **Given:** 5500 mL   **Need:** L

       Plan: mL $\rightarrow$ L

$$\frac{1\ L}{1000\ mL}$$

       Set Up: $5500\ \cancel{mL} \times \dfrac{1\ L}{1000\ \cancel{mL}} = 5.5\ L\ (2SF)$

     c. **Given:** 0.0055 kg   **Need:** g

       Plan: kg $\rightarrow$ g

$$\frac{1000\ g}{1\ kg}$$

       Set Up: $0.0055\ \cancel{kg} \times \dfrac{1000\ g}{1\ \cancel{kg}} = 5.5\ g\ (2SF)$

1.55 **a.** **Given:** 0.750 qt   **Need:** mL

       Plan: qt $\rightarrow$ L $\rightarrow$ mL

$$\frac{1\ L}{1.06\ qt} \quad \frac{1000\ mL}{1\ L}$$

       Set Up: $0.750\ \cancel{qt} \times \dfrac{1\ \cancel{L}}{1.06\ \cancel{qt}} \times \dfrac{1000\ mL}{1\ \cancel{L}} = 710.\ mL\ (3SF)$

     b. **Given:** 11.8 stones   **Need:** kg

       Plan: stones $\rightarrow$ lb $\rightarrow$ kg

$$\frac{14.0\ lb}{1\ stone} \quad \frac{1\ kg}{2.20\ lb}$$

       Set Up: $11.8\ \cancel{stones} \times \dfrac{14.0\ \cancel{lb}}{1\ \cancel{stone}} \times \dfrac{1\ kg}{2.20\ \cancel{lb}} = 75.1\ kg\ (3SF)$

     c. **Given:** 19.5 in.   **Need:** mm

       Plan: in. $\rightarrow$ cm $\rightarrow$ mm

$$\frac{2.54\ cm}{1\ in.} \quad \frac{10\ mm}{1\ cm}$$

       Set Up: $19.5\ \cancel{in.} \times \dfrac{2.54\ \cancel{cm}}{1\ \cancel{in.}} \times \dfrac{10\ mm}{1\ \cancel{cm}} = 495\ mm\ (3SF)$

d. Given: 0.50 μm   **Need:** in.

Plan: μm $\rightarrow$ m $\rightarrow$ cm $\rightarrow$ in.

$$\frac{1\ m}{10^6\ \mu m} \quad \frac{100\ cm}{1\ m} \quad \frac{1\ in.}{2.54\ cm}$$

Set Up: $0.50\ \mu m \times \dfrac{1\ m}{10^6\ \mu m} \times \dfrac{100\ cm}{1\ m} \times \dfrac{1\ in.}{2.54\ cm} = 2.0 \times 10^{-5}$ in. (2SF)

1.57 a. Given: 78.0 ft (length)   **Need:** m

Plan: ft $\rightarrow$ in. $\rightarrow$ cm $\rightarrow$ m

$$\frac{12\ in.}{1\ ft} \quad \frac{2.54\ cm}{1\ in.} \quad \frac{1\ m}{100\ cm}$$

Set Up: $78.0\ ft \times \dfrac{12\ in.}{1\ ft} \times \dfrac{2.54\ cm}{1\ in.} \times \dfrac{1\ m}{100\ cm} = 23.8$ m (length) (3SF)

b. Given: 27.0 ft (width), 23.8 m (length)   **Need:** m^2

Plan: ft $\rightarrow$ in. $\rightarrow$ cm $\rightarrow$ m then length (m), width (m) $\rightarrow$ m^2

$$\frac{12\ in.}{1\ ft} \quad \frac{2.54\ cm}{1\ in.} \quad \frac{1\ m}{100\ cm} \qquad Area = length \times width$$

Set Up: $27.0\ ft \times \dfrac{12\ in.}{1\ ft} \times \dfrac{2.54\ cm}{1\ in.} \times \dfrac{1\ m}{100\ cm} = 8.23$ m (width) (3SF)

then Area = 23.8 m $\times$ 8.23 m = 196 m^2 (3SF)

c. Given: 23.8 m (length)   **Need:** s

Plan: m $\rightarrow$ km $\rightarrow$ h $\rightarrow$ min $\rightarrow$ s

$$\frac{1\ km}{1000\ m} \quad \frac{1\ h}{185\ km} \quad \frac{60\ min}{1\ hr} \quad \frac{60\ s}{1\ min}$$

Set Up: $23.8\ m \times \dfrac{1\ km}{1000\ m} \times \dfrac{1\ h}{185\ km} \times \dfrac{60\ min}{1\ hr} \times \dfrac{60\ s}{1\ min} = 0.463$ s (3SF)

1.59 a. Given: 250 L   **Need:** gal

Plan: L $\rightarrow$ qt $\rightarrow$ gal

$$\frac{1.06\ qt}{1\ L} \quad \frac{1\ gal}{4\ qt}$$

Set Up: $250\ L \times \dfrac{1.06\ qt}{1\ L} \times \dfrac{1\ gal}{4\ qt} = 66$ gal (2SF)

b. Given: 0.024 g   **Need:** tablets

Plan: g $\rightarrow$ mg $\rightarrow$ tablet

$$\frac{1000\ mg}{1\ g} \quad \frac{1\ tablet}{8\ mg}$$

Set Up: $0.024\ g \times \dfrac{1000\ mg}{1\ g} \times \dfrac{1\ tablet}{8\ mg} = 3$ tablets (1SF)

   c. Given: 34-lb child   **Need:** mg ampicillin

      Plan: lb $\rightarrow$ g $\rightarrow$ kg $\rightarrow$ mg ampicillin

$$\frac{454 \text{ g body weight}}{1 \text{ lb body weight}} \quad \frac{1 \text{ kg body weight}}{1000 \text{ g body weight}} \quad \frac{115 \text{ mg ampicillin}}{1 \text{ kg body weight}}$$

      Set Up:

$$34 \text{ lb body weight} \times \frac{454 \text{ g body weight}}{1 \text{ lb body weight}} \times \frac{1 \text{ kg body weight}}{1000 \text{ g body weight}} \times \frac{115 \text{ mg ampicillin}}{1 \text{ kg body weight}}$$

$$= 1.8 \times 10^{3} \text{ mg of ampicillin (2SF)}$$

1.61   Each of the following require a percent factor from the problem information.

   a. Given: 325 g crust   **Need:** g oxygen

      Plan: g crust $\rightarrow$ g oxygen (percent equality: 100.0 g crust = 46.7 g oxygen)

$$\frac{46.7 \text{ g oxygen}}{100.0 \text{ g crust}}$$

      Set Up: $325 \text{ g crust} \times \frac{46.7 \text{ g oxygen}}{100.0 \text{ g crust}} = 152 \text{ g of oxygen (3SF)}$

   b. Given: 1.25 g crust   **Need:** g magnesium

      Plan: g crust $\rightarrow$ g magnesium (percent equality: 100.0 g crust = 2.1 g magnesium)

$$\frac{2.1 \text{ g magnesium}}{100.0 \text{ g crust}}$$

      Set Up: $1.25 \text{ g crust} \times \frac{2.1 \text{ g magnesium}}{100.0 \text{ g crust}} = 0.026 \text{ g of magnesium (2SF)}$

   c. Given: 10.0 oz fertilizer   **Need:** g nitrogen

      Plan: oz $\rightarrow$ lb $\rightarrow$ g $\rightarrow$ g nitrogen (percent equality: 100.0 g fertilizer = 15 g nitrogen)

$$\frac{1 \text{ lb}}{16 \text{ oz}} \quad \frac{454 \text{ g}}{1 \text{ lb}} \quad \frac{15 \text{ g nitrogen}}{100.0 \text{ g crust}}$$

      Set Up: $10.0 \text{ oz fertilizer} \times \frac{1 \text{ lb}}{16 \text{ oz}} \times \frac{454 \text{ g}}{1 \text{ lb}} \times \frac{15 \text{ g nitrogen}}{100.0 \text{ g fertilizer}} = 43 \text{ g of nitrogen (2SF)}$

   d. Given: 5.0 kg pecans   **Need:** lb candy

      Plan: kg pecans $\rightarrow$ kg bars $\rightarrow$ lb (percent equality: 100.0 kg bars = 22.0 kg pecans)

$$\frac{100.0 \text{ kg choc. bars}}{22.0 \text{ kg pecans}} \quad \frac{2.20 \text{ lb}}{1 \text{ kg}}$$

      Set Up: $5.0 \text{ kg pecans} \times \frac{100.0 \text{ kg choc. bars}}{22.0 \text{ kg pecans}} \times \frac{2.20 \text{ lb}}{1 \text{ kg}} = 50. \text{ lb of chocolate bars (2SF)}$

1.63   Because the density of aluminum is 2.70 g/cm^3, silver is 10.5 g/cm^3, and lead is 11.3 g/cm^3, we can identify the unknown metal by calculating its density as follows:

$$\text{Density} = \frac{\text{mass}}{\text{Volume}} = \frac{217 \text{ g metal}}{19.2 \text{ cm}^3 \text{ metal}} = 11.3 \text{ g/cm}^3 \text{ (3SF) The metal is lead.}$$

1.65 Density is the mass of a substance divided by its volume. $\text{Density} = \dfrac{\text{mass (grams)}}{\text{Volume (mL)}}$

The densities of solids and liquids are usually stated in g/mL or g/cm^3, so in some problems the units will need to be converted.

a. $\text{Density} = \dfrac{\text{mass (grams)}}{\text{Volume (mL)}} = \dfrac{24.0 \text{ g}}{20.0 \text{ mL}} = 1.20 \text{ g/mL (3SF)}$

b. Given: 0.250 lb butter, 130. mL   **Need:** density (g/mL)

Plan: lb → g then calculate density

$\dfrac{454 \text{ g}}{1 \text{ lb}}$

Set Up: $0.250 \cancel{\text{ lb}} \times \dfrac{454 \text{ g}}{1 \cancel{\text{ lb}}} = 113.5 \text{ g (3SF allowed) then}$

$\text{Density} = \dfrac{\text{mass}}{\text{Volume}} = \dfrac{113.5 \text{ g}}{130. \text{ mL}} = 0.873 \text{ g/mL (3SF)}$

c. Given: 20.0 mL initial volume, 34.5 mL final volume, 45.0 g   **Need:** density (g/mL)

Plan: calculate volume by difference then calculate density

Set Up: volume of gem: 34.5 mL total − 20.0 mL water = 14.5 mL

density of gem: $\text{Density} = \dfrac{\text{mass}}{\text{Volume}} = \dfrac{45.0 \text{ g}}{14.5 \text{ mL}} = 3.10 \text{ g/mL (3SF)}$

d. Given: 0.100 pt, 115.25 g initial, 182.48 g final   **Need:** density (g/mL)

Plan: pt → qt → L → mL then calculate mass by difference

$\dfrac{1 \text{ qt}}{2 \text{ pt}} \quad \dfrac{1 \text{ L}}{1.06 \text{ qt}} \quad \dfrac{1000 \text{ mL}}{1 \text{ L}}$ then calculate the density

Set Up: $0.100 \cancel{\text{ pt}} \times \dfrac{1 \cancel{\text{ qt}}}{2 \cancel{\text{ pt}}} \times \dfrac{1 \cancel{\text{ L}}}{1.06 \cancel{\text{ qt}}} \times \dfrac{1000 \text{ mL}}{1 \cancel{\text{ L}}} = 47.3 \text{ mL (3SF)}$

mass of syrup = 182.48 g − 115.25 g = 67.23 g

$\text{Density} = \dfrac{\text{mass}}{\text{Volume}} = \dfrac{67.23 \text{ g}}{47.3 \text{ mL}} = 1.42 \text{ g/mL (3SF)}$

1.67 In these problems the density is used as a conversion factor.

a. Given: 1.5 kg   **Need:** L

Plan: kg → g → mL → L

$\dfrac{1000 \text{ g}}{1 \text{ kg}} \quad \dfrac{1 \text{ mL}}{0.79 \text{ g}} \quad \dfrac{1000 \text{ mL}}{1 \text{ L}}$

Set Up: $1.5 \cancel{\text{ kg alcohol}} \times \dfrac{1000 \cancel{\text{ g}}}{1 \cancel{\text{ kg alcohol}}} \times \dfrac{1 \cancel{\text{ mL}}}{0.79 \cancel{\text{ g}}} \times \dfrac{1 \text{ L}}{1000 \cancel{\text{ mL}}} = 1.9 \text{ L (2SF)}$

b. Given: 6.5 mL   **Need:** g

Plan: mL → g

$\dfrac{13.6 \text{ g}}{1 \text{ mL}}$

Set Up: $6.5 \cancel{\text{ mL}} \times \dfrac{13.6 \text{ g}}{1 \cancel{\text{ mL}}} = 88 \text{ g (2SF)}$

c. Given: 225 mL   **Need:** oz

   Plan: mL $\rightarrow$ g $\rightarrow$ lb $\rightarrow$ oz

$$\frac{7.8\text{ g}}{1\text{ mL}}\quad \frac{1\text{ lb}}{454\text{ g}}\quad \frac{16\text{ oz}}{1\text{ lb}}$$

   Set Up: $225\text{ mL} \times \dfrac{7.8\text{ g}}{1\text{ mL}} \times \dfrac{1\text{ lb}}{454\text{ g}} \times \dfrac{16\text{ oz}}{1\text{ lb}} = 62\text{ oz (2SF)}$

d. Given: 12.0 gal   **Need:** kg

   Plan: gal $\rightarrow$ qt $\rightarrow$ mL $\rightarrow$ g $\rightarrow$ kg

$$\frac{4\text{ qt}}{1\text{ gal}}\quad \frac{1000\text{ mL}}{1.06\text{ qt}}\quad \frac{0.66\text{ g}}{1\text{ mL}}\quad \frac{1\text{ kg}}{1000\text{ g}}$$

   Set Up: $12.0\text{ gal} \times \dfrac{4\text{ qt}}{1\text{ gal}} \times \dfrac{1000\text{ mL}}{1.06\text{ qt}} \times \dfrac{0.66\text{ g}}{1\text{ mL}} \times \dfrac{1\text{ kg}}{1000\text{ g}} = 30.\text{ kg (2SF)}$

1.69 Specific gravity is the ratio of the density of the sample to the density of water.

   a. Specific gravity $= \dfrac{\text{density of sample}}{\text{density of H}_2\text{O}} = \dfrac{1.030\text{ g/mL}}{1.00\text{ g/mL}} = 1.030\text{ (3SF)}$

   b. Calculate the density and then the specific gravity.

$$\text{Density} = \frac{\text{mass}}{\text{Volume}} = \frac{45.0\text{ g}}{40.0\text{ mL}} = 1.13\text{ g/mL (3SF)}$$

$$\text{Specific gravity} = \frac{\text{density of sample}}{\text{density of H}_2\text{O}} = \frac{1.13\text{ g/mL}}{1.00\text{ g/mL}} = 1.13\text{ (3SF)}$$

   c. Rearrange the formula for specific gravity, by multiplying both sides of the equation by the density of H$_2$O. (Specific gravity) $\times$ (density of H$_2$O) = density of sample
   0.85 (oil sp gr) $\times$ 1.00 g/mL (H$_2$O density) = 0.85 g/mL (oil density) (2SF)

1.71 In c. both numbers contain 2 significant figures; and in d. both numbers contain 4 significant figures.

1.73 **a.** The number of legs is a counted number; it is exact.
   b. The height is measured with a ruler or tape measure; it is a measured number.
   c. The number of chairs is a counted number; it is exact.
   d. The area is measured with a ruler or tape measure; it is a measured number.

1.75 **a.** length = 6.96 cm; width = 4.75 cm
   b. length = 69.6 mm; width = 47.5 mm
   c. There are three significant figures in the length measurement.
   d. There are three significant figures in the width measurement.
   e. Area = length $\times$ width = 6.96 cm $\times$ 4.75 cm = 33.1 cm^2
   f. Since there are three significant figures in the width and length measurements, there are three significant figures in the area.

1.77 **Given:** 18.5 mL initial volume, 23.1 mL final volume, 8.24 g   **Need:** density (g/mL)

   Plan: calculate volume by difference then calculate density

   Set Up: The volume of the object is 23.1 mL $-$ 18.5 mL = 4.6 mL

The mass is 8.24 g and the density is $\text{Density} = \dfrac{\text{mass}}{\text{Volume}} = \dfrac{8.24\text{ g}}{4.6\text{ mL}} = 1.8\text{ g/mL (2SF)}$

1.79   **a.** 0.000 012 6 L, since the fourth significant digit (the first digit to be dropped) is 5 or greater the last retained digit is increased by 1 when the last digit is dropped.

   b. 3.53×10^2 kg, since the fourth significant digit (the first digit to be dropped) is 5 or greater the last retained digit is increased by 1 when the last digit is dropped. The $\times\ 10^2$ is retained so that the magnitude of the answer is not changed.

   c. 125 000 m, the last three digits are changed to zero since the first nonsignificant digit is 4 or less.

   d. 58.7 g, since the fourth digit is 4 or less, the last two digits are dropped.

   e. 3.00×10^{-3} s, since only one significant figure is shown, two zeros must be added. The $\times\ 10^{-3}$ is retained so that the magnitude of the answer is not changed.

   f. 0.010 8 g, the last two digits are dropped since the first dropped digit is 4 or less.

1.81   This problem requires several conversion factors. Let's take a look first at a possible unit plan. When you write out the unit plan, be sure you know a conversion factor you can use for each step.

   Given: 7500 ft   **Need:** min

   Plan: ft $\rightarrow$ in. $\rightarrow$ cm $\rightarrow$ m $\rightarrow$ min

$$\frac{12\ \text{in.}}{1\ \text{ft}} \quad \frac{2.54\ \text{cm}}{1\ \text{in.}} \quad \frac{1\ \text{m}}{100\ \text{cm}} \quad \frac{1\ \text{min}}{55.0\ \text{m}}$$

   Set Up: $7500\ \text{ft} \times \dfrac{12\ \text{in.}}{1\ \text{ft}} \times \dfrac{2.54\ \text{cm}}{1\ \text{in.}} \times \dfrac{1\ \text{m}}{100\ \text{cm}} \times \dfrac{1\ \text{min}}{55.0\ \text{m}} = 42\ \text{min (2SF)}$

1.83   **Given:** 4.0 lb   **Need:** onions

   Plan: lb $\rightarrow$ g $\rightarrow$ onions

$$\frac{454\ \text{g}}{1\ \text{lb}} \quad \frac{1\ \text{onion}}{115\ \text{g}}$$

   Set Up: $4.0\ \text{lb onions} \times \dfrac{454\ \text{g}}{1\ \text{lb}} \times \dfrac{1\ \text{onion}}{115\ \text{g}} = 16\ \text{onions}$

   Because the number of onions is a counting number, the value for onions, 15.8, is rounded to a whole number, 16.

1.85   **a.** **Given:** 8.0 oz   **Need:** crackers

   Plan: oz $\rightarrow$ crackers

$$\frac{6\ \text{crackers}}{0.50\ \text{oz}}$$

   Set Up: $8.0\ \text{oz} \times \dfrac{6\ \text{crackers}}{0.50\ \text{oz}} = 96\ \text{crackers (2SF)}$

   b. **Given:** 10 crackers   **Need:** oz fat

   Plan: crackers $\rightarrow$ servings $\rightarrow$ g $\rightarrow$ lb $\rightarrow$ oz

$$\frac{1\ \text{serving}}{6\ \text{crackers}} \quad \frac{4\ \text{g fat}}{1\ \text{serving}} \quad \frac{1\ \text{lb}}{454\ \text{g}} \quad \frac{16\ \text{oz}}{1\ \text{lb}}$$

   Set Up: $10\ \text{crackers} \times \dfrac{1\ \text{serving}}{6\ \text{crackers}} \times \dfrac{4\ \text{g fat}}{1\ \text{serving}} \times \dfrac{1\ \text{lb}}{454\ \text{g}} \times \dfrac{16\ \text{oz}}{1\ \text{lb}} = 0.2\ \text{oz of fat (1SF)}$

   c. **Given:** 50 boxes   **Need:** g

   Plan: boxes $\rightarrow$ oz $\rightarrow$ servings $\rightarrow$ mg $\rightarrow$ g

$$\frac{8.0\ \text{oz}}{1\ \text{box}} \quad \frac{1\ \text{serving}}{0.50\ \text{oz}} \quad \frac{140\ \text{mg}}{1\ \text{serving}} \quad \frac{1\ \text{g}}{1000\ \text{mg}}$$

   Set Up: $50\ \text{boxes} \times \dfrac{8.0\ \text{oz}}{1\ \text{box}} \times \dfrac{1\ \text{serving}}{0.50\ \text{oz}} \times \dfrac{140\ \text{mg sodium}}{1\ \text{serving}} \times \dfrac{1\ \text{g}}{1000\ \text{mg}} = 110\ \text{g of sodium (2SF)}$

1.87 **Given:** 0.45 lb **Need:** cents

Plan: lb → kg → pesos → dollar → cents

$$\frac{1\text{ kg}}{2.20\text{ lb}} \quad \frac{48\text{ pesos}}{1\text{ kg}} \quad \frac{1\text{ dollar}}{10.8\text{ pesos}} \quad \frac{100\text{ cents}}{1\text{ dollar}}$$

Set Up: $0.45\text{ lb} \times \dfrac{1\text{ kg}}{2.20\text{ lb}} \times \dfrac{48\text{ pesos}}{1\text{ kg}} \times \dfrac{1\text{ dollar}}{10.8\text{ pesos}} \times \dfrac{100\text{ cents}}{1\text{ dollar}} = 91\text{ cents (2SF)}$

1.89 **Given:** 325 tubes **Need:** kg

Plan: tubes → oz cream → lb cream → kg cream → kg sunscreen

$$\frac{4\text{ oz cream}}{1\text{ tube}} \quad \frac{1\text{ lb cream}}{16\text{ oz cream}} \quad \frac{1\text{ kg cream}}{2.20\text{ lb cream}} \quad \frac{2.50\text{ kg sunscreen}}{100\text{ kg cream}}$$

Set Up: $325\text{ tubes} \times \dfrac{4.0\text{ oz}}{1\text{ tube}} \times \dfrac{1\text{ lb}}{16\text{ oz}} \times \dfrac{1\text{ kg}}{2.20\text{ lb}} \times \dfrac{2.50\text{ kg sunscreen}}{100\text{ kg cream}} = 0.92\text{ kg (2SF)}$

1.91 **Given:** 1.85 g/L **Need:** mg/dL

Plan: g/L → mg/L → mg/dL

$$\frac{1000\text{ mg}}{1\text{ g}} \quad \frac{1\text{ L}}{10\text{ dL}}$$

Set Up: This problem involved two units conversions. Convert g to mg, and convert L in the denominator to dL. $\dfrac{1.85\text{ g}}{1\text{ L}} \times \dfrac{1000\text{ mg}}{1\text{ g}} \times \dfrac{1\text{ L}}{10\text{ dL}} = 185\text{ mg/dL (3SF)}$

1.93 **Given:** 215 mL initial, 285 mL final **Need:** g

Plan: calculate the volume by difference and mL → g

$$\frac{11.3\text{ g}}{1\text{ mL}}$$

Set Up: The difference between the initial volume of the water and its volume with the lead object will give us the volume of the lead object: 285 mL total − 215 mL water = 70. mL lead then

$$70.\text{ mL lead} \times \frac{11.3\text{ g lead}}{1\text{ mL lead}} = 790\text{ g of lead (2SF)}$$

1.95 **Given:** 1.00 L gasoline **Need:** cm³ olive oil

Plan: L gas → mL gas → g gas → g oil → mL oil → cm³ oil

$$\frac{1000\text{ mL gas}}{1\text{ L gas}} \quad \frac{0.66\text{ g gas}}{1\text{ mL gas}} \quad \frac{1\text{ g oil}}{1\text{ g gas}} \quad \frac{1\text{ mL oil}}{0.92\text{ g oil}} \quad \frac{1\text{ cm}^3}{1\text{ mL}}$$

Set Up: $1.00\text{ L gas} \times \dfrac{1000\text{ mL gas}}{1\text{ L gas}} \times \dfrac{0.66\text{ g gas}}{1\text{ mL gas}} \times \dfrac{1\text{ g oil}}{1\text{ g gas}} \times \dfrac{1\text{ mL oil}}{0.92\text{ g oil}} \times \dfrac{1\text{ cm}^3\text{ olive oil}}{1\text{ mL oil}} =$

720 cm³ of olive oil (2SF)

1.97 **a.** **Given:** 45 kg body mass   **Need:** lb fat

Plan: kg mass → kg fat → lb (percent equality: 100.0 kg mass = 3.0 kg fat)

$$\frac{3.0 \text{ kg fat}}{100.0 \text{ kg body mass}} \quad \frac{2.20 \text{ lb fat}}{1 \text{ kg fat}}$$

Set Up: $45 \text{ kg body mass} \times \dfrac{3.0 \text{ kg fat}}{100.0 \text{ kg body mass}} \times \dfrac{2.20 \text{ lb fat}}{1 \text{ kg fat}} = 3.0 \text{ lb of fat (2SF)}$

b. **Given:** 3.0 L fat   **Need:** lb fat

Plan: L → mL → g → lb

$$\frac{1000 \text{ mL}}{1 \text{ L}} \quad \frac{0.94 \text{ g}}{1 \text{ mL}} \quad \frac{2.20 \text{ lb}}{1 \text{ kg}}$$

Set Up: $3.0 \text{ L} \times \dfrac{1000 \text{ mL}}{1 \text{ L}} \times \dfrac{0.94 \text{ g}}{1 \text{ mL}} \times \dfrac{1 \text{ lb}}{454 \text{ g}} = 6.2 \text{ lb (2SF)}$

1.99 **Given:** 27.0 cm^3 **Need:** oz pure silver

Plan: cm^3 → g → g silver → lb → oz (percent equality: 100 g sterling = 92.5 g silver)

$$\frac{10.3 \text{ g alloy}}{1 \text{ cm}^3 \text{ alloy}} \quad \frac{92.5 \text{ g silver}}{100.0 \text{ g alloy}} \quad \frac{1 \text{ lb}}{454 \text{ g}} \quad \frac{16 \text{ oz}}{1 \text{ lb}}$$

Set Up: $27.0 \text{ cm}^3 \times \dfrac{10.3 \text{ g}}{1 \text{ cm}^3} \times \dfrac{92.5 \text{ g silver}}{100.0 \text{ g alloy}} \times \dfrac{1 \text{ lb}}{454 \text{ g}} \times \dfrac{16 \text{ oz}}{1 \text{ lb}} = 9.07 \text{ oz of pure silver (3SF)}$

1.101 **a.** **Given:** 180 lb body mass   **Need:** cups of coffee

Plan: lb body mass → kg body mass → mg caffeine → fl oz coffee → cups coffee

$$\frac{1 \text{ kg body mass}}{2.20 \text{ lb body mass}} \quad \frac{192 \text{ mg caffeine}}{1 \text{ kg body mass}} \quad \frac{6 \text{ fl oz coffee}}{100. \text{ mg caffeine}} \quad \frac{1 \text{ cup coffee}}{12 \text{ fl oz coffee}}$$

Set Up:

$180 \text{ lb body mass} \times \dfrac{1 \text{ kg body mass}}{2.20 \text{ lb body mass}} \times \dfrac{192 \text{ mg caffeine}}{1 \text{ kg body mass}} = 1.571 \times 10^4 \text{ mg of caffeine (2SF allowed)}$

$1.571 \times 10^4 \text{ mg caffeine} \times \dfrac{6 \text{ fl oz coffee}}{100. \text{ mg caffeine}} \times \dfrac{1 \text{ cup coffee}}{12 \text{ fl oz coffee}} = 80 \text{ cups of coffee (1SF)}$

b. **Given:** mg caffeine from part a.   **Need:** cans of cola

Plan: mg caffeine → cans cola

$$\frac{1 \text{ can of cola}}{50. \text{ mg caffeine}}$$

Set Up: $1.571 \times 10^4 \text{ mg caffeine} \times \dfrac{1 \text{ can of cola}}{50. \text{ mg caffeine}} = 310 \text{ cans of cola (2SF)}$

c. **Given:** mg caffeine from part a.   **Need:** No-Doz tablets

Plan: mg caffeine → No-Doz tablets

$$\frac{1 \text{ No-Doz tablet}}{100 \text{ mg caffeine}}$$

Set Up: $1.571 \times 10^4 \text{ mg caffeine} \times \dfrac{1 \text{ No-Doz tablet}}{100. \text{ mg caffeine}} = 160 \text{ No-Doz tablets (2SF)}$

1.103 You should record the mass as 34.075 g. Since your balance will weigh to the nearest 0.001 g, the mass values should be reported to 0.001 g.

1.105 **Given:** 3.0 h **Need:** gal of gasoline

Plan: h → mi → km → L → qt → gal

$$\frac{55 \text{ mi}}{1 \text{ h}} \quad \frac{1 \text{ km}}{0.621 \text{ mi}} \quad \frac{1 \text{ L}}{11 \text{ km}} \quad \frac{1.06 \text{ qt}}{1 \text{ L}} \quad \frac{1 \text{ gal}}{4 \text{ qt}}$$

Set Up: $3.0 \text{ h} \times \dfrac{55 \text{ mi}}{1 \text{ h}} \times \dfrac{1 \text{ km}}{0.621 \text{ mi}} \times \dfrac{1 \text{ L}}{11 \text{ km}} \times \dfrac{1.06 \text{ qt}}{1 \text{ L}} \times \dfrac{1 \text{ gal}}{4 \text{ qt}} = 6.4$ gal of gasoline (2SF)

1.107 **Given:** 1.50 g silicon, 3.00 in diameter **Need:** thickness (mm)

Plan: g → cm³ and d(in) → r(in) → r(cm) then

$$\frac{1 \text{ cm}^3}{2.33 \text{ g silicon}} \quad \frac{2.54 \text{ cm}}{1 \text{ in}}$$

rearrange Volume equation for thickness (cm) → thickness (mm)

$$V = \pi r^2 h \ (\div \ \pi r^2) \ \frac{10 \text{ mm}}{1 \text{ cm}}$$

Set Up: Volume: $1.50 \text{ g} \times \dfrac{1 \text{ cm}^3}{2.33 \text{ g}} = 0.644 \text{ cm}^3$ (3SF)

Radius: $3.00 \text{ in} \times \dfrac{1}{2} \times \dfrac{2.54 \text{ cm}}{1 \text{ in.}} = 3.81 \text{ cm}$ (3SF)

$h = \dfrac{V}{\pi r^2} = \dfrac{0.644 \text{ cm}^3}{3.14 \ (3.81 \text{ cm})^2} = 0.0141 \text{ cm} \times \dfrac{10 \text{ mm}}{1 \text{ cm}} = 0.141 \text{ mm}$ (3SF)

1.109 **Given:** 66.7 yd length, 12 in. wide, 0.000 30 in. depth **Need:** g

Plan: Length: yd → ft → in. → cm and Width and Depth: in. → cm then

$$\frac{3 \text{ ft}}{1 \text{ yd}} \quad \frac{12 \text{ in.}}{1 \text{ ft}} \quad \frac{2.54 \text{ cm}}{1 \text{ in.}} \quad \frac{2.54 \text{ cm}}{1 \text{ in.}} \quad \text{calculate Volume then cm}^3 \rightarrow \text{g}$$

$$V = lwh \ \frac{2.70 \text{ g}}{1 \text{ cm}^3}$$

Set Up: Length: $66.7 \text{ yd} \times \dfrac{3 \text{ ft}}{1 \text{ yd}} \times \dfrac{12 \text{ in.}}{1 \text{ ft}} \times \dfrac{2.54 \text{ cm}}{1 \text{ in.}} = 61\,00 \text{ cm}$ (2SF)

Width: $12 \text{ in.} \times \dfrac{2.54 \text{ cm}}{1 \text{ in.}} = 30. \text{ cm}$ (2SF) Depth: $0.000 \ 30 \text{ in.} \times \dfrac{2.54 \text{ cm}}{1 \text{ in.}} = 0.000 \ 76 \text{ cm}$ (2SF)

Volume = $6100 \text{ cm} \times 30. \text{ cm} \times 0.000 \ 76 \text{ cm} = 140 \text{ cm}^3$ then $140 \text{ cm}^3 \times \dfrac{2.70 \text{ g}}{1 \text{ cm}^3} = 380 \text{ g}$ (2SF)

13

2

Energy and Matter

2.1 As the car climbs the hill, kinetic energy is converted to potential until, at the top of the hill, all of the energy is in the form of potential energy. As it descends the hill, potential energy is being converted into kinetic energy. When the car reaches the bottom, all of its energy is in the form of motion (kinetic energy).

2.3 **a.** Potential energy is stored in the water at the top of the waterfall.
b. Kinetic energy is displayed as the kicked ball moves.
c. Potential energy is stored in the chemical bonds in the coal.
d. Potential energy is stored when the skier is at the top of the hill.

2.5 **a. Given:** 1.1×10^3 J/match, 20 matches   **Need:** kilojoules (kJ)

Plan: match → J → kJ

$$\frac{1.1 \times 10^3 \text{ J}}{1 \text{ match}} \quad \frac{1 \text{ kJ}}{1000 \text{ J}}$$

Set Up: $20 \text{ matches} \times \dfrac{1.1 \times 10^3 \text{ J}}{1 \text{ match}} \times \dfrac{1 \text{ kJ}}{1000 \text{ J}} = 22 \text{ kJ (2SF)}$

b. Given: 1.1×10^3 J/match, 20 matches   **Need:** calories (cal)

Plan: match → J → cal

$$\frac{1.1 \times 10^3 \text{ J}}{1 \text{ match}} \quad \frac{1 \text{ cal}}{4.184 \text{ J}}$$

Set Up: $20 \text{ matches} \times \dfrac{1.1 \times 10^3 \text{ J}}{1 \text{ match}} \times \dfrac{1 \text{ cal}}{4.184 \text{ J}} = 5.3 \times 10^3 \text{ cal (2SF)}$

c. Given: 1.1×10^3 J/match, 20 matches   **Need:** kilocalories (kcal)

Plan: match → J → cal → kcal

$$\frac{1.1 \times 10^3 \text{ J}}{1 \text{ match}} \quad \frac{1 \text{ cal}}{4.184 \text{ J}} \quad \frac{1 \text{ kcal}}{1000 \text{ cal}}$$

Set Up: $20 \text{ matches} \times \dfrac{1.1 \times 10^3 \text{ J}}{1 \text{ match}} \times \dfrac{1 \text{ cal}}{4.184 \text{ J}} \times \dfrac{1 \text{ kcal}}{1000 \text{ cal}} = 5.3 \text{ kcal (2SF)}$

2.7 The Fahrenheit temperature scale is still used in the United States. A normal body temperature is 98.6 °F on this scale. To convert her temperature to the equivalent reading on the Celsius scale, the following calculation must be performed: $T_C = \dfrac{(99.8 \text{ °F} - 32)}{1.8} = \dfrac{67.8}{1.8} \text{ °C} = 37.7 \text{ °C}$
(32 is exact)(3SF) Because a normal body temperature is 37.0 on the Celsius scale, her temperature of 37.7 °C would be a mild fever.

2.9 **a.** 1.8 (37.0 °C) + 32 = 66.6 + 32 = 98.6 °F (1.8 and 32 are exact) (3SF)
b. $\dfrac{(65.3 \text{ °F} - 32)}{1.8} = \dfrac{33.3}{1.8} \text{ °C} = 18.5 \text{ °C}$ (1.8 and 32 are exact) (3SF)
c. −27 °C + 273 = 246 K
d. 62 °C + 273 = 335 K

e. $\dfrac{(114\ °F - 32)}{1.8} = \dfrac{82}{1.8}\ °C = 46\ °C$ (1.8 and 32 are exact) (2SF)

f. $\dfrac{(72\ °F - 32)}{1.8} = \dfrac{40.}{1.8}\ °C = 22\ °C;\ 22\ °C + 273 = 295\ K$ (1.8 and 32 are exact) (3SF)

2.11   **a.** $\dfrac{(106\ °F - 32)}{1.8} = \dfrac{74}{1.8}\ °C = 41\ °C$ (1.8 and 32 are exact) (2SF)

       b. $\dfrac{(103\ °F - 32)}{1.8} = \dfrac{71}{1.8}\ °C = 39\ °C$ (1.8 and 32 are exact) (2SF)

No, there is no need to phone the doctor. The child's temperature is less than 40.0 °C.

2.13   Copper has the lowest specific heat of the samples and will reach the highest temperature.

2.15   **a. Given:**   heat = 312 J; mass = 13.5 g; $\Delta T = 83.6\ °C - 24.2\ °C = 59.4\ °C$

         Need: specific heat (J/g °C)

         Plan: $SH = \dfrac{\text{heat}}{\text{mass} \times \Delta T}$

         Set Up: Specific Heat $(SH) = \dfrac{312\ \text{J}}{13.5\ \text{g} \times 59.4\ °C} = \dfrac{0.389\ \text{J}}{\text{g} °C}$ (3SF)

         b. Given: heat = 345 J; mass = 48.2 g; $\Delta T = 57.9\ °C - 35.0\ °C = 22.9\ °C$

         Need: specific heat (J/g °C)

         Plan: $SH = \dfrac{\text{heat}}{\text{mass} \times \Delta T}$

         Set Up: Specific Heat $(SH) = \dfrac{345\ \text{J}}{48.2\ \text{g} \times 22.9\ °C} = \dfrac{0.313\ \text{J}}{\text{g} °C}$ (3SF)

2.17   **a. Given:**   specific heat = 1.00 cal/g °C; mass = 25 g; $\Delta T = 25\ °C - 15\ °C = 10.\ °C$

         Need: heat (cal)

         Plan: heat = mass $\times \Delta T \times SH$

         Set Up: $25\ \cancel{g} \times \dfrac{1.00\ \text{cal}}{\cancel{g}\ \cancel{°C}} \times 10.\ \cancel{°C} = 250\ \text{cal}$ (2SF)

         b. Given: specific heat = 1.00 cal/g °C; mass = 150 g; $\Delta T = 75\ °C - 0\ °C = 75\ °C$

         Need: heat (cal)

         Plan: heat = mass $\times \Delta T \times SH$

         Set Up: $150\ \cancel{g} \times \dfrac{1.00\ \text{cal}}{\cancel{g}\ \cancel{°C}} \times 75\ \cancel{°C} = 11\ 000\ \text{cal}$ (2SF)

         c. Given: specific heat = 1.00 cal/g °C; mass = 150 g; $\Delta T = 77\ °C - 15\ °C = 62\ °C$

         Need: heat (kcal)

Plan: heat = mass $\times \Delta T \times SH$ then cal → kcal

$$\frac{1 \text{ kcal}}{1000 \text{ cal}}$$

Set Up: $150 \text{ g} \times \dfrac{1.00 \text{ cal}}{\text{g} \, ^{\circ}\text{C}} \times 62 \, ^{\circ}\text{C} \times \dfrac{1 \text{ kcal}}{1000 \text{ cal}} = 9.3 \text{ kcal (2SF)}$

2.19 **a. Given:** specific heat = 4.184 J/g °C; mass = 25.0 g; $\Delta T = 25.7 \,^{\circ}\text{C} - 12.5 \,^{\circ}\text{C} = 13.2 \,^{\circ}\text{C}$

    Need: heat (cal)

    Plan: heat = mass $\times \Delta T \times SH$ then J → cal

$$\frac{1 \text{ cal}}{4.184 \text{ J}}$$

    Set Up: $25.0 \text{ g} \times 13.2 \,^{\circ}\text{C} \times \dfrac{4.184 \text{ J}}{\text{g} \,^{\circ}\text{C}} = 1380 \text{ J}$ and $1380 \text{ J} \times \dfrac{1 \text{ cal}}{4.184 \text{ J}} = 330. \text{ cal (3SF)}$

    b. Given: specific heat = 0.385 J/g °C; mass = 38.0 g; $\Delta T = 246 \,^{\circ}\text{C} - 122 \,^{\circ}\text{C} = 124 \,^{\circ}\text{C}$

    Need: heat (cal)

    Plan: heat = mass $\times \Delta T \times SH$ then J → cal

$$\frac{1 \text{ cal}}{4.184 \text{ J}}$$

    Set Up: $38.0 \text{ g} \times 124 \,^{\circ}\text{C} \times \dfrac{0.385 \text{ J}}{\text{g} \,^{\circ}\text{C}} = 1810 \text{ J}$ and $1810 \text{ J} \times \dfrac{1 \text{ cal}}{4.184 \text{ J}} = 434 \text{ cal (3SF)}$

    c. Given: specific heat = 2.46 J/g °C; mass = 15.0 g; $\Delta T = 60.5 \,^{\circ}\text{C} - (-42.0 \,^{\circ}\text{C}) = 102.5 \,^{\circ}\text{C}$

    Need: heat (cal)

    Plan: heat = mass $\times \Delta T \times SH$ then J → cal

$$\frac{1 \text{ cal}}{4.184 \text{ J}}$$

    Set Up: $15.0 \text{ g} \times 102.5 \,^{\circ}\text{C} \times \dfrac{2.46 \text{ J}}{\text{g} \,^{\circ}\text{C}} = 3780 \text{ J}$ and $3780 \text{ J} \times \dfrac{1 \text{ cal}}{4.184 \text{ J}} = 904 \text{ cal (3SF)}$

    d. Given: specific heat = 0.452 J/g °C; mass = 112 g; $\Delta T = 118 \,^{\circ}\text{C} - 55 \,^{\circ}\text{C} = 63 \,^{\circ}\text{C}$

    Need: heat (cal)

    Plan: heat = mass $\times \Delta T \times SH$ then J → cal

$$\frac{1 \text{ cal}}{4.184 \text{ J}}$$

    Set Up: $112 \text{ g} \times 63 \,^{\circ}\text{C} \times \dfrac{0.452 \text{ J}}{\text{g} \,^{\circ}\text{C}} = 3200 \text{ J}$ and $3200 \text{ J} \times \dfrac{1 \text{ cal}}{4.184 \text{ J}} = 760 \text{ cal (2SF)}$

2.21 **a. Given:** specific heat = 0.129 J/g °C; heat = 225 J; $\Delta T = 47.0 \,^{\circ}\text{C} - 15.0 \,^{\circ}\text{C} = 32.0 \,^{\circ}\text{C}$

    Need: mass (g)

    Plan: heat = mass $\times \Delta T \times SH$ divide both sides of the equation by $\Delta T \times SH$ to get

$$\text{mass} = \frac{\text{heat}}{\Delta T \times SH}$$

    Set Up: $\dfrac{225 \text{ J}}{32.0 \,^{\circ}\text{C} \times \dfrac{0.129 \text{ J}}{\text{g} \,^{\circ}\text{C}}} = 54.5 \text{ g of gold (3SF)}$

b. Given: specific heat = 0.452 J/g °C; heat = 8.40 kJ; $\Delta T = 168.0\,°C - 82.0\,°C = 86.0\,°C$

Need: mass (g)

Plan: kJ → J then heat = mass × ΔT × SH divide both sides of the equation by $\Delta T \times SH$

to get mass = $\dfrac{\text{heat}}{\Delta T \times SH}$

$\dfrac{1000\ \text{J}}{1\ \text{kJ}}$

Set Up: $\dfrac{8.40\ \cancel{kJ} \times \dfrac{1000\ \cancel{J}}{1\ \cancel{kJ}}}{86.0\ \cancel{°C} \times \dfrac{0.452\ \cancel{J}}{g\ \cancel{°C}}} = 216$ g of iron (3SF)

c. Given: specific heat = 0.897 J/g °C; heat = 8.80 kJ; $\Delta T = 26.8\,°C - 12.5\,°C = 14.3\,°C$

Need: mass (g)

Plan: kJ → J then heat = mass × ΔT × SH divide both sides of the equation by $\Delta T \times SH$

to get mass = $\dfrac{\text{heat}}{\Delta T \times SH}$

$\dfrac{1000\ \text{J}}{1\ \text{kJ}}$

Set Up: $\dfrac{8.80\ \cancel{kJ} \times \dfrac{1000\ \cancel{J}}{1\ \cancel{kJ}}}{14.3\ \cancel{°C} \times \dfrac{0.897\ \cancel{J}}{g\ \cancel{°C}}} = 686$ g of aluminum (3SF)

d. Given: specific heat = 0.523 J/g °C; heat = 14 200 J; $\Delta T = 185\,°C - 42\,°C = 143\,°C$

Need: mass (g)

Plan: heat = mass × ΔT × SH divide both sides of the equation by $\Delta T \times SH$ to get

mass = $\dfrac{\text{heat}}{\Delta T \times SH}$

Set Up: $\dfrac{14\ 200\ \cancel{J}}{143\ \cancel{°C} \times \dfrac{0.523\ \cancel{J}}{g\ \cancel{°C}}} = 190.$ g of titanium (3SF)

2.23 a. Given: specific heat = 1.00 cal/g °C; mass = 505 g; $\Delta T = 35.7\,°C - 25.2\,°C = 10.5\,°C$

Need: heat in kJ and kcal

Plan: heat = mass × ΔT × SH then cal → kcal and kcal → kJ

$\dfrac{1\ \text{kcal}}{1000\ \text{cal}}\quad \dfrac{4.184\ \text{kJ}}{1\ \text{kcal}}$

Set Up: $505\ \cancel{g} \times \dfrac{1.00\ \cancel{cal}}{\cancel{g}\ \cancel{°C}} \times 10.5\ \cancel{°C} \times \dfrac{1\ \text{kcal}}{1000\ \cancel{cal}} = 5.30$ kcal

and $5.30\ \cancel{kcal} \times \dfrac{4.184\ \text{kJ}}{1\ \cancel{kcal}} = 22.2$ kJ (3SF)

b. Given: specific heat = 1.00 cal/g °C; mass = 4980 g; $\Delta T = 62.4\,°C - 20.6\,°C = 41.8\,°C$

Need: heat in kJ and kcal

Plan: heat = mass $\times \Delta T \times SH$ then cal $\rightarrow$ kcal and kcal $\rightarrow$ kJ

$$\frac{1 \text{ kcal}}{1000 \text{ cal}} \quad \frac{4.184 \text{ kJ}}{1 \text{ kcal}}$$

Set Up: $4980 \text{ g} \times \dfrac{1.00 \text{ cal}}{\text{g} \, ^\circ\text{C}} \times 41.8 \, ^\circ\text{C} \times \dfrac{1 \text{ kcal}}{1000 \text{ cal}} = 208 \text{ kcal}$

and $208 \text{ kcal} \times \dfrac{4.184 \text{ kJ}}{1 \text{ kcal}} = 870. \text{ kJ (3SF)}$

2.25   **a.** Because the orange juice contains both carbohydrate and protein, two calculations will be needed.

Given: 26 g of carbohydrate, 0 g of fat, 2 g of protein   **Need:**   Cal

Plan: g $\rightarrow$ kcal $\rightarrow$ Cal then total all of the Calories

$$\frac{4 \text{ kcal}}{1 \text{ g of carbohydrate}} \quad \frac{4 \text{ kcal}}{1 \text{ g of protein}} \quad \frac{1 \text{ Cal}}{1 \text{ kcal}}$$

Set Up: $26 \text{ g of carbohydrate} \times \dfrac{4 \text{ kcal}}{1 \text{ g of carbohydrate}} \times \dfrac{1 \text{ Cal}}{1 \text{ kcal}} = 100 \text{ Cal}$

and $2 \text{ g of protein} \times \dfrac{4 \text{ kcal}}{1 \text{ g of protein}} \times \dfrac{1 \text{ Cal}}{1 \text{ kcal}} = 8 \text{ Cal}$ then

Total: $100 \text{ Cal} + 8 \text{ Cal} = 108 \text{ Cal} = 110 \text{ Cal (rounded)}$

b. With only carbohydrate present, a single calculation is all that is required.

Given: 72 kcal, 0 g of fat, 0 g of protein   **Need:**   g of carbohydrate

Plan: kcal $\rightarrow$ g

$$\frac{1 \text{ g of carbohydrate}}{4 \text{ kcal}}$$

Set Up: $72 \text{ kcal} \times \dfrac{1 \text{ g of carbohydrate}}{4 \text{ kcal}} = 18 \text{ g of carbohydrate}$

c. With only fat present, a single calculation is all that is required.

Given: 0 g of carbohydrate, 14 g of fat, 0 g of protein   **Need:**   Cal

Plan: g $\rightarrow$ kcal $\rightarrow$ Cal then total all of the Calories

$$\frac{9 \text{ kcal}}{1 \text{ g fat}} \quad \frac{1 \text{ Cal}}{1 \text{ kcal}}$$

Set Up: $14 \text{ g of fat} \times \dfrac{9 \text{ kcal}}{1 \text{ g of fat}} \times \dfrac{1 \text{ Cal}}{1 \text{ kcal}} = 130 \text{ Cal}$

d. Three calculations are needed.

Given: 30. g of carbohydrate, 15 g of fat, 5 g of protein   **Need:**   Cal

Plan: g $\rightarrow$ kcal $\rightarrow$ Cal then total all of the Calories

$$\frac{4 \text{ kcal}}{1 \text{ g of carbohydrate}} \quad \frac{9 \text{ kcal}}{1 \text{ g of fat}} \quad \frac{4 \text{ kcal}}{1 \text{ g of protein}} \quad \frac{1 \text{ Cal}}{1 \text{ kcal}}$$

Set Up: $30. \text{ g of carbohydrate} \times \dfrac{4 \text{ kcal}}{1 \text{ g of carbohydrate}} \times \dfrac{1 \text{ Cal}}{1 \text{ kcal}} = 120 \text{ Cal},$

$15 \text{ g of fat} \times \dfrac{9 \text{ kcal}}{1 \text{ g of fat}} \times \dfrac{1 \text{ Cal}}{1 \text{ kcal}} = 144 \text{ Cal, and}$

$$5 \text{ g of protein} \times \frac{4 \text{ kcal}}{1 \text{ g of protein}} \times \frac{1 \text{ Cal}}{1 \text{ kcal}} = 20 \text{ Cal then}$$

$$\text{Total}: 120 \text{ Cal} + 144 \text{ Cal} + 20 \text{ Cal} = 284 \text{ Cal} = 280 \text{ Cal (rounded)}$$

2.27 Three calculations are needed:

Given: 16 g of carbohydrate, 12 g of fat, 9 g of protein   **Need:** kcal and kJ

Plan: g → kcal → Cal then total all of the Calories and kcal → kJ

$$\frac{4 \text{ kcal}}{1 \text{ g of carbohydrate}} \quad \frac{9 \text{ kcal}}{1 \text{ g of fat}} \quad \frac{4 \text{ kcal}}{1 \text{ g of protein}} \quad \frac{1 \text{ Cal}}{1 \text{ kcal}} \quad \frac{4.184 \text{ kJ}}{1 \text{ kcal}}$$

Set Up: $9 \text{ g of protein} \times \frac{4 \text{ kcal}}{1 \text{ g of protein}} = 36 \text{ kcal}$, $12 \text{ g of fat} \times \frac{9 \text{ kcal}}{1 \text{ g of fat}} = 108 \text{ kcal}$, and

$$16 \text{ g of carbohydrate} \times \frac{4 \text{ kcal}}{1 \text{ g of carbohydrate}} = 64 \text{ kcal then}$$

$$\text{Total}: 36 \text{ kcal} + 108 \text{ kcal} + 64 \text{ kcal} = 208 \text{ kcal} = 210 \text{ kcal (rounded) and}$$

$$208 \text{ kcal} \times \frac{4.184 \text{ kJ}}{1 \text{ kcal}} = 870 \text{ kJ (rounded)}$$

2.29 *Elements* are the simplest type of pure substance. *Compounds* contain two or more elements in the same ratio.
   a. Baking soda ($NaHCO_3$) is a compound since it contains four elements (Na, H, C, and O).
   b. Oxygen (O_2) is an element since it contains only one type of atom (O).
   c. Ice (H_2O) is a compound since it contains two elements (H and O).
   d. Aluminum foil (Al) is an element since it contains only one type of atom (Al).

2.31 A *homogeneous mixture* has a uniform composition; a *heterogeneous mixture* does not have a uniform composition throughout the mixture.
   a. Vegetable soup is a heterogeneous mixture since it has chunks of vegetables.
   b. Salt water is a homogeneous mixture since it is uniform.
   c. Tea is a homogeneous mixture since it is uniform.
   d. Tea with ice and a slice of lemon is a heterogeneous mixture since it has chunks of ice and lemon.
   e. Water and sand in an aquarium is a heterogeneous mixture since it has a layer of sand and a layer of water.
   f. Fruit salad is a heterogeneous mixture since it has chunks of fruit.

2.33 **a.** A gas takes the shape and volume of its container. Thus, a gas has no definite volume or shape.
   b. The particles in a gas have little attraction between them and do not interact.
   c. A solid has a definite volume or shape.

2.35 A physical property is a characteristic of the substance such as color, shape, odor, luster, size, melting point, and density. A chemical property is a characteristic that indicates the ability of a substance to form another substance, describing action.
   a. Color and physical state are physical properties.
   b. The ability to react is a chemical property.
   c. The melting point is a physical property.
   d. Milk souring describes chemical reactions and so is a chemical property.

2.37 A physical change describes a change in a physical property that retains the identity of the substance. A chemical change occurs when the atoms of the initial substances rearrange to form new substances.
   a. Water vapor condensing is a physical change since the physical form of the water changes, but not the substance.
   b. Cesium metal reacting is a chemical change since new substances form.

    c. Gold melting is a physical change, since the shape changes, but not the substance.

    d. Cutting a puzzle is a physical change, since the shape changes, but not the substance.

    e. Dissolving sugar is a physical change, since the size of the sugar particles change, but no new substances are formed.

2.39   **a.** The high reactivity of fluorine is a chemical property, since it describes that new substances will be formed.

    b. The physical state of fluorine is a physical property.

    c. The color of fluorine is a physical property.

    d. The reactivity of fluorine with hydrogen is a chemical property, since it describes that new substances will be formed.

    e. The melting point of fluorine is a physical property.

2.41   **a.** Melting is described by the conversion of a solid to a liquid.

    b. Sublimation is described by the conversion of a solid directly to a vapor.

    c. Freezing is described by the conversion of a liquid to a solid.

    d. Deposition is described as the conversion of a vapor directly to a solid.

2.43   **a. Given:**   65 g of ice melting   **Need:**   heat (cal) absorbed or released

        Plan: g → cal heat is absorbed since the ice is melting

$$\frac{80.\ \text{cal}}{1\ \text{g}}$$

        Set Up: $65\ \cancel{\text{g of ice}} \times \dfrac{80.\ \text{cal}}{1\ \cancel{\text{g of ice}}} = 5200$ cal absorbed (2SF)

    b. Given: 17 g of ice melting   **Need:**   heat (cal) absorbed or released

        Plan: g → cal heat is absorbed since the ice is melting

$$\frac{80.\ \text{cal}}{1\ \text{g}}$$

        Set Up: $17\ \cancel{\text{g of ice}} \times \dfrac{80.\ \cancel{\text{cal}}}{1\ \cancel{\text{g of ice}}} = 1400$ cal absorbed (2SF)

    c. Given: 225 g of water freezing   **Need:**   heat (kcal) absorbed or released

        Plan: g → cal → kcal heat is released since the water is freezing

$$\frac{80.\ \text{cal}}{1\ \text{g}} \quad \frac{1\ \text{kcal}}{1000\ \text{cal}}$$

        Set Up: $225\ \cancel{\text{g of water}} \times \dfrac{80.\ \cancel{\text{cal}}}{1\ \cancel{\text{g of water}}} \times \dfrac{1\ \text{kcal}}{1000\ \cancel{\text{cal}}} = 18$ kcal released (2SF)

2.45   **a.** Condensation is described by the conversion of a vapor to a liquid.

    b. Evaporation is described by the conversion of a liquid to a vapor.

    c. Boiling is described by the conversion of a liquid to a vapor at temperatures at or above the boiling point.

    d. Condensation is described by the conversion of a vapor to a liquid.

2.47   **a. Given:**   10.0 g of water vaporizing   **Need:**   heat (cal) absorbed or released

        Plan: g → cal heat is absorbed since the water is vaporizing

$$\frac{540\ \text{cal}}{1\ \text{g}}$$

        Set Up: $10.0\ \cancel{\text{g of water}} \times \dfrac{540\ \text{cal}}{1\ \cancel{\text{g of water}}} = 5400$ cal absorbed (2SF)

b. Given: 50.0 g of water vaporizing   **Need:** heat (kcal) absorbed or released

     Plan: g → cal → kcal heat is absorbed since the water is vaporizing

$$\frac{540 \text{ cal}}{1 \text{ g}} \quad \frac{1 \text{ kcal}}{1000 \text{ cal}}$$

     Set Up: $50.0 \text{ g of water} \times \dfrac{540 \text{ cal}}{1 \text{ g of water}} \times \dfrac{1 \text{ kcal}}{1000 \text{ cal}} = 27 \text{ kcal absorbed (2SF)}$

c. Given: 8.0 kg of vapor condensing   **Need:** heat (kcal) absorbed or released

     Plan: g → kg → cal → kcal heat is released since the water is condensing

$$\frac{1000 \text{ g}}{1 \text{ kg}} \quad \frac{540 \text{ cal}}{1 \text{ g}} \quad \frac{1 \text{ kcal}}{1000 \text{ cal}}$$

     Set Up: $8.0 \text{ kg of steam} \times \dfrac{1000 \text{ g}}{1 \text{ kg}} \times \dfrac{540 \text{ cal}}{1 \text{ g of steam}} \times \dfrac{1 \text{ kcal}}{1000 \text{ cal}} = 4300 \text{ kcal released (2SF)}$

2.49

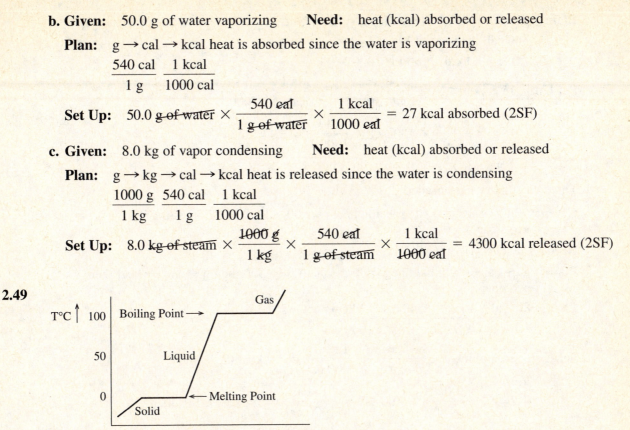

2.51   **a. Given:** specific heat = 1.00 cal/g °C; mass = 20.0 g; $\Delta T = 72\,°C - 15\,°C = 57\,°C$

     Need: heat (cal)

     Plan: heat = mass $\times \Delta T \times SH$

     Set Up: $20.0 \text{ g} \times \dfrac{1.00 \text{ cal}}{\text{g °C}} \times 57\,°C = 1100 \text{ cal (2SF)}$

   b. Two calculations are needed:

     Given: 50.0 g ice at 0 °C; specific heat = 1.00 cal/g °C; $\Delta T = 65\,°C - 0\,°C = 65\,°C$

     Need: heat (cal)

     Plan: g → cal then heat = mass $\times \Delta T \times SH$ then add energies

$$\frac{80. \text{ cal}}{1 \text{ g}}$$

     Set Up: $50.0 \text{ g of ice} \times \dfrac{80. \text{ cal}}{1 \text{ g of ice}} = 4000 \text{ cal (2SF)}$ and

     $50.0 \text{ g} \times \dfrac{1.00 \text{ cal}}{\text{g °C}} \times 65\,°C = 3300 \text{ cal}$ then

     Total: 4000 cal + 3300 cal = 7300 cal (2SF)

   c. Two calculations are needed:

     Given: 15 g of vapor condensing; specific heat = 4.184 J/g °C;

           $\Delta T = 100.\,°C - 0\,°C = 100.\,°C$

     Need: heat (kJ)

Plan: $g \rightarrow cal \rightarrow J \rightarrow kJ$ then heat = mass $\times \Delta T \times SH$ $J \rightarrow kJ$ then add energies

$$\frac{540 \text{ cal}}{1 \text{ g}} \quad \frac{4.184 \text{ J}}{1 \text{ cal}} \quad \frac{1 \text{ kJ}}{1000 \text{ J}} \quad \frac{1 \text{ kJ}}{1000 \text{ J}}$$

Set Up: $15 \text{ g of steam} \times \dfrac{540 \text{ cal}}{1 \text{ g of steam}} \times \dfrac{4.184 \text{ J}}{1 \text{ cal}} \times \dfrac{1 \text{ kJ}}{1000 \text{ J}} = 34 \text{ kJ}$ then

$$15 \text{ g} \times \frac{4.18 \text{ J}}{\text{g °C}} \times 100. \text{ °C} \times \frac{1 \text{ kJ}}{1000 \text{ J}} = 6.3 \text{ kJ then}$$

Total: 34 kJ + 6.3 kJ = 40. kJ (2SF)

d. Three calculations are needed:

Given: 24 g of ice at 0 °C; specific heat = 1.00 cal/g °C; $\Delta T = 100. °C - 0 °C = 100. °C$ to steam

Need: heat (kcal)

Plan: $g \rightarrow cal \rightarrow kcal$ then heat = mass $\times \Delta T \times SH$ then $g \rightarrow cal \rightarrow kcal$ then add energies

$$\frac{80. \text{ cal}}{1 \text{ g}} \quad \frac{1 \text{ kcal}}{1000 \text{ cal}} \quad \frac{540 \text{ cal}}{1 \text{ g}} \quad \frac{1 \text{ kcal}}{1000 \text{ cal}}$$

Set Up: $24 \text{ g of ice} \times \dfrac{80. \text{ cal}}{1 \text{ g of ice}} \times \dfrac{1 \text{ kcal}}{1000 \text{ cal}} = 1.9 \text{ kcal (2SF) then}$

$$24 \text{ g} \times \frac{1.00 \text{ cal}}{\text{g °C}} \times 100. \text{ °C} \times \frac{1 \text{ kcal}}{1000 \text{ cal}} = 2.4 \text{ kcal (2SF) then}$$

$$24 \text{ g of water} \times \frac{540 \text{ cal}}{1 \text{ g of water}} \times \frac{1 \text{ kcal}}{1000 \text{ cal}} = 13 \text{ kcal (2SF) then}$$

Total: 1.9 kcal + 2.4 kcal + 13 kcal = 17 kcal (2SF)

2.53 **a.** 10 °C is warmer since 0 °C = 32 °F.
b. 30 °C is warmer since 0 °C = 32 °F.
c. 32 °F is warmer since 0 °C = 32 °F.
d. 200 °C is warmer since 0 °C = 273 K.

2.55 $1.8(45 °C) + 32 = (81 + 32) °F = 113 °F$ (1.8 and 32 are exact) (3SF) and
$45 °C + 273 = 318 \text{ K (3SF)}$

2.57 **Given:** cheeseburger: 31 g of protein, 29 g of fat, 34 g of carbohydrate; fries: 3 g of protein, 11 g of fat, 26 g of carbohydrate; shake: 11 g of protein, 9 g of fat, 6 g of carbohydrate;

Need: kcal

Plan: total gram of each type then $g \rightarrow kcal$ then total all of the kcal

$$\frac{4 \text{ kcal}}{1 \text{ g of protein}} \quad \frac{9 \text{ kcal}}{1 \text{ g of fat}} \quad \frac{4 \text{ kcal}}{1 \text{ g of carbohydrate}}$$

Set Up: protein = 31 g + 3 g + 11 g = 45 g $\quad 45 \text{ g of protein} \times \dfrac{4 \text{ kcal}}{1 \text{ g of protein}} = 180 \text{ kcal,}$

fat = 29 g + 11 g + 9 g = 49 g. $\quad 49 \text{ g of fat} \times \dfrac{9 \text{ kcal}}{1 \text{ g of fat}} = 441 \text{ kcal, and}$

carbohydrate = 34 g + 26 g + 6 g = 66 g.

$$66 \text{ g of carbohydrate} \times \frac{4 \text{ kcal}}{1 \text{ g of carbohydrate}} = 264 \text{ kcal then}$$

Total: 180 kcal + 441 kcal + 264 kcal = 885 kcal = 890 kcal (rounded)

a. Given: kcal from meal   **Need:** hours of sleeping to burn off

Plan: kcal → h

$$\frac{1\ h}{60\ kcal}$$

Set Up: $890\ kcal \times \dfrac{1\ h}{60\ kcal} = 15\ h$ of sleeping (2SF)

b. Given: kcal from meal   **Need:** hours of running to burn off

Plan: kcal → h

$$\frac{1\ h}{750\ kcal}$$

Set Up: $890\ kcal \times \dfrac{1\ h}{750\ kcal} = 1.2\ h$ of running (2SF)

2.59 Mixtures **b.** and **c.** are not the same throughout and are heterogeneous. Mixture **a.** is homogeneous because it has the same composition everywhere.

2.61 **a.** As perspiration evaporates, it removes heat from the body, cooling the body.
b. Clothes dry more quickly on a hot summer day than on a cold winter day because the temperature is higher. The water molecules have more kinetic energy as the temperature increases. On a hot day, there are more molecules with sufficient energy to become water vapor.

2.63 **a.** $-60\ ^\circ C$
b. $60\ ^\circ C$
c. A represents the solid state. B represents the change from solid to liquid or melting of the substance. C represents the liquid state as temperature increases. D represents the change from liquid to gas or boiling of the liquid. E represents a gas.
d. At $-80\ ^\circ C$, solid; at $-40\ ^\circ C$, liquid; at $25\ ^\circ C$, liquid; at $80\ ^\circ C$, gas.

2.65 Liquid water has a higher specific heat ($1.00\ cal/g\ ^\circ C$) than sand, which means that a large amount of energy is required to cause a significant temperature change. Sand, on the other hand, has a low specific heat ($0.19\ cal/g\ ^\circ C$). Even a small amount of energy will cause a significant temperature change in the sand.

2.67 Both water condensation (formation of rain) and deposition (formation of snow) from the gaseous moisture in the air are exothermic processes (heat is released). The heat released in either of these processes warms the surrounding air, and so the air temperature is in fact raised.

2.69 **a.** $1.8(58.0\ ^\circ C) + 32 = (104 + 32)\ ^\circ F = 136\ ^\circ F$ (1.8 and 32 are exact) (3SF)

b. $1.8(-89.2\ ^\circ C) + 32 = (-161 + 32)\ ^\circ F = -129\ ^\circ F$ (1.8 and 32 are exact) (3SF)

2.71 **Given:** specific heat = 4.184 J/g °C; mass = 883 g; $\Delta T = 27\ ^\circ C - 4\ ^\circ C = 23\ ^\circ C$

Need: heat (kJ)

Plan: heat = mass $\times \Delta T \times SH$ then J → kJ

$$\frac{1\ kJ}{1000\ J}$$

Set Up: $883\ g \times \dfrac{4.184\ J}{g\ ^\circ C} \times 23\ ^\circ C \times \dfrac{1\ kJ}{1000\ J} = 85\ kJ$ (2SF)

2.73   **a. Given:**   1200 kcal diet, 15% calories from protein, 45% calories from carbohydrates

Need: g of protein, g of carbohydrate, and g of fat

Plan: kcal diet → kcal food type → g food type

$$\frac{15 \text{ kcal of protein}}{1 \text{ kcal of diet}} \quad \frac{45 \text{ kcal of carbohydrate}}{1 \text{ kcal of diet}} \quad \frac{40 \text{ kcal of fat}}{1 \text{ kcal of diet}} \quad \frac{1 \text{ g of protein}}{4 \text{ kcal}} \quad \frac{1 \text{ g of carbohydrate}}{4 \text{ kcal}} \quad \frac{1 \text{ g of fat}}{9 \text{ kcal}}$$

Set Up: $1200 \text{ kcal of diet} \times \dfrac{15 \text{ kcal of protein}}{100 \text{ kcal of diet}} \times \dfrac{1 \text{ g of protein}}{4 \text{ kcal of protein}} = 45 \text{ g of protein,}$

$1200 \text{ kcal of diet} \times \dfrac{45 \text{ kcal of carbohydrate}}{100 \text{ kcal of diet}} \times \dfrac{1 \text{ g of carbohydrate}}{4 \text{ kcal of carbohydrate}} = 140 \text{ g of carbohydrate,}$

and $2600 \text{ kcal of diet} \times \dfrac{40 \text{ kcal of fat}}{100 \text{ kcal of diet}} \times \dfrac{1 \text{ g of fat}}{9 \text{ kcal of fat}} = 120 \text{ g of fat (2SF)}$

b. Given: 1900 kcal diet, 15% calories from protein, 45% calories from carbohydrates

Need: g of protein, g of carbohydrates, and g of fat

Plan: kcal diet → kcal food type → g food type

$$\frac{15 \text{ kcal of protein}}{1 \text{ kcal of diet}} \quad \frac{45 \text{ kcal of carbohydrate}}{1 \text{ kcal of diet}} \quad \frac{40 \text{ kcal of fat}}{1 \text{ kcal of diet}} \quad \frac{1 \text{ g of protein}}{4 \text{ kcal}} \quad \frac{1 \text{ g of carbohydrate}}{4 \text{ kcal}} \quad \frac{1 \text{ g of fat}}{9 \text{ kcal}}$$

Set Up: $1900 \text{ kcal of diet} \times \dfrac{15 \text{ kcal of protein}}{100 \text{ kcal of diet}} \times \dfrac{1 \text{ g of protein}}{4 \text{ kcal of protein}} = 71 \text{ g of protein,}$

$1900 \text{ kcal of diet} \times \dfrac{45 \text{ kcal of carbohydrate}}{100 \text{ kcal of diet}} \times \dfrac{1 \text{ g of carbohydrate}}{4 \text{ kcal of carbohydrate}} = 210 \text{ g of carbohydrate,}$

and $1900 \text{ kcal of diet} \times \dfrac{40 \text{ kcal of fat}}{100 \text{ kcal of diet}} \times \dfrac{1 \text{ g of fat}}{9 \text{ kcal of fat}} = 84 \text{ g of fat (2SF)}$

c. Given: 2600 kcal diet, 15% calories from protein, 45% calories from carbohydrates

Need: g of protein, g of carbohydrate, and g of fat

Plan: kcal diet → kcal food type → g food type

$$\frac{15 \text{ kcal of protein}}{1 \text{ kcal of diet}} \quad \frac{45 \text{ kcal of carbohydrate}}{1 \text{ kcal of diet}} \quad \frac{40 \text{ kcal of fat}}{1 \text{ kcal of diet}} \quad \frac{1 \text{ g of protein}}{4 \text{ kcal}} \quad \frac{1 \text{ g of carbohydrate}}{4 \text{ kcal}} \quad \frac{1 \text{ g of fat}}{9 \text{ kcal}}$$

Set Up: $2600 \text{ kcal of diet} \times \dfrac{15 \text{ kcal of protein}}{100 \text{ kcal of diet}} \times \dfrac{1 \text{ g of protein}}{4 \text{ kcal of protein}} = 98 \text{ g of protein,}$

$2600 \text{ kcal of diet} \times \dfrac{45 \text{ kcal of carbohydrate}}{100 \text{ kcal of diet}} \times \dfrac{1 \text{ g of carbohydrate}}{4 \text{ kcal of carbohydrate}} = 290 \text{ g of carbohydrate,}$

and $2600 \text{ kcal of diet} \times \dfrac{40 \text{ kcal of fat}}{100 \text{ kcal of diet}} \times \dfrac{1 \text{ g of fat}}{9 \text{ kcal of fat}} = 120 \text{ g of fat (2SF)}$

2.75 **Given:** 1 lb of body fat; 15% (m/m) water in body fat   **Need:**   kcal to burn off

Plan: Because each gram of body fat contains 15% water, a person actually loses 85 grams of fat per hundred grams of body fat. (We considered 1 lb of fat as exactly 1 lb.)

$$\text{lb body fat} \rightarrow \text{g body fat} \rightarrow \text{g fat} \rightarrow \text{kcal}$$

$$\frac{454 \text{ g of body fat}}{1 \text{ lb of body fat}} \quad \frac{85 \text{ g of fat}}{100 \text{ g of body fat}} \quad \frac{9 \text{ kcal}}{1 \text{ g of fat}}$$

Set Up: $1 \text{ lb of body fat} \times \dfrac{454 \text{ g of body fat}}{1 \text{ lb of body fat}} \times \dfrac{85 \text{ g of fat}}{100 \text{ g of body fat}} \times \dfrac{9 \text{ kcal}}{1 \text{ g of fat}} = 3500 \text{ kcal (2SF)}$

2.77 **a.** Popcorn in a bag is a solid.   **b.** Water in a garden hose is a liquid.
c. A computer mouse is a solid.   **d.** Air in a tire is a gas.
e. Hot tea is a liquid.

2.79

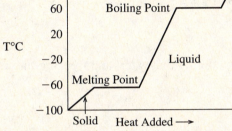

a. Chloroform is a solid at −75 °C.
b. At −64 °C the solid melts.
c. Chloroform is a liquid at −18 °C.
d. Chloroform is a gas at 80 °C.
e. Both solid and liquid will be present at 61 °C.

2.81 **Given:** specific heat = 1.00 cal/g °C; mass = 725 g; $\Delta T = 65\,°C - 37\,°C = 28\,°C$

Need: heat (kcal)

Plan: heat = mass × ΔT × SH then cal → kcal

$$\frac{1 \text{ kcal}}{1000 \text{ cal}}$$

Set Up: $725 \text{ g} \times \dfrac{1.00 \text{ cal}}{\text{g °C}} \times 28\,°C \times \dfrac{1 \text{ kcal}}{1000 \text{ cal}} = 20. \text{ kcal (2SF)}$

2.83 **Given:** 45 g of steam condensing; specific heat = 1.00 cal/g °C; $\Delta T = 100.\,°C - 15\,°C = 85\,°C$

Need: heat (kcal)

Plan: g → cal then heat = mass × ΔT × SH then add energies cal → kcal

$$\frac{540 \text{ cal}}{1 \text{ g}} \quad \frac{1 \text{ kcal}}{1000 \text{ cal}}$$

Set Up: $45 \text{ g of steam} \times \dfrac{540 \text{ cal}}{1 \text{ g of steam}} = 24\,000 \text{ cal or } 2.4 \times 10^4 \text{ cal then}$

$45 \text{ g} \times \dfrac{1.00 \text{ cal}}{\text{g °C}} \times 85\,°C = 3800 \text{ cal or } 3.8 \times 10^3 \text{ cal then}$

Total : $24\,000 \text{ cal} + 3800 \text{ cal} = 28\,000 \text{ cal or } 2.8 \times 10^4 \text{ cal then}$

$28\,000 \text{ cal} \times \dfrac{1 \text{ kcal}}{1000 \text{ cal}} = 28 \text{ kcal (2SF)}$

2.85 **Given:** alloy: mass = 25 g; ΔT = 98 °C − 27 °C = 71 °C

water: specific heat = 1.00 cal/g °C; mass = 50. g; ΔT = 27 °C − 15 °C = 12 °C

Need: specific heat of alloy (cal/g °C)

Plan: The heat lost by the alloy is gained by the water. Calculate the heat lost by the water using heat = mass × ΔT × SH and use to calculate the specific heat of the alloy.

$$SH = \frac{\text{heat}}{\text{mass} \times \Delta T}$$

Set Up: water: 50. g × 12 °C × $\dfrac{1.00 \text{ cal}}{\text{g °C}}$ = 600 cal (6.0 × 10^2 cal)(2SF) then

alloy: specific heat = $\dfrac{600 \text{ cal}}{(25 \text{ g})(71 °C)}$ = 0.34 cal/g °C (2SF)

2.87 **Given:** 35.0 g of steam condensing; specific heat = 4.184 J/g °C; ΔT = 100. °C − 0 °C = 100. °C

Need: heat (kJ)

Plan: Three steps are needed: condensing the steam; cooling the water; and freezing the water.

$$\frac{2260 \text{ J}}{1 \text{ g}} \quad \frac{334 \text{ J}}{1 \text{ g}} \quad \frac{1 \text{ kJ}}{1000 \text{ J}}$$

Set Up: condense steam: 35.0 g × $\dfrac{2260 \text{ J}}{\text{g}}$ = 79 100 J;

cool water: 35.0 g × 100 °C × $\dfrac{4.184 \text{ J}}{\text{g °C}}$ = 14 600 J;

freeze water: 35.0 g × $\dfrac{334 \text{ J}}{1 \text{ g}}$ = 11 700 J

Total: 79 100 J + 14 600 J + 11 700 J = 105 400 J (to 100s place)

105 400 J × $\dfrac{1 \text{ kJ}}{1000 \text{ J}}$ = 105.4 kJ

2.89 **a. Given:** specific heat = 4.184 J/g °C; heat = 8250 J; ΔT = 92.6 °C − 18.3 °C = 74.3 °C

Need: mass (g)

Plan: heat = mass × ΔT × SH divide both sides of the equation by ΔT × SH to get

mass = $\dfrac{\text{heat}}{\Delta T \times SH}$

Set Up: $\dfrac{8250 \text{ J}}{74.3 \text{ °C} \times \dfrac{4.184 \text{ J}}{\text{g °C}}}$ = 26.5 g (3SF)

b. Given: specific heat = 0.129 J/g °C; heat = 225 J; ΔT = 47.0 °C − 15.0 °C = 32.0 °C

Need: mass (g)

Plan: heat = mass × ΔT × SH divide both sides of the equation by ΔT × SH to get

$$mass = \frac{heat}{\Delta T \times SH}$$

Set Up: $\dfrac{225\ \cancel{J}}{32.0\ \cancel{°C} \times \dfrac{0.129\ \cancel{J}}{g\ \cancel{°C}}} = 54.5\ g\ (3SF)$

c. Given: specific heat = 0.452 J/g °C; heat = 1580 J; mass = 20.0 g

Need: ΔT

Plan: heat = mass × ΔT × SH divide both sides of the equation by mass × SH to get

$$\Delta T = \frac{heat}{mass \times SH}$$

Set Up: $\dfrac{1580\ \cancel{J}}{20.0\ \cancel{g} \times \dfrac{0.452\ \cancel{J}}{\cancel{g}\ °C}} = 175\ °C\ (3SF)$

d. Given: heat = 28 cal; mass = 8.50 g; ΔT = 24 °C − 12 °C = 12 °C

Need: specific heat (cal/g °C)

Plan: $SH = \dfrac{heat}{mass \times \Delta T}$

Set Up: Specific Heat $(SH) = \dfrac{28\ cal}{8.50\ g \times 12\ °C} = \dfrac{0.27\ cal}{g\ °C}\ (2SF)$

2.91 Given: lead: mass = 3.0 kg; specific heat = 0.13 J/g °C; ΔT = 300. °C − 0 °C = 300. °C

Need: mass of ice melted (g)

Plan: The heat lost by the lead is gained by the ice. Calculate the heat lost by the lead using
kg → g and heat = mass × ΔT × SH = heat gained by the ice J → cal → g

$$\frac{1000\ g}{1\ kg} \quad \frac{1\ cal}{4.184\ J} \quad \frac{1\ g}{80.\ cal}$$

Set Up: $3.0\ \cancel{kg} \times \dfrac{1000\ \cancel{g}}{1\ \cancel{kg}} \times \dfrac{0.13\ J}{\cancel{g}\ \cancel{°C}} \times 300.\ \cancel{°C} = 117000\ J$ (not rounded) available to melt ice

$117000\ \cancel{J} \times \dfrac{1\ \cancel{cal}}{4.184\ \cancel{J}} \times \dfrac{1\ g}{80.\ \cancel{cal}} = 350\ g$ of ice (2SF)

Answers to Combining Ideas from Chapters 1 and 2

CI.1 **a.** There are 4 significant figures in 20.17 lb.

b. $20.17 \text{ lb} \times \dfrac{1 \text{ kg}}{2.20 \text{ lb}} = 9.17 \text{ kg (3SF)}$

c. $9.17 \text{ kg} \times \dfrac{1000 \text{ g}}{1 \text{ kg}} \times \dfrac{1 \text{ cm}^3}{19.3 \text{ g}} = 475 \text{ cm}^3 \text{ (3SF)}$

d. $1.8(1064 \text{ °C}) + 32 \text{ °C} = 1947 \text{ °F (4SF)}$

$1064 \text{ °C} + 273 = 1337 \text{ K (4SF)}$

e. $\Delta T = T_{\text{final}} - T_{\text{initial}} = 1064 \text{ °C} - 500. \text{ °C} = 564 \text{ °C} = \text{temperature change}$

$9.17 \text{ kg} \times \dfrac{1000 \text{ g}}{1 \text{ kg}} \times \dfrac{0.129 \text{ J}}{\text{g °C}} \times 564 \text{ °C} \times \dfrac{1 \text{ kJ}}{1000 \text{ J}} = 667 \text{ kJ to raise the temperature}$

$9.17 \text{ kg} \times \dfrac{1000 \text{ g}}{1 \text{ kg}} \times \dfrac{63.6 \text{ J}}{\text{g}} \times \dfrac{1 \text{ kJ}}{1000 \text{ J}} = 583 \text{ kJ to melt}$

Total energy = 667 kJ + 583 kJ = 1250. kJ (4SF)

$1250. \text{ kJ} \times \dfrac{1 \text{ kcal}}{4.184 \text{ kJ}} = 298.8 \text{ kcal (4SF)}$

f. $9.17 \text{ kg} \times \dfrac{1000 \text{ g}}{1 \text{ kg}} \times \dfrac{1 \text{ ozt}}{31.1 \text{ g}} \times \dfrac{\$895}{1 \text{ ozt}} = \$2.64 \times 10^5 = \$264\,000 \text{ (3SF)}$

CI.3 **a.** Sample B has its own shape.

b. The volumes of both A and B remain the same.

c. A is liquid water represented by diagram 2. In liquid water, the water particles are in a random arrangement, but close together. B is solid water represented by diagram 1. In solid water, the water particles are fixed in a definite arrangement.

d. freezing; freezing point; 0 °C; physical; melting; melting point; 0 °C; physical

e. The solid water particles break apart from their fixed arrangement to have a more random arrangement, but they are still close together.

f. $\Delta T = T_{\text{final}} - T_{\text{initial}} = 45 \text{ °C} - 0 \text{ °C} = 45 \text{ °C temperature change}$

$19.8 \text{ g} \times 45 \text{ °C} \times \dfrac{4.184 \text{ J}}{\text{g °C}} = 3700 \text{ J to lower the temperature}$

$19.8 \text{ g} \times \dfrac{80. \text{ cal}}{1 \text{ g}} \times \dfrac{4.184 \text{ J}}{1 \text{ cal}} = 6600 \text{ J to freeze}$

Total = 3700 J + 6600 J = 10 300 J (3SF)

CI.5 **a.** $0.250 \text{ lb} \times \dfrac{454 \text{ g}}{1 \text{ lb}} \times \dfrac{1 \text{ cm}^3}{7.86 \text{ g}} = 14.4 \text{ cm}^3 \text{ (2SF)}$

b. $30 \text{ nails} \times \dfrac{14.4 \text{ cm}^3}{75 \text{ nails}} = 5.76 \text{ cm}^3 \text{ (2SF)}$

17.6 mL water + 5.76 mL = 2.34 mL new water level (3SF)

c. $125 \text{ °C} - 16 \text{ °C} = 109 \text{ °C} = \text{temperature change}$

$0.250 \text{ lb} \times \dfrac{454 \text{ g}}{1 \text{ lb}} \times 109 \text{ °C} \times \dfrac{0.450 \text{ J}}{\text{g °C}} = 5570 \text{ J or } 5.57 \times 10^3 \text{ J (3SF)}$

3.1   **a.** Cu is the symbol for copper.   **b.** Si is the symbol for silicon.
     c. K is the symbol for potassium.   **d.** N is the symbol for nitrogen.
     e. Fe is the symbol for iron.   **f.** Ba is the symbol for barium.
     g. Pb is the symbol for lead.   **h.** Sr is the symbol for strontium.

3.3   **a.** Carbon is the element with the symbol C.   **b.** Chlorine is the element with the symbol Cl.
     c. Iodine is the element with the symbol I.   **d.** Mercury is the element with the symbol Hg.
     e. Fluorine is the element with the symbol F.   **f.** Argon is the element with the symbol Ar.
     g. Zinc is the element with the symbol Zn.   **h.** Nickel is the element with the symbol Ni.

3.5   **a.** Sodium (Na) and chlorine (Cl) are in NaCl.
     b. Calcium (Ca), sulfur (S), and oxygen (O) are in $CaSO_4$.
     c. Carbon (C), hydrogen (H), chlorine (Cl), nitrogen (N), and oxygen (O) are in $C_{15}H_{22}ClNO_2$.
     d. Calcium (Ca), carbon (C), and oxygen (O) are in $CaCO_3$.

3.7   **a.** C, N, and O are in Period 2.
     b. He is the element at the top of Group 8A (18).
     c. The alkali metals are the elements in Group 1A (1).
     d. Period 2 is the horizontal row of elements that ends with neon (Ne).

3.9   **a.** Ca is an alkaline earth metal.   **b.** Fe is a transition element.
     c. Xe is a noble gas.   **d.** Na is an alkali metal.
     e. Cl is a halogen.

3.11   **a.** C is Group 4A, Period 2.   **b.** He is a noble gas in Period 1.
     c. Na is an alkali metal in Period 3.   **d.** Ca is Group 2, Period 4.
     e. Al is Group 13, Period 3.

3.13   On the periodic table, *metals* are located to the left of the heavy zigzag line, *nonmetals* are elements to the right, and metalloids B, Si, Ge, As, Sb, Te, Po, and At are located along the line.
     a. Ca is a metal.   **b.** S is a nonmetal.
     c. Metals are shiny.   **d.** Nonmetals do not conduct heat.
     e. Group 8A elements are nonmetals.   **f.** P is a nonmetal.
     g. B is a metalloid.   **h.** Ag is a metal.

3.15   **a.** The electron has the smallest mass.   **b.** The proton has a 1+ charge.
     c. The electron is found outside the nucleus.   **d.** The neutron is electrically neutral.

3.17   Rutherford determined that positively charged particles called protons are located in a very small, dense region of the atoms called the nucleus.

3.19   All of the statements are true except for selection **d.** A proton is attracted to an electron, not to a neutron.

3.21   Your hair is more likely to fly away on a dry day; because the hair strands repel one another, there must be like electrical charges on each strand.

3.23   **a.** The atomic number is the same as the number of protons in an atom.
     b. Both are needed since the number of neutrons is the mass number minus the atomic number.
     c. The mass number is the number of particles in the nucleus.
     d. The atomic number is the same as the number of electrons in a neutral atom.

3.25 The atomic number defines the element and is found above the symbol of the element in the periodic table.

    a. Lithium, Li, has an atomic number of 3.   **b.** Fluorine, F, has an atomic number of 9.

    c. Calcium, Ca, has an atomic number of 20.   **d.** Zinc, Zn, has an atomic number of 30.

    e. Neon, Ne, has an atomic number of 10.   **f.** Silicon, Si, has an atomic number of 14.

    g. Iodine, I, has an atomic number of 53.   **h.** Oxygen, O, has an atomic number of 8.

3.27 The number of protons in an atom is the same as the atomic number.

    a. There are 12 protons in a magnesium atom.   **b.** There are 30 protons in a zinc atom.

    c. There are 53 protons in an iodine atom.   **d.** There are 19 protons in a potassium atom.

3.29 The atomic number is the same as the number of protons in an atom and the number of electrons in a neutral atom; the atomic number defines the element. The number of neutrons is the (mass number) − (atomic number).

Name of Element	Symbol	Atomic Number	Mass Number	Number of Protons	Number of Neutrons	Number of Electrons
Aluminum	Al	13	27	13	$27 - 13 = 14$	13
Magnesium	Mg	12	$12 + 12 = 24$	12	12	12
Potassium	K	19	$19 + 20 = 39$	19	20	19
Sulfur	S	16	$16 + 15 = 31$	16	15	16
Iron	Fe	26	56	26	$56 - 26 = 30$	26

3.31   **a.** Since the atomic number of silicon is 14, every Si atom has 14 protons. An atom of silicon (mass number 30) has 16 neutrons ($30 - 14 = 16$ n). Neutral atoms have the same number of protons and electrons. Therefore, 14 protons, 16 neutrons, 14 electrons.

    b. Since the atomic number of cobalt is 27, every Co atom has 27 protons. An atom of cobalt (mass number 60) has 33 neutrons ($60 - 27 = 33$ n). Neutral atoms have the same number of protons and electrons. Therefore, 27 protons, 33 neutrons, 27 electrons.

    c. Since the atomic number of selenium is 34, every Se atom has 34 protons. An atom of selenium (mass number 80) has 46 neutrons ($80 - 34 = 46$ n). Neutral atoms have the same number of protons and electrons. Therefore, 34 protons, 46 neutrons, 34 electrons.

    d. Since the atomic number of fluorine is 9, every F atom has 9 protons. An atom of fluorine (mass number 19) has 10 neutrons ($19 - 9 = 10$ n). Neutral atoms have the same number of protons and electrons. Therefore, 9 protons, 10 neutrons, 9 electrons.

3.33   **a.** Since the number of protons is 15, the atomic number is 15 and the element symbol is P. The mass number is the sum of the number of protons and the number of neutrons, $15 + 16 = 31$. The symbol for this isotope is $^{31}_{15}P$.

    b. Since the number of protons is 35, the atomic number is 35 and the element symbol is Br. The mass number is the sum of the number of protons and the number of neutrons, $35 + 45 = 80$. The symbol for this isotope is $^{80}_{35}Br$.

    c. Since the number of electrons is 13, there must be 13 protons in a neutral atom. Since the number of protons is 13, the atomic number is 13 and the element symbol is Al. The mass number is the sum of the number of protons and the number of neutrons, $13 + 14 = 27$. The symbol for this isotope is $^{27}_{13}Al$.

    d. Since the element is chlorine, the element symbol is Cl, atomic number is 17, and the number of protons is 17. The mass number is the sum of the number of protons and the number of neutrons, $17 + 18 = 35$. The symbol for this isotope is $^{35}_{17}Cl$.

    e. Since the element is mercury, the element symbol is Hg; the atomic number, and the number of protons, is 80. The mass number is the sum of the number of protons and the number of neutrons, $80 + 122 = 202$. The symbol for this isotope is $^{202}_{80}Hg$.

3.35 **a.** Since element is sulfur, the element symbol is S, the atomic number is 16, and the number of protons is 16. The symbols for the isotopes with mass numbers of 32, 33, 34, and 36, are $^{32}_{16}$S, $^{33}_{16}$S, $^{34}_{16}$S, and $^{36}_{16}$S, respectively.

b. They all have the same atomic number (the same number of protons and electrons).

c. They have different numbers of neutrons, which is reflected in their mass numbers.

d. The atomic mass of sulfur on the periodic table is the weighted average atomic mass of all the naturally occurring isotopes of sulfur.

e. Since the average atomic mass of S is 32.07 amu, the isotope with a mass number of 32$\left(^{32}_{16}S\right)$ is the most abundant.

3.37 Since the atomic mass of copper is closer to 63 amu, there are more atoms of $^{63}_{29}$Cu.

3.39 $^{69}_{31}$Ga $68.93 \times \dfrac{60.11}{100} = 41.43$ amu

$^{71}_{31}$Ga $70.92 \times \dfrac{39.89}{100} = 28.29$ amu

Atomic mass of Ga $= \overline{69.72}$ amu   (4SF)

3.41 **a.** A 1*s* orbital is spherical.   **b.** A 2*p* orbital has two lobes.

c. A 5*s* orbital is spherical.

3.43 **a.** All *s* orbitals are spherical.

b. A 3*s* sublevel and a 3*p* sublevel are in the energy level $n = 3$.

c. All *p* sublevels contain three *p* orbitals.

d. The 3*p* orbitals all have two lobes and are in energy level $n = 3$.

3.45 **a.** There are five orbitals in the 3*d* sublevel.

b. There is one sublevel in the $n = 1$ principal energy level: 1*s*.

c. There is one orbital in the 6*s* sublevel.

d. There are nine orbitals in the $n = 3$ energy level: one 3*s* orbital, three 3*p* orbitals, and five 3*d* orbitals.

3.47 **a.** Any orbital can hold a maximum of two electrons. Thus, a 2*p* orbital can hold a maximum of two electrons.

b. The 3*p* sublevel contains three *p* orbitals, each of which can hold a maximum of two electrons, which gives a maximum of six electrons in the 3*p* sublevel.

c. Using $2n^2$, the calculation for the maximum number of electrons in the $n = 4$ energy level is $2(4)^2 = 2(16) = 32$ electrons.

d. The 5*d* sublevel contains five *d* orbitals, each of which can hold a maximum of two electrons, which gives a maximum of 10 electrons in the 5*d* sublevel.

3.49 Determine the number of electrons and then fill orbitals in the following order: $1s^2 2s^2 2p^6 3s^2 3p^6$

a. Boron is atomic number 5 and so it has 5 electrons. Fill orbitals as

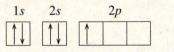

b. Aluminum is atomic number 13 and so it has 13 electrons. Fill orbitals as

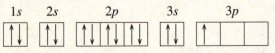

c. Phosphorus is atomic number 15 and so it has 15 electrons. Fill orbitals as

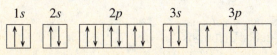

d. Argon is atomic number 18 and so it has 18 electrons. Fill orbitals as

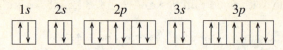

3.51 Determine the number of electrons and then fill orbitals in the following order: $1s^2 2s^2 2p^6 3s^2 3p^6 4s^2 3d^{10} 4p^6$.

    a. Nitrogen (N) is atomic number 7 and so it has 7 electrons. Fill orbitals as $1s^2 2s^2 2p^3$.

    b. Sodium (Na) is atomic number 11 and so it has 11 electrons. Fill orbitals as $1s^2 2s^2 2p^6 3s^1$.

    c. Sulfur (S) is atomic number 16 and so it has 16 electrons. Fill orbitals as $1s^2 2s^2 2p^6 3s^2 3p$.

    d. Arsenic (As) is atomic number 33 and so it has 33 electrons. Fill orbitals as $1s^2 2s^2 2p^6 3s^2 3p^6 4s^2\, 3d^{10} 4p^3$.

    e. Iron (Fe) is atomic number 26 and so it has 26 electrons. Fill orbitals as $1s^2 2s^2 2p^6 3s^2 3p^6 4s^2 3d^6$.

3.53 Determine the number of electrons and then fill orbitals in the following order: $1s^2 2s^2 2p^6 3s^2 3p^6 4s^2\, 3d^{10} 4p^6$. The abbreviated electron configuration consists of the symbol of the preceding noble gas followed by the electron configuration in the next period: $[\text{He}] = 1s^2$ (2 electrons) and $[\text{Ne}] = 1s^2 2s^2 2p^6$ (10 electrons), $[\text{Ar}] = 1s^2 2s^2 2p^6 3s^2 3p^6$ (18 electrons), $[\text{Kr}] = 1s^2 2s^2 2p^6 3s^2 3p^6 4s^2 3d^{10} 4p^6$ (36 electrons), and $[\text{Xe}] = 1s^2 2s^2 2p^6 3s^2 3p^6 4s^2 3d^{10} 4p^6 5s^2 4d^{10} 5p^6$ (54 electrons).

    a. Magnesium (Mg) is atomic number 12 and so it has 12 electrons. There are 2 electrons beyond [Ne], so the abbreviated configuration is $[\text{Ne}]3s^2$.

    b. Sulfur (S) is atomic number 16 and so it has 16 electrons. There are 6 electrons beyond [Ne], so the abbreviated configuration is $[\text{Ne}]3s^2 3p^4$.

    c. Aluminum (Al) is atomic number 13 and so it has 13 electrons. There are 3 electrons beyond [Ne], so the abbreviated configuration is $[\text{Ne}]3s^2 3p^1$.

    d. Titanium (Ti) is atomic number 22 and so it has 22 electrons. There are 4 electrons beyond [Ar], so the abbreviated configuration is $[\text{Ar}]4s^2 3d^2$.

    e. Barium (Ba) is atomic number 56 and so it has 56 electrons. There are 2 electrons beyond [Xe], so the abbreviated configuration is $[\text{Xe}]6s^2$.

3.55 Count the electrons in the electron configuration. This number of electrons is the same as the atomic number of the element.

    a. There are 16 electrons in the electron configuration $(2 + 2 + 6 + 2 + 4 = 16)$. S has two electrons in the 3s and four electrons in the 3p sublevels.

    b. There are 27 electrons in the electron configuration $(2 + 2 + 6 + 2 + 6 + 2 + 7 = 27)$. Co (ends in $3d^7$).

    c. There are 14 electrons in the electron configuration $(10 + 2 + 2 = 14)$. Si has two electrons in the 3s and two electrons in the 3p sublevels.

    d. There are 36 electrons in the electron configuration $(18 + 2 + 10 + 5 = 36)$. Br (ends in $4p^5$).

3.57 **a.** Al has three electrons in the third energy level: $3s^2 3p^1$.

    b. C has two 2p electrons.

    c. Ar completes the 3p sublevel: $3p^6$.

    d. Zr has two 4d electrons.

3.59 **a.** Zn is the tenth element in the 3d block; it has ten 3d electrons.

    b. Na has an electron in the 3s block; the 2p block in Na is complete with six electrons.

    c. As is the third element in the 4p block; it has three 4p electrons.

    d. Rb is the first element in the 5s block; Rb has one 5s electron.

3.61 **a.** An element with two valence electrons is in Group 2A (2).

    b. An element with five valence electrons is in Group 5A (15).

    c. An element with six valence electrons is in Group 6A (16).

3.63 **a.** Aluminum in Group 3A (13) has three valence electrons.

    b. Any element in Group 5A (15) has five valence electrons.

    c. Each halogen in Group 7A (17) has seven valence electrons.

3.65 The number of dots is equal to the number of valence electrons, as indicated by the group number.

    a. Sulfur has six valence electrons: $\cdot \overset{\cdot\cdot}{\underset{\cdot\cdot}{S}} :$; Group 6a (16)

    b. Nitrogen has five valence electrons: $\cdot \overset{\cdot\cdot}{N} \cdot$; Group 5A (15)

    c. Calcium has two valence electrons: $\overset{\cdot}{Ca}\cdot$; Group 2A (2)

    d. Sodium has one valence electron: $Na \cdot$; Group 1A (1)

    e. Barium has two valence electrons: $\cdot Ba \cdot$; Group 2A (2)

3.67   **a.** Group 1A (1) elements have one valence electron $M \cdot$
    b. Group 2A (2) elements have two valence electrons $\cdot M \cdot$

3.69   **a.** The atomic radius of representative elements decreases from Group 1A (1) to 8A (18): Mg, Al, Si.
    b. The atomic radius of representative elements increases going down a group: I, Br, Cl.
    c. The atomic radius of representative elements decreases from Group 1A (1) to 8A (18): Sr, Sb, I.

3.71 The atomic radius of representative elements decreases going across a period from Group 1A (1) to 8A (18) and increases going down a group.
    a. In Period 3, Na, which is on the left, is larger than Cl.
    b. In Group 1A (1), Rb, which is farther down the group, is larger than Na.
    c. In Period 3, Na, which is on the left, is larger than Mg.

3.73   **a.** The ionization energy decreases going down a group: Br, Cl, F.
    b. Going across a period from left to right, the ionization energy generally increases: Na, Al, Cl.
    c. The ionization energy decreases going down a group: Cs, K, Na.

3.75   **a.** Br, which is above I in Group 7A (17), has a higher ionization energy than I.
    b. Ionization energy increases from Group 2A (2) to Group 6A (16), which gives S a higher ionization energy than Mg.
    c. Ionization energy increases from Group 4A (14) to Group 5A (15), which gives P a higher ionization energy than Si.

3.77 Statements **b.** and **c.** are true. According to Dalton's atomic theory, atoms of an element are different than atoms of other elements, and atoms do not appear and disappear in a chemical reaction.

3.79   **a.** The weighted average of the sum of the number of protons (1) and the number of neutrons (2) in the atoms of an element is the atomic mass.
    b. The number of protons (1) is the atomic number.
    c. The protons (1) are positively charged.
    d. The electrons (3) are negatively charged.
    e. The number of neutrons (2) is the mass number − atomic number.

3.81   **a.** $^{16}_{8}X$, $^{17}_{8}X$, and $^{18}_{8}X$ all have eight protons.

    b. $^{16}_{8}X$, $^{17}_{8}X$, and $^{18}_{8}X$ are all isotopes of oxygen.

    c. $^{16}_{8}X$ and $^{16}_{9}X$ have mass number 16, whereas $^{18}_{8}X$ and $^{18}_{10}X$ have mass number 18.

    d. $^{16}_{8}X$ (16 − 8 = 8) and $^{18}_{10}X$ (18 − 10 = 8) both have eight neutrons.

3.83   **a.** Mg, magnesium is in Group 2A, Period 3.   **b.** Br, bromine is in Group 7A, Period 4.
    c. Al, aluminum is in Group 13, Period 3.   **d.** O, oxygen is in Group 16, Period 2.

3.85   **a.** False. A proton has a positive charge.
    b. False. The neutron has about the same mass as a proton.
    c. True.
    d. False. The nucleus is the tiny, dense central core of an atom.
    e. True.

3.87 **a.** Since the atomic number of aluminum is 13, every Al atom has 13 protons. An atom of aluminum (mass number 27) has 14 neutrons ($27 - 13 = 14$ n). Neutral atoms have the same number of protons and electrons. Therefore, 13 protons, 14 neutrons, 13 electrons.

b. Since the atomic number of chromium is 24, every Cr atom has 24 protons. An atom of chromium (mass number 52) has 28 neutrons ($52 - 24 = 28$ n). Neutral atoms have the same number of protons and electrons. Therefore, 24 protons, 28 neutrons, 24 electrons.

c. Since the atomic number of sulfur is 16, every S atom has 16 protons. An atom of sulfur (mass number 34) has 18 neutrons ($34 - 16 = 18$ n). Neutral atoms have the same number of protons and electrons. Therefore, 16 protons, 18 neutrons, 16 electrons.

d. Since the atomic number of iron is 26, every Fe atom has 26 protons. An atom of iron (mass number 56) has 30 neutrons ($56 - 26 = 30$ n). Neutral atoms have the same number of protons and electrons. Therefore, 26 protons, 30 neutrons, 26 electrons.

e. Since the atomic number of xenon is 54, every Xe atom has 54 protons. An atom of xenon (mass number 136) has 82 neutrons ($136 - 54 = 82$ n). Neutral atoms have the same number of protons and electrons. Therefore, 54 protons, 82 neutrons, 54 electrons.

3.89

Name	Nuclear Symbol	Number of Protons	Number of Neutrons	Number of Electrons
Sulfur	$^{34}_{16}S$	16	$34 - 16 = 18$	16
Zinc	$^{30+40}_{30}Zn$ or $^{70}_{30}Zn$	30	40	30
Magnesium	$^{12+14}_{12}Mg$ or $^{26}_{12}Mg$	12	14	12
Radon	$^{220}_{86}Rn$	86	$220 - 86 = 134$	86

3.91 **a.** On the periodic table, the $3p$ sublevel block follows the $3s$ sublevel block.
b. On the periodic table, the $5s$ sublevel block follows the $4p$ sublevel block.
c. On the periodic table, the $4p$ sublevel block follows the $3d$ sublevel block.
d. On the periodic table, the $4s$ sublevel block follows the $3p$ sublevel block.

3.93 **a.** Iron is the sixth element in the $3d$ block; iron has six $3d$ electrons.
b. Barium has a completely filled $5p$ sublevel, which is six $5p$ electrons.
c. Iodine has a completely filled $4d$ sublevel, which is ten $4d$ electrons.
d. Barium has a filled $6s$ sublevel or $6s$ block, which is two $6s$ electrons.

3.95 Ca, Sr, and Ba all have two valence electrons, ns^2, which places them in Group 2A (2).

3.97 **a.** Phosphorus, in Group 5A (15), has an electron configuration that ends with $3s^23p^3$.
b. Lithium is the alkali metal that is highest in Group 1A (1) and has the smallest atomic radius. [H in Group 1A (1) is a nonmetal.]
c. Cadmium in Period 5 has a complete $4d$ sublevel with 10 electrons.
d. Nitrogen, at the top of Group 5A (15), has the highest ionization energy in that group.
e. Sodium, the first element in Period 3, has the largest atomic radius of that period.

3.99 Calcium has a greater net nuclear charge than K, so Ca has a higher ionization energy than K. The least-tightly-bound electron in Ca is farther from the nucleus than in Mg and needs less energy to remove.

3.101 **a.** Na is on the far left of the heavy zigzag line; Na is a metal.
b. Na, at the beginning of Period 3, has the largest atomic radius.
c. F, at the top of Group 7A (17) and to the far right in Period 2, has the highest ionization energy.
d. Na has the lowest ionization energy and loses an electron most easily.
e. Cl is found in Period 3 in Group 7A (17).

3.103   **a.** K and Mg are on the far left of the heavy zigzag line; K and Mg are metals.
  b. Si is on the heavy zigzag line; Si is a metalloid.
  c. K is in Group 1A (1); K is an alkali metal.
  d. Atomic size decreases towards the right and top of the periodic table so, Ar is the smallest atom.
  e. S has an electron arrangement $1s^2 2s^2 2p^6 3s^2 3p^4$.

3.105   **a.** Since the atomic number of iron is 26, every Fe atom has 26 protons. An atom of iron (mass number 56) has 30 neutrons ($56 - 26 = 30$ n). Neutral atoms have the same number of protons and electrons. Therefore, 26 protons, 30 neutrons, 26 electrons.
  b. Since the atomic number of iron is 26, every Fe atom has 26 protons. An atom of iron with 25 neutrons has a mass number of $26 + 25 = 51$. Therefore the symbol is $^{51}_{26}$Fe.
  c. Since the mass number is 51 and the number of neutrons is 27, the number of protons is $51 - 27 = 24$ p. Atoms with 24 protons have an atomic number of 24 and are chromium atoms. The symbol is $^{51}_{24}$Cr.

3.107   **Given:** 1 inch, sodium atoms (3.14×10^{-8} cm diameter)   **Need:** number of Na atoms

  Plan: in. → cm → Na atoms

$$\frac{2.54 \text{ cm}}{1 \text{ in.}} \quad \frac{1 \text{ atom}}{3.14 \times 10^{-8} \text{ cm}}$$

  Set Up: $1 \text{ in.} \times \dfrac{2.54 \text{ cm}}{1 \text{ in.}} \times \dfrac{1 \text{ atom}}{3.14 \times 10^{-8} \text{ cm}} = 8.09 \times 10^7$ atoms (3SF)

3.109   (4SF)

$$^{204}_{82}\text{Pb} \quad 203.97 \times \frac{1.40}{100} = 2.86 \text{ amu}$$

$$^{206}_{82}\text{Pb} \quad 205.97 \times \frac{24.10}{100} = 49.64 \text{ amu}$$

$$^{207}_{82}\text{Pb} \quad 206.98 \times \frac{22.10}{100} = 45.74 \text{ amu}$$

$$^{208}_{82}\text{Pb} \quad 207.98 \times \frac{52.40}{100} = 109.0 \text{ amu}$$

  Atomic mass of Pb $= \overline{207.2 \text{ amu}}$ (4SF)

3.111   **a.** X is a metal (in Group 2A (2)); Y and Z are nonmetals (top half of Group 4A (14)).
  b. X has the largest atomic radius, since it is closest to the bottom left of the periodic table.
  c. Y and Z have similar properties since both have six valence electrons and are in Group 6A (16).
  d. Y has the highest ionization energy, since it is closest to the top right of the periodic table.
  e. Y has the smallest atomic radius, since it is closest to the top right of the periodic table.

3.113   **a.** X and Y are metals, and Z is a nonmetal.
  b. Z, since it is closest to the top right of the periodic table.
  c. X and Y are both metals and so have the most similar properties.
  d. Z has the highest ionization energy, since it is closest to the top right of the periodic table and is a noble gas.
  e. X has a half-filled $3d$ sublevel.

4.1   **a.** An α-particle and a helium nucleus both contain two protons and two neutrons. However, an α-particle has no electrons and carries a 2+ charge. Alpha particles are emitted from unstable nuclei during radioactive decay.
   b. α, $_{2}^{4}\text{He}$
   c. Alpha particles may be emitted from unstable nuclei to form more stable, lower energy nuclei.

4.3   **a.** $_{19}^{39}\text{K}$, $_{19}^{40}\text{K}$, $_{19}^{41}\text{K}$
   b. Each isotope has 19 protons and 19 electrons, but they differ in the number of neutrons present. Potassium-39 has 20 neutrons, potassium-40 has 21 neutrons, and potassium-41 has 22 neutrons.

4.5

Medical Use	Atomic Symbol	Mass Number	Number of Protons	Number of Neutrons
Heart imaging	$_{81}^{201}\text{Tl}$	201	81	120
Radiation therapy	$_{27}^{60}\text{Co}$	60	27	33
Abdominal scan	$_{31}^{67}\text{Ga}$	67	31	36
Hyperthyroidism	$_{53}^{131}\text{I}$	131	53	78
Leukemia treatment	$_{15}^{32}\text{P}$	32	15	17

4.7   **a.** α, $_{2}^{4}\text{He}$ **b.** $_{0}^{1}\text{n}$, n **c.** β, $_{-1}^{0}e$ **d.** $_{7}^{15}\text{N}$ **e.** $_{53}^{125}\text{I}$

4.9   **a.** β (or e^{-})   **b.** α (or $_{2}^{4}\text{He}$)   **c.** n (or $_{0}^{1}\text{n}$)   **d.** sodium-24   **e.** carbon-14

4.11   **a.** Because β-particles are lighter and move faster than α-particles, they can penetrate farther into solid material.
   b. Radiation breaks bonds and forms reactive species that cause undesirable reactions in the cells.
   c. Radiation technicians leave the room to increase their distance from the radiation source. A thick wall or one that contains lead also shields them.
   d. Wearing gloves shields the skin from α and β radiation.

4.13   The mass number of the radioactive atom is reduced by 4 when an alpha particle ($_{2}^{4}\text{He}$) is emitted. The unknown product will have an atomic number that is 2 less than the atomic number of the radioactive atom.
   a. $_{84}^{208}\text{Po} \rightarrow {}_{82}^{204}\text{Pb} + {}_{2}^{4}\text{He}$ **b.** $_{90}^{232}\text{Th} \rightarrow {}_{88}^{228}\text{Ra} + {}_{2}^{4}\text{He}$
   c. $_{102}^{251}\text{No} \rightarrow {}_{100}^{247}\text{Fm} + {}_{2}^{4}\text{He}$ **d.** $_{86}^{220}\text{Rn} \rightarrow {}_{84}^{216}\text{Po} + {}_{2}^{4}\text{He}$

4.15   The mass number of the radioactive atom is not changed when a beta particle ($_{-1}^{0}e$) is emitted. The unknown product will have an atomic number that is 1 higher than the atomic number of the radioactive atom.
   a. $_{11}^{25}\text{Na} \rightarrow {}_{12}^{25}\text{Mg} + {}_{-1}^{0}e$ **b.** $_{8}^{20}\text{O} \rightarrow {}_{9}^{20}\text{F} + {}_{-1}^{0}e$
   c. $_{38}^{92}\text{Sr} \rightarrow {}_{39}^{92}\text{Y} + {}_{-1}^{0}e$ **d.** $_{19}^{42}\text{K} \rightarrow {}_{20}^{42}\text{Ca} + {}_{-1}^{0}e$

4.17 The mass number of the radioactive atom is not changed when a positron ($_{+1}^{0}e$) is emitted. The unknown product will have an atomic number that is 1 less than the atomic number of the radioactive atom.

a. $_{14}^{26}Si \rightarrow _{13}^{26}Al + _{+1}^{0}e$ **b.** $_{27}^{54}Co \rightarrow _{26}^{54}Fe + _{+1}^{0}e$

c. $_{37}^{77}Rb \rightarrow _{36}^{77}Kr + _{+1}^{0}e$ **d.** $_{45}^{93}Rh \rightarrow _{44}^{93}Ru + _{+1}^{0}e$

4.19 Balance mass numbers and the number of protons in each nuclear equation.

a. $_{13}^{28}Al \rightarrow _{14}^{28}Si + _{-1}^{0}e$? $= _{14}^{28}Si$ **b.** $_{36}^{87}Kr \rightarrow _{36}^{86}Kr + _{0}^{1}n$? $= _{36}^{86}Kr$

c. $_{29}^{66}Cu \rightarrow _{30}^{66}Zn + _{-1}^{0}e$? $= _{-1}^{0}e$ **d.** $_{92}^{238}U \rightarrow _{2}^{4}He + _{90}^{234}Th$? $= _{92}^{238}U$

e. $_{80}^{188}Hg \rightarrow _{79}^{188}Au + _{+1}^{0}e$? $= _{79}^{188}Au$

4.21 Balance mass numbers and the number of protons in each nuclear equation.

a. $_{4}^{9}Be + _{0}^{1}n \rightarrow _{4}^{10}Be$? $= _{4}^{10}Be$

b. $_{16}^{32}S + _{-1}^{0}e \rightarrow _{15}^{32}P$? $= _{-1}^{0}e$

c. $_{13}^{27}Al + _{0}^{1}n \rightarrow _{11}^{24}Na + _{2}^{4}He$? $= _{13}^{27}Al$

d. $_{13}^{27}Al + _{2}^{4}He \rightarrow _{15}^{30}P + _{0}^{1}n$? $= _{15}^{30}P$

4.23 **a.** When radiation enters the Geiger counter, it ionizes a gas in the detection tube. The ions created in the tube move toward an electrode of opposite charge. This flow of charge produces an electric current, which is detected by the instrument.

b. The becquerel (Bq) is the SI unit for activity. The curie (Ci) is the original unit for activity of radioactive samples.

c. The SI unit for absorbed dose is the gray (Gy). The rad (radiation absorbed dose) is a unit of radiation absorbed per gram of sample. It is the older unit.

d. A kilogray is 1000 gray, which is equivalent to 100 000 rads.

4.25 $70.0 \text{ kg} \times \dfrac{4.20 \text{ } \mu\text{Ci}}{1 \text{ kg}} = 294 \text{ } \mu\text{Ci} \text{ (3SF)}$

4.27 While flying a plane, a pilot is exposed to higher levels of background radiation because there is less atmosphere to act as a shield against cosmic radiation.

4.29 Half-life is the time required for one-half of a radioactive sample to decay.

4.31 **a.** After one half-life, one-half of the sample would be radioactive: $80.0 \text{ mg} \times \frac{1}{2} = 40.0 \text{ mg. (3SF)}$
b. After two half-lives, one-fourth of the sample would still be radioactive:

$80.0 \text{ mg} \times \frac{1}{2} \times \frac{1}{2} = 80.0 \text{ mg} \times \frac{1}{4} = 20.0 \text{ mg (3SF)}$

c. $18 \text{ h} \times \dfrac{1 \text{ half-life}}{6.0 \text{ h}} = 3.0 \text{ half-lives}$

$80.0 \text{ mg} \times \frac{1}{2} \times \frac{1}{2} \times \frac{1}{2} = 80.0 \text{ mg} \times \frac{1}{8} = 10.0 \text{ mg (3SF)}$

d. $24 \text{ h} \times \dfrac{1 \text{ half-life}}{6.0 \text{ h}} = 4.0 \text{ half-lives}$

$80.0 \text{ mg} \times \frac{1}{2} \times \frac{1}{2} \times \frac{1}{2} \times \frac{1}{2} = 80.0 \text{ mg} \times \frac{1}{16} = 5.00 \text{ mg (3SF)}$

4.33 The radiation level in a radioactive sample is cut in half with each half-life. We must first determine the number of half-lives: $\frac{1}{4} = \frac{1}{2} \times \frac{1}{2}$ or 2 half-lives.

Because each half-life is 65 days, it will take 130 days for the radiation level of strontium-85 to fall to one-fourth of its original value: 2 half-lives × 65 days/half-life = 130 days. (2SF)

To determine the amount of time for the strontium-85 to drop to one-eighth of its original activity, we calculate the number of half-lives: $\frac{1}{8} = \frac{1}{2} \times \frac{1}{2} \times \frac{1}{2}$ or 3 half-lives.

Because each half-life is 65 days, it will take 195 days for the radiation level of strontium-85 to fall to one-eighth of its original value:

3 half-lives × 64 days/half-life = 195 days = 200 days (2SF).

4.35 **a.** Because the elements calcium and phosphorus are part of bone, any calcium and/or phosphorus atom, regardless of isotope, will be carried to and become part of the bony structures in the body. Once there, the radiation emitted by the radioisotope can be used for diagnosis or treatment of bone diseases.

b. $^{89}_{38}Sr \rightarrow ^{89}_{39}Y + ^{0}_{-1}e$ Strontium (Sr) acts much like calcium (Ca) because both are Group 2A (2) elements. The body will accumulate radioactive strontium in bones in the same way that it incorporates calcium. Once the strontium isotope is absorbed by the bone, the beta radiation will destroy cancer cells.

4.37 $4.0 \text{ mL} \times \dfrac{45 \,\mu Ci}{1 \text{ mL}} = 180 \,\mu Ci$ (2SF)

4.39 Nuclear fission is the splitting of a large atom into smaller fragments with a simultaneous release of large amounts of energy.

4.41 $^{235}_{92}U + ^{1}_{0}n \rightarrow ^{131}_{50}Sn + ^{103}_{42}Mo + 2^{1}_{0}n + energy$

4.43 **a.** fission   **b.** fusion   **c.** fission   **d.** fusion

4.45 **a.** $^{11}_{6}C$ **b.**

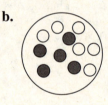

4.47

4.49 Half of a radioactive sample decays with each half-life:

$\frac{1}{2}$ lives   (1)   (2)   (3)
                      5740 y   5740 y   5740 y
6.4 μCi $\longrightarrow$ 3.2 μCi $\longrightarrow$ 1.6 μCi $\longrightarrow$ 0.80 μCi

Therefore, the activity of carbon-14 drops to 0.80 μCi in three half-lives or 3 × 5740 years, which makes the age of the painting 17 200 years.

4.51 **a.** Sodium-25 has 11 protons and $25 - 11 = 14$ neutrons.
b. Nickel-61 has 28 protons and $61 - 28 = 33$ neutrons.
c. Rubidium-84 has 37 protons and $84 - 37 = 47$ neutrons.
d. Silver-110 has 47 protons and $110 - 47 = 63$ neutrons.

4.53 **a.** In alpha decay (α), a helium nucleus is emitted from a radioisotope. In beta decay (β), a neutron in an unstable nucleus is converted to a proton and electron, which is emitted as a beta particle. In gamma emission (γ), high-energy radiation is emitted from the nucleus of a radioisotope.
b. Alpha radiation is abbreviated as α and $^{4}_{2}He$. Beta radiation is abbreviated as β, $^{0}_{-1}\beta$, and $^{0}_{-1}e$. Gamma radiation is abbreviated as γ and $^{0}_{0}\gamma$.

4.55 **a.** gamma radiation   **b.** positron emission   **c.** alpha decay

4.57 **a.** $^{225}_{90}\text{Th} \rightarrow {}^{221}_{88}\text{Ra} + {}^{4}_{2}\text{He}$ **b.** $^{210}_{83}\text{Bi} \rightarrow {}^{206}_{81}\text{Tl} + {}^{4}_{2}\text{He}$

     c. $^{137}_{55}\text{Cs} \rightarrow {}^{137}_{56}\text{Ba} + {}^{0}_{-1}e$ **d.** $^{126}_{50}\text{Sn} \rightarrow {}^{126}_{51}\text{Sb} + {}^{0}_{-1}e$

     e. $^{13}_{7}\text{N} \rightarrow {}^{13}_{6}\text{C} + {}^{0}_{+1}e$

4.59 **a.** $^{14}_{7}\text{N} + {}^{4}_{2}\text{He} \rightarrow {}^{17}_{8}\text{O} + {}^{1}_{1}\text{H}$ **b.** $^{27}_{13}\text{Al} + {}^{4}_{2}\text{He} \rightarrow {}^{30}_{14}\text{Si} + {}^{1}_{1}\text{H}$

     c. $^{235}_{92}\text{U} + {}^{1}_{0}\text{n} \rightarrow {}^{90}_{38}\text{Sr} + 3{}^{1}_{0}\text{n} + {}^{143}_{54}\text{Xe}$

4.61 **a.** $^{16}_{8}\text{O} + {}^{16}_{8}\text{O} \rightarrow {}^{4}_{2}\text{He} + {}^{28}_{14}\text{Si}$ **b.** $^{249}_{98}\text{Cf} + {}^{18}_{8}\text{O} \rightarrow {}^{263}_{106}\text{Sg} + 4{}^{1}_{0}\text{n}$

     c. $^{222}_{86}\text{Rn} \rightarrow {}^{4}_{2}\text{He} + {}^{218}_{84}\text{Po}$

     d. Then polonium-218 decays as follows: $^{218}_{84}\text{Po} \rightarrow {}^{4}_{2}\text{He} + {}^{214}_{82}\text{Pb}$

4.63 Half of a radioactive sample decays with each half-life:

$\frac{1}{2}$ lives   (1)   (2)

1.2 g $\longrightarrow$ 0.60 g $\longrightarrow$ 0.30 g

Therefore, the amount of phosphorus-32 will drop to 0.30 g in two half-lives, which is 28 days. One half-life is 14 days: 28 days/2 half-lives = 14 days/half-life.

4.65 **a.** $^{131}_{53}\text{I} \rightarrow {}^{0}_{-1}e + {}^{131}_{47}\text{Xe}$

     b. First we must determine the number of half-lives:

$$40 \text{ days} \times \frac{1 \text{ half-life}}{8.0 \text{ days}} = 5.0 \text{ half-lives}$$

Now we can calculate the number of grams of iodine-131 remaining:

$$12.0 \text{ g} \times \left(\tfrac{1}{2} \times \tfrac{1}{2} \times \tfrac{1}{2} \times \tfrac{1}{2} \times \tfrac{1}{2}\right) = 12.0 \text{ g} \times \tfrac{1}{32} = 0.375 \text{ g (3SF)}$$

     c. One-half of a radioactive sample decays with each half-life:

$\frac{1}{2}$ lives   (1)   (2)   (3)   (4)

48 g $\longrightarrow$ 24 g $\longrightarrow$ 12 g $\longrightarrow$ 6.0 g $\longrightarrow$ 3.0 g

When 3.0 g remain, four half-lives must have passed. Because each half-life is 8.0 days, we can calculate the number of days that the sample required to decay to 3.0 g:

$$4 \text{ half-lives} \times \frac{8.0 \text{ days}}{1 \text{ half-life}} = 32 \text{ days}$$

4.67 First, calculate the number of half-lives that have passed since the nurse was exposed:

$$36 \text{ h} \times \frac{1 \text{ half-life}}{12 \text{ h}} = 3.0 \text{ half-lives}$$

Because the activity of a radioactive sample is cut in half with each half-life, the activity must have been double its present value before each half-life. For 3.0 half-lives, we need to double the value 3 times: $2.0 \ \mu\text{Ci} \times (2 \times 2 \times 2) = 16 \ \mu\text{Ci}$ (2SF).

4.69 First, calculate the number of half-lives:

$$24 \text{ h} \times \frac{1 \text{ half-life}}{6.0 \text{ h}} = 4.0 \text{ half-lives}$$

And now calculate the amount of technetium-99$^\text{m}$ that remains after 4 half-lives have passed:

$$120 \text{ mg} \times \left(\tfrac{1}{2} \times \tfrac{1}{2} \times \tfrac{1}{2} \times \tfrac{1}{2}\right) = 120 \text{ mg} \times \tfrac{1}{16} = 7.5 \text{ mg. (2SF)}$$

4.71 Irradiating foods kills bacteria that are responsible for food-borne illnesses and food spoilage. As a result, shelf life of the food is extended.

4.73 Nuclear fission is the splitting of a large atom into smaller fragments with a simultaneous release of large amounts of energy. Nuclear fusion occurs when two (or more) nuclei combine (fuse) to form a larger species, with a simultaneous release of large amounts of energy.

4.75 Fusion reactions naturally occur in stars, such as our sun.

4.77 **a.** gamma radiation   **b.** positron emission
      c. beta decay   **d.** alpha decay

4.79 **a.** $^{238}_{92}U \rightarrow {}^{234}_{90}Th + {}^{4}_{2}He$ **b.** $^{234}_{90}Th \rightarrow {}^{234}_{91}Pa + {}^{0}_{-1}e$

      c. $^{226}_{88}Ra \rightarrow {}^{222}_{86}Rn + {}^{4}_{2}He$

4.81 half-life = 4.5 days ^{47}Ca 4.0 μCi after 18 days

$$18 \text{ days} \times \frac{1 \text{ half-life}}{4.5 \text{ days}} = 4.0 \text{ half-lives (2SF) Initially, the sample had an activity of 64 } \mu\text{Ci.}$$

$$64\ \mu\text{Ci} \xrightarrow{(1)} 32\ \mu\text{Ci} \xrightarrow{(2)} 16\ \mu\text{Ci} \xrightarrow{(3)} 8.0\ \mu\text{Ci} \xrightarrow{(4)} 4.0\ \mu\text{Ci}$$

4.83 **a.** $^{180}_{80}Hg \rightarrow {}^{176}_{78}Pt + {}^{4}_{2}He$ **b.** $^{126}_{50}Sn \rightarrow {}^{126}_{51}Sb + {}^{0}_{-1}e$

      c. $^{49}_{25}Mn \rightarrow {}^{49}_{24}Cr + {}^{0}_{+1}e$

Compounds and Their Bonds

5.1 Atoms with one, two, or three valence electrons will lose those electrons.
   a. one   **b.** two   **c.** three   **d.** one   **e.** two

5.3   **a.** Li^+ **b.** F^- **c.** Mg^{2+} **d.** Fe^{3+}

5.5   **a.** 8 protons, 10 electrons   **b.** 19 protons, 18 electrons
      c. 35 protons, 36 electrons   **d.** 16 protons, 18 electrons

5.7   **a.** Cl^- **b.** K^+ **c.** O^{2-} **d.** Al^{3+}

5.9   **a.** K   **b.** Cl^- **c.** Ca   **d.** K^+

5.11 **a.** (Li and Cl)   and   **c.** (K and O) will form ionic compounds.

5.13 **a.** Na_2O **b.** $AlBr_3$ **c.** BaO   **d.** $MgCl_2$ **e.** Al_2S_3

5.15 **a.** the ions Na^+ and S^{2-} combine to form Na_2S
      b. the ions K^+ and N^{3-} combine to form K_3N
      c. the ions Al^{3+} and I^- combine to form AlI_3
      d. the ions Li^+ and O^{2-} combine to form Li_2O

5.17 **a.** aluminum oxide   **b.** calcium chloride
      c. sodium oxide   **d.** magnesium nitride
      e. potassium iodide

5.19 The Roman numeral is used to specify the positive charge on the transition metal in the compound. It is necessary for most transition metal compounds because many transition metals can exist as more than one cation; transition metals have variable ionic charges. For example, iron forms Fe^{2+} and Fe^{3+} ions, which are named iron(II) and iron(III).

5.21 **a.** iron(II)   **b.** copper(II)   **c.** zinc   **d.** lead(IV)   **e.** chromium(III)

5.23 **a.** tin(II) chloride   **b.** iron(II) oxide   **c.** copper(I) sulfide
      d. copper(II) sulfide   **e.** chromium(III) bromide   **f.** zinc chloride

5.25 **a.** Au^{3+} **b.** Fe^{3+} **c.** Pb^{4+} **d.** Sn^{2+}

5.27 **a.** $MgCl_2$ **b.** Na_2S **c.** Cu_2O **d.** Zn_3P_2
      e. AuN   **f.** $CrCl_2$

5.29 **a.** HCO_3^- **b.** NH_4^+ **c.** PO_4^{3-} **d.** HSO_4^-

5.31 **a.** sulfate   **b.** carbonate   **c.** phosphate   **d.** nitrate

5.33

	OH^-	NO_2^-	CO_3^{2-}	HSO_4^-	PO_4^{3-}
Li^+	LiOH	$LiNO_2$	Li_2CO_3	$LiHSO_4$	Li_3PO_4
Cu^{2+}	$Cu(OH)_2$	$Cu(NO_2)_2$	$CuCO_3$	$Cu(HSO_4)_2$	$Cu_3(PO_4)_2$
Ba^{2+}	$Ba(OH)_2$	$Ba(NO_2)_2$	$BaCO_3$	$Ba(HSO_4)_2$	$Ba_3(PO_4)_2$

5.35 **a.** CO_3^{2-}, sodium carbonate **b.** NH_4^+, ammonium chloride
c. PO_4^{3-}, lithium phosphate **d.** NO_2^-, copper(II) nitrite
e. SO_3^{2-}, iron(II) sulfite

5.37 **a.** $Ba(OH)_2$ **b.** Na_2SO_4 **c.** $Fe(NO_3)_2$ **d.** $Zn_3(PO_4)_2$ **e.** $Fe_2(CO_3)_3$

5.39 The nonmetallic elements that are not noble gases are likely to form covalent bonds.

5.41 **a.** Each H atom has one valence electron, for a total of two valence electrons in the molecule. In H_2, there is one bonding pair and no (0) lone pairs.
b. The Br atom has seven valence electrons and the H atom has one valence electron, for a total of eight valence electrons in the molecule. The Br atom achieves an octet by sharing a valence electron with one H atom to give eight valence electrons; the H atom has two valence electrons. The molecule has one bonding pair and there are three lone pairs on the Br atom.
c. Each Br atom has seven valence electrons, for a total of 14 valence electrons in the molecule. Each Br atom achieves an octet by sharing one valence electron with the other Br atom. There is one bonding pair between the Br atoms, and six lone pairs (three lone pairs for each Br atom).

5.43 **a.** HF ($8e^-$) H:F: or H—F:

b. SF_2 (20 e^-) :F:S:F: or :F—S—F:

c. NBr_3 ($26e^-$) :Br:N:Br: or :Br—N—Br: (with :Br: above)

d. CH_3OH (14 e^-) H:C:O:H or H—C—O—H (with H above and below)

e. N_2H_4 (14 e^-) H:N:N:H or H—N—N—H (with H H above)

5.45 When using all the valence electrons does not give complete octets, it is necessary to write multiple bonds.

5.47 Resonance occurs when we can write two or more electron–dot formulas for the same molecule or ion.

5.49 **a.** CO (10 e^-) :C:::O: or :C≡O:

b. H_2CCH_2 (12 e^-) H:C::C:H or H—C=C—H (with H H above)

c. H_2CO (12 e^-) H:C:H or H—C—H (with :O: above)

5.51 $ClNO_2$:Cl—N—O: ⟷ :Cl—N=O: (with :O: above)

5.53 **a.** phosphorus tribromide **b.** carbon tetrabromide
c. silicon dioxide **d.** dinitrogen trioxide
e. silicon tetrabromide **f.** phosphorus pentachloride

5.55   **a.** CCl_4 **b.** CO   **c.** PCl_3 **d.** N_2O_4
        e. BF_3 **f.** SF_6

5.57   **a.** This is an ionic compound with Al^{3+} ion and the sulfate SO_4^{2-} polyatomic ion. The correct name is aluminum sulfate.
        b. This is an ionic compound with Ca^{2+} ion and the carbonate CO_3^{2-} polyatomic ion. The correct name is calcium carbonate.
        c. This is a covalent compound because it contains two nonmetals. Using prefixes, it is named dinitrogen monoxide.
        d. This is an ionic compound with sodium ion Na^+ and the PO_4^{3-} polyatomic ion. The correct name is sodium phosphate.
        e. This ionic compound contains two polyatomic ions, ammonium NH_4^+ and sulfate SO_4^{2-}. It is named ammonium sulfate.
        f. This is an ionic compound containing the variable metal ion Fe^{3+} and oxide ion O^{2-}. It is named using the Roman numeral as iron(III) oxide.

5.59   The electronegativity increases going from left to right across a period.

5.61   A nonpolar covalent bond would have an electronegativity difference of 0.0 to 0.4.

5.63   **a.** Electronegativity increases going up a group: K, Na, Li.
        b. Electronegativity increases going across a period: Na, P, Cl.
        c. Electronegativity increases going across a period and at the top of a group: Ca, Br, O.

5.65   **a.** Si—Br electronegativity difference 1.0, polar covalent
        b. Li—F electronegativity difference 3.0, ionic
        c. Br—F electronegativity difference 1.2, polar covalent
        d. Br—Br electronegativity difference 0, nonpolar covalent
        e. N—P electronegativity difference 0.9, polar covalent
        f. C—O electronegativity difference 1.0, polar covalent

5.67   **a.** $\overset{\delta^+ \ \ \delta^-}{N—F}$ **b.** $\overset{\delta^+ \ \ \delta^-}{Si—Br}$ **c.** $\overset{\delta^+ \ \ \delta^-}{C—O}$ **d.** $\overset{\delta^+ \ \ \delta^-}{P—Br}$ **e.** $\overset{\delta^+ \ \ \delta^-}{B—Cl}$

5.69   Tetrahedral. Four atoms bonded to the central atom with four electron pairs form a tetrahedron.

5.71   The four electron groups in PCl_3 have a tetrahedral arrangement, but three bonded atoms and a lone pair around a central atom give a pyramidal shape. The arrangement of electron pairs determines the angles between the pairs, whereas the number of bonded atoms determines the shape of the molecule.

5.73   In the electron-dot formula of PH_3, the central atom P has three bonded atoms and one lone pair, which give PH_3 a pyramidal shape with bond angles slightly less than 109°. In the molecule NH_3, the central atom N is also bonded to three atoms and one lone pair. Thus, NH_3 also has a pyramidal shape with bond angles slightly less than 109°.

5.75   **a.** The central oxygen atom has four electron pairs with two bonded to fluorine atoms. Its shape is bent with a bond angle slightly less than 109°.
        b. The central atom C has four electron pairs bonded to four chlorine atoms; CCl_4 has a tetrahedral shape.
        c. The central carbon atom has two bonded atoms and no lone pairs. The shape is linear.
        d. The central Se atom has two bonded atoms and one lone pair. Its shape is bent with a bond angle slightly less than 120°.

5.77 Cl_2 is a nonpolar molecule because there is a nonpolar covalent bond between the two Cl atoms, which have identical electronegativity values. In H—Cl, the bond is a polar bond, which is a dipole and makes HCl a polar molecule.

5.79 **a.** single H—Br bond; polar **b.** dipoles do not cancel; polar
c. four dipoles cancel; nonpolar **d.** three dipoles cancel; nonpolar

5.81 **a.** An attraction between the positive end of one polar molecule and the negative end of another polar molecule is called dipole–dipole attraction.
b. An ionic bond is an attraction between positive and negative ions.
c. The weak attractions that occur between temporary dipoles in nonpolar CCl_4 molecules are dispersion forces.
d. The attraction between H and F, O, or N in a dipole is a hydrogen bond.
e. The weak attractions that occur between temporary dipoles in nonpolar Cl_2 molecules are dispersion forces.

5.83 **a.** Hydrogen bonding occurs between dipoles containing H and F, O, or N.
b. Dispersion forces occur between temporary dipoles in nonpolar molecules.
c. Dipole–dipole attractions occur between dipoles in polar molecules.
d. Dispersion forces occur between temporary dipoles in nonpolar molecules.
e. Dispersion forces occur between temporary dipoles in nonpolar molecules.

5.85 **a.** HF; hydrogen bonds are stronger than dipole–dipole attractions of HBr.
b. NaF; ionic bonds are stronger than the hydrogen bonds in HF.
c. $MgBr_2$; ionic bonds are stronger than the dipole–dipole attractions in PBr_3.
d. CH_3OH can form hydrogen bonds and has a higher boiling point than CH_4.

5.87 **a.** If a sodium atom loses its valence electron, its second energy level has a complete octet.
b. A neon atom has the same electron arrangement as a sodium ion.
c. Group 1A (1) and Group 2A (2) elements do not have a stable octet until each has lost one or two electrons, respectively. Electrically charged ions are formed when electrons are lost, and these positively charged ions are attracted to negatively charged ions, resulting in the formation of compounds. Group 8A (18) elements have stable octets that remain electrically neutral and have no tendency to form compounds.

5.89 **a.** P^{3-} ion **b.** O atom **c.** Zn^{2+} ion **d.** Fe^{3+} ion **e.** Li^+ ion **f.** N^{3-} ion

5.91 **a.** 2– pyramidal, polar **b.** 1– bent, polar **c.** 3– tetrahedral, nonpolar

5.93

Period	Electron-Dot Symbols	Formula of Compound	Name of Compound
3	·X· and ·Ÿ·	Mg_3P_2	Magnesium phosphide
3	·Ẋ· and ·Ÿ·	Al_2S_3	Aluminum sulfide
5	·X· and ·Ÿ·	SrI_2	Strontium iodide

5.95

Electron Configurations		Symbols of Ions		Formula of Compound	Name of Compound
Cation	Anion	Cation	Anion		
$1s^22s^1$	$1s^22s^22p^63s^23p^4$	Li^+	S^{2-}	Li_2S	Lithium sulfide
$1s^22s^22p^63s^23p^64s^2$	$1s^22s^22p^63s^23p^3$	Ca^{2+}	P^{3-}	Ca_3P_2	Calcium phosphide
$1s^22s^22p^63s^1$	$1s^22s^22p^63s^23p^5$	Na^+	Cl^-	NaCl	Sodium chloride

5.97 **a.** Chlorine in Group 7A (17) gains one electron to form chloride ion Cl^-.
b. Potassium in Group 1A (1) loses one electron to form potassium ion K^+.
c. Oxygen in Group 6A (16) gains two electrons to form oxide ion O^{2-}.
d. Aluminum in Group 3A (3) loses three electrons to form aluminum ion Al^{3+}.

5.99 **a.** potassium ion   **b.** sulfide ion   **c.** calcium ion   **d.** nitride ion

5.101 **a.** Ions: Au^{3+} and $Cl^- \rightarrow AuCl_3$ **b.** Ions: Pb^{4+} and $O^{2-} \rightarrow PbO_2$
c. Ions: Ag^+ and $Cl^- \rightarrow AgCl$ **d.** Ions: Ca^{2+} and $N^{3-} \rightarrow Ca_3N_2$
e. Ions: Cu^+ and $P^{3-} \rightarrow Cu_3P$ **f.** Ions: Cr^{2+} and $Cl^- \rightarrow CrCl_2$

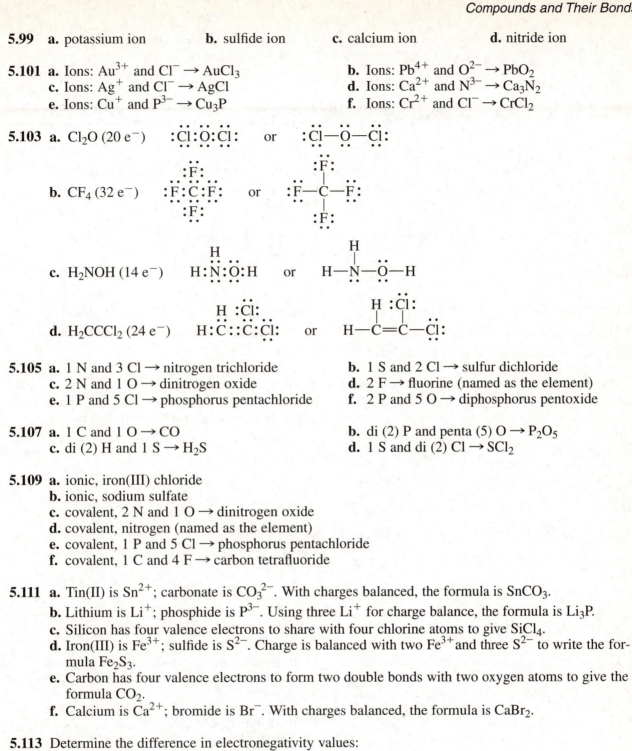

5.103 **a.** Cl_2O (20 e$^-$)

b. CF_4 (32 e$^-$)

c. H_2NOH (14 e$^-$)

d. H_2CCCl_2 (24 e$^-$)

5.105 **a.** 1 N and 3 Cl $\rightarrow$ nitrogen trichloride   **b.** 1 S and 2 Cl $\rightarrow$ sulfur dichloride
c. 2 N and 1 O $\rightarrow$ dinitrogen oxide   **d.** 2 F $\rightarrow$ fluorine (named as the element)
e. 1 P and 5 Cl $\rightarrow$ phosphorus pentachloride   **f.** 2 P and 5 O $\rightarrow$ diphosphorus pentoxide

5.107 **a.** 1 C and 1 O $\rightarrow$ CO   **b.** di (2) P and penta (5) O $\rightarrow P_2O_5$
c. di (2) H and 1 S $\rightarrow H_2S$ **d.** 1 S and di (2) Cl $\rightarrow SCl_2$

5.109 **a.** ionic, iron(III) chloride
b. ionic, sodium sulfate
c. covalent, 2 N and 1 O $\rightarrow$ dinitrogen oxide
d. covalent, nitrogen (named as the element)
e. covalent, 1 P and 5 Cl $\rightarrow$ phosphorus pentachloride
f. covalent, 1 C and 4 F $\rightarrow$ carbon tetrafluoride

5.111 **a.** Tin(II) is Sn^{2+}; carbonate is CO_3^{2-}. With charges balanced, the formula is $SnCO_3$.
b. Lithium is Li^+; phosphide is P^{3-}. Using three Li^+ for charge balance, the formula is Li_3P.
c. Silicon has four valence electrons to share with four chlorine atoms to give $SiCl_4$.
d. Iron(III) is Fe^{3+}; sulfide is S^{2-}. Charge is balanced with two Fe^{3+} and three S^{2-} to write the formula Fe_2S_3.
e. Carbon has four valence electrons to form two double bonds with two oxygen atoms to give the formula CO_2.
f. Calcium is Ca^{2+}; bromide is Br^-. With charges balanced, the formula is $CaBr_2$.

5.113 Determine the difference in electronegativity values:
a. C—O (1.0)   C—N is less (0.5)
b. N—F (1.0)   N—Br is less (0.2)
c. S—Cl (0.5)   Br—Cl is less (0.2)
d. Br—I (0.3)   Br—Cl is less (0.2)
e. N—F (1.0)   N—O is less (0.5)

5.115 A dipole arrow points from the atom with the lower electronegativity value (more positive) to the atom in the bond that has the higher electronegativity value (more negative).
a. Si has the lower electronegativity value of 1.8, making Si the positive end of the dipole. The Cl atom has a higher electronegativity value of 3.0.

Si—Cl

b. C has the lower electronegativity value of 2.5, making C the positive end of the dipole. The N atom has a higher electronegativity value of 3.0.

$$C{-}N$$
$\longleftarrow{\longrightarrow}$

c. Cl has the lower electronegativity value of 3.0, making Cl the positive end of the dipole. The F atom has a higher electronegativity value of 4.0.

$$F{-}Cl$$
$\longleftarrow{\longrightarrow}$

d. C has the lower electronegativity value of 2.5, making C the positive end of the dipole. The F atom has a higher electronegativity value of 4.0.

$$C{-}F$$
$\longleftarrow{\longrightarrow}$

e. N has the lower electronegativity value of 3.0, making N the positive end of the dipole. The O atom has a higher electronegativity value of 3.5.

$$N{-}O$$
$\longleftarrow{\longrightarrow}$

5.117 a. polar covalent (Cl 3.0 − Si 1.8 = 1.2)   **b.** nonpolar covalent (C 2.5 − C 2.5 = 0.0)
c. ionic (Cl 3.0 − Na 0.9 = 2.1)   **d.** nonpolar covalent (C 2.5 − H 2.1 = 0.4)
e. nonpolar covalent (F 4.0 − F 4.0 = 0.0)

5.119 a. In a molecule that has a trigonal planar shape, the dipoles cancel, making the molecule nonpolar.
b. In a molecule with a bent shape and one lone pair, the dipoles do not cancel. The molecule is polar.
c. In a linear molecule with identical atoms, any dipoles cancel, making the molecule nonpolar.

5.121 a. NF_3 :F—N—F: trigonal pyramidal
                              |
                            :F:

b. $SiBr_4$:Br—Si—Br: tetrahedral
                          |
                        :Br:

c. $BeCl_2$:Cl—Be—Cl: linear

d. SO_2 (:O=S—O:) ⟷ (:O—S=O:)   bent (120°)

5.123 a. bent; dipoles do not cancel; polar   **b.** pyramidal; dipoles do not cancel; polar
c. pyramidal; dipoles do not cancel; polar   **d.** tetrahedral; dipoles do not cancel; polar
e. tetrahedral; dipoles cancel; nonpolar

5.125 a. hydrogen bond (3)   **b.** dipole–dipole attraction (2)
c. dispersion forces (4)   **d.** ionic (1)

5.127 a. X is in Group 1A (1); Y is in Group 6A (16)   **b.** ionic
c. X^+, Y^{2-} **d.** X_2Y **e.** XCl   **f.** YCl_2

5.129 a. Sn^{4+} **b.** 50 protons, 46 electrons   **c.** SnO_2 **d.** $Sn_3(PO_4)_4$

5.131 a. iron(II) chloride   **b.** dichlorine heptoxide
c. nitrogen   **d.** calcium phosphate
e. phosphorus trichloride   **f.** aluminum nitrate
g. lead(IV) chloride   **h.** magnesium carbonate
i. nitrogen dioxide   **j.** tin(II) sulfate
k. barium nitrate   **l.** copper(II) sulfide

6

Chemical Reactions and Quantities

6.1 An equation is balanced when there are equal numbers of atoms of each element on the reactant as on the product side.
   a. not balanced   **b.** balanced   **c.** not balanced   **d.** balanced

6.3 Place coefficients in front of formulas until you make the atoms of each element equal on each side of the equation. Try starting with the formula that has subscripts.
   a. $N_2(g) + O_2(g) \rightarrow 2NO(g)$ **b.** $2HgO(s) \rightarrow 2Hg(l) + O_2(g)$
   c. $4Fe(s) + 3O_2(g) \rightarrow 2Fe_2O_3(s)$ **d.** $2Na(s) + Cl_2(g) \rightarrow 2NaCl(s)$

6.5 **a.** There are two NO_3 in the product. Balance by placing a 2 before $AgNO_3$.

   $$Mg(s) + 2AgNO_3(aq) \rightarrow Mg(NO_3)_2(aq) + 2Ag(s)$$

   b. Start with the formula $Al_2(SO_4)_3$. Balance the Al by writing 2 Al, and balance the SO_4 by writing 3 $CuSO_4$.

   $$2Al(s) + 3CuSO_4(aq) \rightarrow 3Cu(s) + Al_2(SO_4)_3(aq)$$

   c. $Pb(NO_3)_2(aq) + 2NaCl(aq) \rightarrow PbCl_2(s) + 2NaNO_3(aq)$
   d. $2Al(s) + 6HCl(aq) \rightarrow 2AlCl_3(aq) + 3H_2(g)$

6.7 **a.** This is a decomposition reaction because a single reactant splits into two simpler substances.
   b. This is a single replacement reaction because I_2 in BaI_2 is replaced by Br_2.

6.9 **a.** combination reaction   **b.** single replacement reaction   **c.** decomposition reaction
   d. double replacement reaction   **e.** double replacement reaction

6.11 **a.** Since this is a combination reaction, the product is a single compound.

   $$Mg(s) + Cl_2(g) \rightarrow MgCl_2(s)$$

   b. Since this is a decomposition reaction, the product is two species.

   $$2HBr(g) \rightarrow H_2(g) + Br_2(g)$$

   c. Since this is a single replacement reaction, the two metals change places.

   $$Mg(s) + Zn(NO_3)_2(aq) \rightarrow Zn(s) + Mg(NO_3)_2(aq)$$

   d. Since this is a double replacement reaction, the cations change places and the anions change places.

   $$K_2S(aq) + Pb(NO_3)_2(aq) \rightarrow 2KNO_3(aq) + PbS(s)$$

6.13 Oxidation involves a loss of electrons (electrons as a product); and reduction involves a gain of electrons (electrons as reactant).
   a. reduction   **b.** oxidation   **c.** reduction   **d.** reduction

6.15 **a.** Zinc (Zn) is oxidized because it loses electrons to form Zn^{2+}; chlorine (Cl_2) is reduced.
   b. Bromide ion ($2Br^-$) is oxidized to $Br_2{}^0$; chlorine (Cl_2) is reduced to 2 Cl^- (gains electrons).
   c. Oxide ion (O^{2-}) is oxidized to $O_2{}^0$ (loses electrons); lead(II) ion (Pb^{2+}) is reduced.
   d. Sn^{2+} ion is oxidized to Sn^{4+} (loses electrons); Fe^{3+} ion is reduced to Fe^{2+} (gains electrons).

6.17 **a.** $Fe^{3+} + e^- \rightarrow Fe^{2+}$ is a reduction.   **b.** $Fe^{2+} \rightarrow Fe^{3+} + e^-$ is an oxidation.

6.19 Linoleic acid gains hydrogen atoms and is reduced.

6.21 A mole is the amount of a substance that contains 6.02×10^{23} items. For example, one mole of water contains 6.02×10^{23} molecules of water.

6.23 **a.** $0.200 \text{ mole of Ag} \times \dfrac{6.02 \times 10^{23} \text{ Ag atoms}}{1 \text{ mole of Ag}} = 1.20 \times 10^{23} \text{ Ag atoms (3SF)}$

b. $0.750 \text{ mole of } C_3H_8O \times \dfrac{6.02 \times 10^{23} \, C_3H_8O \text{ molecules}}{1 \text{ mole of } C_3H_8O} = 4.52 \times 10^{23} \, C_3H_8O \text{ molecules (3SF)}$

c. $2.88 \times 10^{23} \text{ atoms Au} \times \dfrac{1 \text{ mole of Au}}{6.02 \times 10^{23} \text{ atoms Au}} = 0.478 \text{ mole of Au (3SF)}$

6.25 The subscripts indicate the moles of each element in one mole of that compound.

a. $1.0 \text{ mole of quinine} \times \dfrac{24 \text{ moles of H}}{1 \text{ mole of quinine}} = 24 \text{ moles of H (2SF)}$

b. $5.0 \text{ moles of quinine} \times \dfrac{20 \text{ moles of C}}{1 \text{ mole of quinine}} = 1.0 \times 10^2 \text{ moles of C (2SF)}$

c. $0.020 \text{ mole of quinine} \times \dfrac{2 \text{ moles of N}}{1 \text{ mole of quinine}} = 0.040 \text{ mole of N (2SF)}$

6.27 **a.** $0.500 \text{ mole of C} \times \dfrac{6.02 \times 10^{23} \text{ C atoms}}{1 \text{ mole of C}} = 3.01 \times 10^{23} \text{ C atoms (3SF)}$

b. $1.28 \text{ moles of } SO_2 \times \dfrac{6.02 \times 10^{23} \, SO_2 \text{ molecules}}{1 \text{ mole of } SO_2} = 7.71 \times 10^{23} \, SO_2 \text{ molecules (3SF)}$

c. $5.22 \times 10^{22} \text{ atoms of Fe} \times \dfrac{1 \text{ mole of Fe}}{6.02 \times 10^{23} \text{ atoms of Fe}} = 0.0867 \text{ mole of Fe (3SF)}$

d. $8.50 \times 10^{24} \, C_2H_5OH \text{ molecules} \times \dfrac{1 \text{ mole of } C_2H_5OH}{6.02 \times 10^{23} \, C_2H_5OH \text{ molecules}} = 14.1 \text{ moles of } C_2H_5OH$

(3SF)

6.29 1 mole of H_3PO_4 molecules contains 3 moles of H atoms, 1 mole of P atoms, and 4 moles of O atoms.

a. $2.00 \text{ moles of } H_3PO_4 \times \dfrac{3 \text{ moles of H}}{1 \text{ mole of } H_3PO_4} = 6.00 \text{ moles of H (3SF)}$

b. $2.00 \text{ moles of } H_3PO_4 \times \dfrac{4 \text{ moles of O}}{1 \text{ mole of } H_3PO_4} = 8.00 \text{ moles of O (3SF)}$

c. $2.00 \text{ moles of } H_3PO_4 \times \dfrac{1 \text{ mole of P}}{1 \text{ mole of } H_3PO_4} \times \dfrac{6.02 \times 10^{23} \text{ atoms P}}{1 \text{ mole of P}} = 1.20 \times 10^{24} \text{ P atoms (3SF)}$

d. $2.00 \text{ moles of } H_3PO_4 \times \dfrac{4 \text{ moles of O}}{1 \text{ mole of } H_3PO_4} \times \dfrac{6.02 \times 10^{23} \text{ atoms O}}{1 \text{ mole of O}} = 4.82 \times 10^{24} \text{ O atoms (3SF)}$

6.31 **a.** 1 mole of K and 1 mole of Cl: $39.1 \text{ g} + 35.5 \text{ g} = 74.6 \text{ g/mole of KCl (3SF)}$
b. 2 moles of Fe and 3 moles of O:

$2(55.9 \text{ g}) + 3(16.0 \text{ g}) = 111.8 \text{ g} + 48.0 \text{ g} = 159.8 \text{ g/mole of } Fe_2O_3 \text{ (4SF)}$

c. 2 moles of Li and 1 mole of C and 3 moles of O:

$2(6.9 \text{ g}) + 12.0 \text{ g} + 3(16.0 \text{ g}) = 13.8 \text{ g} + 12.0 \text{ g} + 48.0 \text{ g} = 73.8 \text{ g/mole of } Li_2CO_3 \text{ (3SF)}$

d. 2 moles of Al and 3 moles of S and 12 moles of O:

$2(27.0 \text{ g}) + 3(32.1 \text{ g}) + 12(16.0 \text{ g}) = 54.0 \text{ g} + 96.3 \text{ g} + 192.0 \text{ g} = 342.3 \text{ g/mole of } Al_2(SO_4)_3$

(4SF)

e. 1 mole of Mg and 2 moles of O and 2 moles of H:

$24.3\ g + 2(16.0\ g) + 2(1.0\ g) = 24.3\ g + 32.0\ g + 2.0\ g = 58.3\ g/mole\ of\ Mg(OH)_2$ (3SF)

f. 16 moles of C and 19 moles of H and 3 of moles N and 5 moles of O and 1 mole of S:

$16(12.0\ g) + 19(1.0\ g) + 3(14.0\ g) + 5(16.0\ g) + 32.1\ g =$

$192.0\ g + 19.0\ g + 42.0\ g + 80.0\ g + 32.1\ g = 365.1\ g/mole\ of\ C_{16}H_{19}N_3O_5S$ (4SF)

6.33 **a.** $2.00\ \cancel{moles\ of\ Na} \times \dfrac{23.0\ g\ of\ Na}{1\ \cancel{mole\ of\ Na}} = 46.0\ g\ of\ Na$ (3SF)

b. $2.80\ \cancel{moles\ of\ Ca} \times \dfrac{40.1\ g\ of\ Ca}{1\ \cancel{mole\ of\ Ca}} = 112\ g\ of\ Ca$ (3SF)

c. $0.125\ \cancel{mole\ of\ Sn} \times \dfrac{118.7\ g\ of\ Sn}{1\ \cancel{mole\ of\ Sn}} = 14.8\ g\ of\ Sn$ (3SF)

d. $1.76\ \cancel{moles\ of\ Cu} \times \dfrac{63.6\ g\ of\ Cu}{1\ \cancel{mole\ of\ Cu}} = 112\ g\ of\ Cu$ (3SF)

6.35 **a.** $0.500\ \cancel{mole\ of\ NaCl} \times \dfrac{58.5\ g\ of\ NaCl}{1\ \cancel{mole\ of\ NaCl}} = 29.3\ g\ of\ NaCl$ (3SF)

b. $1.75\ \cancel{moles\ of\ Na_2O} \times \dfrac{62.0\ g\ of\ Na_2O}{1\ \cancel{mole\ of\ Na_2O}} = 109\ g\ of\ Na_2O$ (3SF)

c. $0.225\ \cancel{mole\ of\ H_2O} \times \dfrac{18.0\ g\ of\ H_2O}{1\ \cancel{mole\ of\ H_2O}} = 4.05\ g\ of\ H_2O$ (3SF)

d. $4.42\ \cancel{mole\ of\ CO_2} \times \dfrac{44.0\ g\ of\ CO_2}{1\ \cancel{mole\ of\ CO_2}} = 194\ g\ of\ CO_2$ (3SF)

6.37 **a.** $5.00\ \cancel{moles\ of\ MgSO_4} \times \dfrac{120.4\ g\ of\ MgSO_4}{1\ \cancel{mole\ of\ MgSO_4}} = 602\ g\ of\ MgSO_4$ (3SF)

b. $0.25\ \cancel{mole\ of\ CO_2} \times \dfrac{44.0\ g\ of\ CO_2}{1\ \cancel{mole\ of\ CO_2}} = 11\ g\ of\ CO_2$ (2SF)

6.39 **a.** $50.0\ \cancel{g\ of\ Ag} \times \dfrac{1\ mole\ of\ Ag}{107.9\ \cancel{g\ of\ Ag}} = 0.463\ mole\ of\ Ag$ (3SF)

b. $0.200\ \cancel{g\ of\ C} \times \dfrac{1\ mole\ of\ C}{12.0\ \cancel{g\ of\ C}} = 0.0167\ mole\ of\ C$ (3SF)

c. $15.0\ \cancel{g\ of\ NH_3} \times \dfrac{1\ mole\ of\ NH_3}{17.0\ \cancel{g\ of\ NH_3}} = 0.882\ mole\ of\ NH_3$ (3SF)

d. $75.0\ \cancel{g\ of\ SO_2} \times \dfrac{1\ mole\ of\ SO_2}{64.1\ \cancel{g\ of\ SO_2}} = 1.17\ moles\ of\ SO_2$ (3SF)

6.41 **a.** $25\ \cancel{g\ of\ S} \times \dfrac{1\ mole\ of\ S}{32.1\ \cancel{g\ of\ S}} = 0.78\ mole\ of\ S$ (2SF)

b. $125\ \cancel{g\ of\ SO_2} \times \dfrac{1\ \cancel{mole\ of\ SO_2}}{64.1\ \cancel{g\ of\ SO_2}} \times \dfrac{1\ mole\ of\ S}{1\ \cancel{mole\ of\ SO_2}} = 1.95\ moles\ of\ S$ (3SF)

c. $2.0\ \cancel{moles\ of\ Al_2S_3} \times \dfrac{3\ moles\ of\ S}{1\ \cancel{mole\ of\ Al_2S_3}} = 6.0\ moles\ of\ S$ (2SF)

6.43 **a.** $40.0\ \cancel{g\ of\ N} \times \dfrac{1\ \cancel{mole\ of\ N}}{14.0\ \cancel{g\ of\ N}} \times \dfrac{6.02 \times 10^{23}\ atoms\ of\ N}{1\ \cancel{mole\ of\ N}} = 1.72 \times 10^{24}\ atoms\ of\ N$ (3SF)

b. $1.5 \text{ moles of } N_2O_4 \times \dfrac{2 \text{ moles of N}}{1 \text{ mole of } N_2O_4} \times \dfrac{6.02 \times 10^{23} \text{ atoms of N}}{1 \text{ mole of N}} = 1.8 \times 10^{24} \text{ atoms of N (2SF)}$

c. $2.0 \text{ moles of } N_2 \times \dfrac{2 \text{ mole of N}}{1 \text{ mole of } N_2} \times \dfrac{6.02 \times 10^{23} \text{ atoms of N}}{1 \text{ mole of N}} = 2.4 \times 10^{24} \text{ atoms of N (2SF)}$

6.45 a. $\dfrac{2 \text{ moles of } SO_2}{1 \text{ mole of } O_2} \text{ and } \dfrac{1 \text{ mole of } O_2}{2 \text{ moles of } SO_2};$ $\qquad$ $\dfrac{2 \text{ moles of } SO_2}{2 \text{ moles of } SO_3} \text{ and } \dfrac{2 \text{ moles of } SO_3}{2 \text{ moles of } SO_2};$

$\dfrac{1 \text{ mole of } O_2}{2 \text{ moles of } SO_3} \text{ and } \dfrac{2 \text{ moles of } SO_3}{1 \text{ mole of } O_2}$

b. $\dfrac{4 \text{ moles of P}}{5 \text{ moles of } O_2} \text{ and } \dfrac{5 \text{ moles of } O_2}{4 \text{ moles of P}};$ $\qquad$ $\dfrac{4 \text{ moles of P}}{2 \text{ moles of } P_2O_5} \text{ and } \dfrac{2 \text{ moles of } P_2O_5}{4 \text{ moles of P}};$

$\dfrac{5 \text{ moles of } O_2}{2 \text{ moles of } P_2O_5} \text{ and } \dfrac{2 \text{ moles of } P_2O_5}{5 \text{ moles of } O_2}$

6.47 a. $2.0 \text{ moles of } H_2 \times \dfrac{1 \text{ mole of } O_2}{2 \text{ moles of } H_2} = 1.0 \text{ mole of } O_2 \text{ (2SF)}$

b. $5.0 \text{ moles of } O_2 \times \dfrac{2 \text{ moles of } H_2}{1 \text{ mole of } O_2} = 10. \text{ moles of } H_2 \text{ (2SF)}$

c. $2.5 \text{ moles of } O_2 \times \dfrac{2 \text{ moles of } H_2O}{1 \text{ mole of } O_2} = 5.0 \text{ moles of } H_2O \text{ (2SF)}$

6.49 a. $0.500 \text{ mole of } SO_2 \times \dfrac{5 \text{ moles of C}}{2 \text{ moles of } SO_2} = 1.25 \text{ moles of C (3SF)}$

b. $1.2 \text{ moles of C} \times \dfrac{4 \text{ moles of CO}}{5 \text{ moles of C}} = 0.96 \text{ mole of CO (2SF)}$

c. $0.50 \text{ mole of } CS_2 \times \dfrac{2 \text{ moles of } SO_2}{1 \text{ mole of } CS_2} = 1.0 \text{ mole of } SO_2 \text{ (2SF)}$

d. $2.5 \text{ moles of C} \times \dfrac{1 \text{ mole of } CS_2}{5 \text{ moles of C}} = 0.50 \text{ mole of } CS_2 \text{ (2SF)}$

6.51 a. $2.50 \text{ moles of Na} \times \dfrac{2 \text{ moles of } Na_2O}{4 \text{ moles of Na}} \times \dfrac{62.0 \text{ g of } Na_2O}{1 \text{ mole of } Na_2O} = 77.5 \text{ g of } Na_2O \text{ (3SF)}$

b. $18.0 \text{ g of Na} \times \dfrac{1 \text{ mole of Na}}{23.0 \text{ g of Na}} \times \dfrac{1 \text{ mole of } O_2}{4 \text{ moles of Na}} \times \dfrac{32.0 \text{ g of } O_2}{1 \text{ mole of } O_2} = 6.26 \text{ g of } O_2 \text{ (3SF)}$

c. $75.0 \text{ g of } Na_2O \times \dfrac{1 \text{ mole of } Na_2O}{62.0 \text{ g of } Na_2O} \times \dfrac{1 \text{ mole of } O_2}{2 \text{ moles of } Na_2O} \times \dfrac{32.0 \text{ g of } O_2}{1 \text{ mole of } O_2} = 19.4 \text{ g of } O_2 \text{ (3SF)}$

6.53 a. $8.00 \text{ moles of } NH_3 \times \dfrac{3 \text{ moles of } O_2}{4 \text{ moles of } NH_3} \times \dfrac{32.0 \text{ g of } O_2}{1 \text{ mole of } O_2} = 192 \text{ g of } O_2 \text{ (3SF)}$

b. $6.50 \text{ g of } O_2 \times \dfrac{1 \text{ mole of } O_2}{32.0 \text{ g of } O_2} \times \dfrac{2 \text{ moles of } N_2}{3 \text{ moles of } O_2} \times \dfrac{28.0 \text{ g of } N_2}{1 \text{ mole of } N_2} = 3.79 \text{ g of } N_2 \text{ (3SF)}$

c. $34.0 \text{ g of } NH_3 \times \dfrac{1 \text{ mole of } NH_3}{17.0 \text{ g of } NH_3} \times \dfrac{6 \text{ moles of } H_2O}{4 \text{ moles of } NH_3} \times \dfrac{18.0 \text{ g of } H_2O}{1 \text{ mole of } H_2O} = 54.0 \text{ g of } H_2O \text{ (3SF)}$

6.55 a. $28.0 \text{ g of NO}_2 \times \dfrac{1 \text{ mole of NO}_2}{46.0 \text{ g of NO}_2} \times \dfrac{1 \text{ mole of H}_2\text{O}}{3 \text{ moles of NO}_2} \times \dfrac{18.0 \text{ g of H}_2\text{O}}{1 \text{ mole of H}_2\text{O}} = 3.65 \text{ g of H}_2\text{O (3SF)}$

b. $15.8 \text{ g of NO}_2 \times \dfrac{1 \text{ mole of NO}_2}{46.0 \text{ g of NO}_2} \times \dfrac{1 \text{ mole of NO}}{3 \text{ moles of NO}_2} \times \dfrac{30.0 \text{ g of NO}}{1 \text{ mole of NO}} = 3.43 \text{ g of NO (3SF)}$

c. $8.25 \text{ g of NO}_2 \times \dfrac{1 \text{ mole of NO}_2}{46.0 \text{ g of NO}_2} \times \dfrac{2 \text{ moles of HNO}_3}{3 \text{ moles of NO}_2} \times \dfrac{63.0 \text{ g of HNO}_3}{1 \text{ mole of HNO}_3} = 7.53 \text{ g of HNO}_3$ (3SF)

6.57 a. $2PbS(s) + 3O_2(g) \rightarrow 2PbO(s) + 2SO_2(g)$

b. $0.125 \text{ mole of PbS} \times \dfrac{3 \text{ moles of O}_2}{2 \text{ moles of PbS}} \times \dfrac{32.0 \text{ g of O}_2}{1 \text{ mole of O}_2} = 6.00 \text{ g of O}_2 \text{ (3SF)}$

c. $65.0 \text{ g of PbS} \times \dfrac{1 \text{ mole of PbS}}{239.3 \text{ g of PbS}} \times \dfrac{2 \text{ moles of SO}_2}{2 \text{ moles of PbS}} \times \dfrac{64.1 \text{ g of SO}_2}{1 \text{ mole of SO}_2} = 17.4 \text{ g of SO}_2 \text{ (3SF)}$

d. $128 \text{ g of PbO} \times \dfrac{1 \text{ mole of PbO}}{223.2 \text{ g of PbO}} \times \dfrac{2 \text{ moles of PbS}}{2 \text{ moles of PbO}} \times \dfrac{239.3 \text{ g of PbS}}{1 \text{ mole of PbS}} = 137 \text{ g of PbS (3SF)}$

6.59 a. $40.0 \text{ g of C} \times \dfrac{1 \text{ mole of C}}{12.0 \text{ g of C}} \times \dfrac{1 \text{ mol of CS}_2}{5 \text{ moles of C}} \times \dfrac{76.2 \text{ g of CS}_2}{1 \text{ mole of CS}_2} = 50.8 \text{ g of CS}_2$

$\dfrac{36.0 \text{ g of CS}_2 \text{ (actual)}}{50.8 \text{ g of CS}_2 \text{ (theoretical)}} \times 100\% = 70.9 \text{ (3SF)}$

b. $32.0 \text{ g of SO}_2 \times \dfrac{1 \text{ mole of SO}_2}{64.1 \text{ g of SO}_2} \times \dfrac{1 \text{ mole of CS}_2}{2 \text{ moles of SO}_2} \times \dfrac{76.2 \text{ g of CS}_2}{1 \text{ mole of CS}_2} = 19.0 \text{ g of CS}_2$

$\dfrac{12.0 \text{ g of CS}_2 \text{ (actual)}}{19.0 \text{ g of CS}_2 \text{ (theoretical)}} \times 100\% = 63.1\% \text{ (3SF)}$

6.61 $50.0 \text{ g of Al} \times \dfrac{1 \text{ mole of Al}}{27.0 \text{ g of Al}} \times \dfrac{2 \text{ moles of Al}_2\text{O}_3}{4 \text{ moles of Al}} \times \dfrac{102.0 \text{ g of Al}_2\text{O}_3}{1 \text{ mole of Al}_2\text{O}_3} = 94.4 \text{ g of Al}_2\text{O}_3$

Use the percent yield to convert theoretical to actual:

$94.4 \text{ g of Al}_2\text{O}_3 \times \dfrac{75.0 \text{ g of Al}_2\text{O}_3}{100 \text{ g of Al}_2\text{O}_3} = 70.8 \text{ g of Al}_2\text{O}_3 \text{ (actual) (3SF)}$

6.63 $30.0 \text{ g of C} \times \dfrac{1 \text{ mole of C}}{12.0 \text{ g of C}} \times \dfrac{2 \text{ moles of CO}}{3 \text{ moles of C}} \times \dfrac{28.0 \text{ g of CO}}{1 \text{ mole of CO}} = 46.7 \text{ g of CO}$

$\dfrac{28.2 \text{ g of CO (actual)}}{46.7 \text{ g of CO (theoretical)}} \times 100\% = 60.4\% \text{ (3SF)}$

6.65 a. With 8 drivers available, only 8 taxis can be used to pick up passengers.
b. Seven taxis are in working condition to be driven.

6.67 a. $3.0 \text{ moles of N}_2 \times \dfrac{2 \text{ moles of NH}_3}{1 \text{ mole of N}_2} = 6.0 \text{ moles of NH}_3$

$5.0 \text{ moles of H}_2 \times \dfrac{2 \text{ moles of NH}_3}{3 \text{ moles of H}_2} = 3.3 \text{ moles of NH}_3 \text{ (smaller moles of product)}$

The limiting reactant is 5.0 moles of H_2. (2SF)

b. $8.0 \text{ moles of N}_2 \times \dfrac{2 \text{ moles of NH}_3}{1 \text{ mole of N}_2} = 16 \text{ moles of NH}_3$

$4.0 \text{ moles of H}_2 \times \dfrac{2 \text{ moles of NH}_3}{3 \text{ moles of H}_2} = 2.7 \text{ moles of NH}_3 \text{ (smaller moles of product)}$

The limiting reactant is 4.0 moles of H_2. (2SF)

c. $3.0 \text{ moles of N}_2 \times \dfrac{2 \text{ moles of NH}_3}{1 \text{ mole of N}_2} = 6.0 \text{ moles of NH}_3 \text{ (smaller moles of product)}$

$12.0 \text{ moles of H}_2 \times \dfrac{2 \text{ moles of NH}_3}{3 \text{ moles of N}_2} = 8.0 \text{ moles of NH}_3$

The limiting reactant is 3.0 moles of N_2. (2SF)

6.69 **a.** $2.00 \text{ moles of SO}_2 \times \dfrac{2 \text{ moles of SO}_3}{2 \text{ moles of SO}_2} = 2.00 \text{ moles of SO}_3 \text{ (smaller moles of product)}$

$2.00 \text{ moles of O}_2 \times \dfrac{2 \text{ moles of SO}_3}{1 \text{ mole of O}_2} = 4.00 \text{ moles of SO}_3$

2.00 moles of SO_3 produced. (3SF)

b. $2.00 \text{ moles of Fe} \times \dfrac{1 \text{ mole of Fe}_3O_4}{3 \text{ moles of Fe}} = 0.667 \text{ mole of Fe}_3O_4$

$2.00 \text{ moles of H}_2O \times \dfrac{1 \text{ mole of Fe}_3O_4}{4 \text{ moles of H}_2O} = 0.500 \text{ mole of Fe}_3O_4 \text{ (smaller moles of product)}$

0.500 mole of Fe_3O_4 produced. (3SF)

c. $2.00 \text{ moles of C}_7H_{16} \times \dfrac{7 \text{ moles of CO}_2}{1 \text{ mole of C}_7H_{16}} = 14.0 \text{ moles of CO}_2$

$2.00 \text{ moles of O}_2 \times \dfrac{7 \text{ moles of CO}_2}{11 \text{ moles of O}_2} = 1.27 \text{ moles of CO}_2 \text{ (smaller moles of product)}$

1.27 moles of CO_2 produced. (3SF)

6.71 **a.** $20.0 \text{ g of Al} \times \dfrac{1 \text{ mole of Al}}{27.0 \text{ g of Al}} \times \dfrac{2 \text{ moles of AlCl}_3}{2 \text{ moles of Al}} = 0.741 \text{ mole of AlCl}_3$

$20.0 \text{ g of Cl}_2 \times \dfrac{1 \text{ mole of Cl}_2}{71.0 \text{ g of Cl}_2} \times \dfrac{2 \text{ moles of AlCl}_3}{3 \text{ moles of Cl}_2}$

$= 0.188 \text{ mole of AlCl}_3 \text{ (smaller moles of product)}$

0.188 mole of $AlCl_3$ produced. (3SF)

b. $20.0 \text{ g of NH}_3 \times \dfrac{1 \text{ mole of NH}_3}{17.0 \text{ g of NH}_3} \times \dfrac{6 \text{ moles of H}_2O}{4 \text{ moles of NH}_3} = 1.76 \text{ moles of H}_2O$

$20.0 \text{ g of O}_2 \times \dfrac{1 \text{ mole of O}_2}{32.0 \text{ g of O}_2} \times \dfrac{6 \text{ moles of H}_2O}{5 \text{ moles of O}_2} = 0.750 \text{ mole of AlCl}_3 \text{ (smaller moles of product)}$

0.750 mole of $AlCl_3$ produced. (3SF)

c. $20.0 \text{ g of CS}_2 \times \dfrac{1 \text{ mole of CS}_2}{76.2 \text{ g of CS}_2} \times \dfrac{2 \text{ moles of SO}_2}{1 \text{ mole of CS}_2} = 0.525 \text{ mole of SO}_2$

$20.0 \text{ g of O}_2 \times \dfrac{1 \text{ mole of O}_2}{32.0 \text{ g of O}_2} \times \dfrac{2 \text{ moles of SO}_2}{3 \text{ moles of O}_2} = 0.417 \text{ mole of SO}_2 \text{ (smaller moles of product)}$

0.417 mole of SO_2 produced. (3SF)

6.73 **a.** The activation energy is the energy required to break the bonds of the reacting molecules.
b. In exothermic reactions, the energy of the products is lower than the reactants.
c.

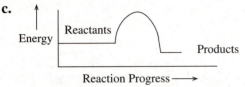

6.75 **a.** An exothermic reaction releases energy.
b. An endothermic reaction has a higher energy level for the products than the reactants.
c. Metabolism is an exothermic reaction, providing energy for the body.

6.77 **a.** Heat is released, which makes the reaction exothermic with $\Delta H = -210$ kcal.
b. Heat is absorbed, which makes the reaction endothermic with $\Delta H = +65.3$ kJ.
c. Heat is released, which makes the reaction exothermic with $\Delta H = -205$ kcal.

6.79 $125 \text{ g of Cl}_2 \times \dfrac{1 \text{ mole of Cl}_2}{70.9 \text{ g of Cl}_2} \times \dfrac{157 \text{ kcal}}{2 \text{ moles of Cl}_2} = 138 \text{ kcal released (3SF)}$

6.81 **a.** 1, 1, 2; combination reaction **b.** 2, 2, 1; decomposition reaction

6.83 **a.** $2NO(g) + O_2(g) \rightarrow 2NO_2(g)$ **b.** combination reaction

6.85 **a.** $2NI_3(s) \rightarrow N_2(g) + 3I_2(g)$ **b.** decomposition reaction

6.87 **a.** $2Cl_2(g) + O_2(g) \rightarrow 2OCl_2(g)$ **b.** combination reaction

6.89 **(1)** **a.** S_2Cl_2 **b.** $2(32.1 \text{ g}) + 2(35.5 \text{ g}) = 135.2 \text{ g/mole of } S_2Cl_2$

c. $10.0 \text{ g of } S_2Cl_2 \times \dfrac{1 \text{ mole of } S_2Cl_2}{135.2 \text{ g of } S_2Cl_2} = 0.0740 \text{ mole of } S_2Cl_2 \text{ (3SF)}$

(2) **a.** C_6H_6 **b.** $6(12.0 \text{ g}) + 6(1.0 \text{ g}) = 78.0 \text{ g/mole of } C_6H_6$

c. $10.0 \text{ g of } C_6H_6 \times \dfrac{1 \text{ mole of } C_6H_6}{78.0 \text{ g of } C_6H_6} = 0.128 \text{ mole of } C_6H_6 \text{ (3SF)}$

6.91 **a.** $10(12.0 \text{ g}) + 8(1.0 \text{ g}) + 2(14.0 \text{ g}) + 2(16.0 \text{ g}) + 2(32.1 \text{ g}) = 252.2 \text{ g/mole}$

b. $25.0 \text{ g of } C_{10}H_8N_2O_2S_2 \times \dfrac{1 \text{ mole of } C_{10}H_8N_2O_2S_2}{252.1 \text{ g of } C_{10}H_8N_2O_2S_2} = 0.0992 \text{ mole of } C_{10}H_8N_2O_2S_2 \text{ (3SF)}$

c. $0.0992 \text{ mole of } C_{10}H_8N_2O_2S_2 \times \dfrac{10 \text{ mole of C}}{1 \text{ mole of } C_{10}H_8N_2O_2S_2} = 0.992 \text{ mole of C (3SF)}$

6.93 **a.** $37.6 \text{ g of Cu} \times \dfrac{1 \text{ mole of Cu}}{63.6 \text{ g of Cu}} \times \dfrac{2 \text{ moles of CuO}}{2 \text{ moles of Cu}} \times \dfrac{79.6 \text{ g of CuO}}{1 \text{ mole of CuO}} = 47.1 \text{ g of CuO (3SF)}$

b. $37.6 \text{ g of Cu} \times \dfrac{1 \text{ mole of Cu}}{63.6 \text{ g of Cu}} \times \dfrac{1 \text{ mole of } O_2}{2 \text{ moles of Cu}} = 0.296 \text{ mole of } O_2 \text{ (3SF)}$

6.95   **a.** $NH_3(g) + HCl(g) \rightarrow NH_4Cl(s)$ combination
     b. $Fe_3O_4(s) + 4H_2(g) \rightarrow 3\,Fe(s) + 4H_2O(g)$ single replacement
     c. $2Sb(s) + 3Cl_2(g) \rightarrow 2SbCl_3(s)$ combination
     d. $2NI_3(s) \rightarrow N_2(g) + 3I_2(g)$ decomposition
     e. $2KBr(aq) + Cl_2(aq) \rightarrow 2KCl(aq) + Br_2(l)$ single replacement
     f. $Al_2(SO_4)_3(aq) + 6NaOH(aq) \rightarrow 3Na_2SO_4(aq) + 2Al(OH)_3(s)$ double replacement

6.97   **a.** $Zn^{2+} + 2e^- \rightarrow Zn$ reduction
     b. $Al \rightarrow Al^{3+} + 3e^-$ oxidation
     c. $Pb \rightarrow Pb^{2+} + 2e^-$ oxidation
     d. $Cl_2 + 2e^- \rightarrow 2Cl^-$ reduction

6.99   **a.** $3 \times C$ (12.0 g/mole) $+ 6 \times H$ (1.0 g/mole) $+ 3 \times O$ (16.0 g/mole) $= 90.1$ g/mole (3SF)

     b. $0.500 \text{ mole of } C_3H_6O_3 \times \dfrac{6.02 \times 10^{23} \text{ molecules}}{1 \text{ mole of } C_3H_6O_3} = 3.01 \times 10^{23}$ molecules (3SF)

     c. $1.50 \text{ moles of } C_3H_6O_3 \times \dfrac{3 \text{ moles of C}}{1 \text{ mole of } C_3H_6O_3} \times \dfrac{6.02 \times 10^{23} \text{ atoms}}{1 \text{ mole of C}} = 2.71 \times 10^{24}$ C atoms (3SF)

     d. $4.5 \times 10^{24} \text{ O atoms} \times \dfrac{1 \text{ mole of O}}{6.02 \times 10^{23} \text{ O atoms}} \times \dfrac{1 \text{ mole of } C_3H_6O_3}{3 \text{ moles of O}} \times \dfrac{90.0 \text{ moles of } C_3H_6O_3}{1 \text{ mole of } C_3H_6O_3}$

       $= 230$ moles of $C_3H_6O_3$ (2SF)

6.101   **a.** $1 \text{ mole of Fe} \times \dfrac{55.9 \text{ g}}{1 \text{ mole of Fe}} = 55.9$ g

       $1 \text{ mole of S} \times \dfrac{32.1 \text{ g}}{1 \text{ mole of S}} = 32.1$ g

       $4 \text{ moles of O} \times \dfrac{16.0 \text{ g}}{1 \text{ mole of O}} = \dfrac{64.0 \text{ g}}{152.0 \text{ g}}$ (4SF)

     b. $1 \text{ mole of Ca} \times \dfrac{40.1 \text{ g}}{1 \text{ mole of Ca}} = 40.1$ g

       $2 \text{ moles of I} \times \dfrac{126.9 \text{ g}}{1 \text{ mole of I}} = 253.8$ g

       $6 \text{ moles of O} \times \dfrac{16.0 \text{ g}}{1 \text{ mole of O}} = \dfrac{96.0 \text{ g}}{389.9 \text{ g}}$ (4SF)

     c. $5 \text{ moles of C} \times \dfrac{12.0 \text{ g}}{1 \text{ mole of C}} = 60.0$ g

       $8 \text{ moles of H} \times \dfrac{1.0 \text{ g}}{1 \text{ mole of H}} = 8.0$ g

       $1 \text{ mole of N} \times \dfrac{14.0 \text{ g}}{1 \text{ mole of N}} = 14.0$ g

       $1 \text{ mole of Na} \times \dfrac{23.0 \text{ g}}{1 \text{ mole of Na}} = 23.0$ g

       $4 \text{ moles of O} \times \dfrac{16.0 \text{ g}}{1 \text{ mole of O}} = \dfrac{64.0 \text{ g}}{169.0 \text{ g}}$ (4SF)

6.103 a. $0.150 \text{ mole of K} \times \dfrac{39.1 \text{ g of K}}{1 \text{ mole of K}} = 5.87 \text{ g of K (3SF)}$

b. $0.150 \text{ mole of Cl}_2 \times \dfrac{71.0 \text{ g of Cl}_2}{1 \text{ mole of Cl}_2} = 10.7 \text{ g of Cl}_2 \text{ (3SF)}$

c. $0.150 \text{ mole of Na}_2\text{CO}_3 \times \dfrac{106.0 \text{ g of Na}_2\text{CO}_3}{1 \text{ mole of Na}_2\text{CO}_3} = 15.9 \text{ g of Na}_2\text{CO}_3 \text{ (3SF)}$

6.105 a. $25.0 \text{ g of CO}_2 \times \dfrac{1 \text{ mole of CO}_2}{44.0 \text{ g of CO}_2} = 0.568 \text{ mole of CO}_2 \text{ (3SF)}$

b. $25.0 \text{ g of Al(OH)}_3 \times \dfrac{1 \text{ mole of Al(OH)}_3}{78.0 \text{ g of Al(OH)}_3} = 0.321 \text{ mole of Al(OH)}_3 \text{ (3SF)}$

c. $25.0 \text{ g of MgCl}_2 \times \dfrac{1 \text{ mole of MgCl}_2}{95.3 \text{ g of MgCl}_2} = 0.262 \text{ mole of MgCl}_2 \text{ (3SF)}$

6.107 a. $124 \text{ g of C}_2\text{H}_6\text{O} \times \dfrac{1 \text{ mole of C}_2\text{H}_6\text{O}}{46.0 \text{ g of C}_2\text{H}_6\text{O}} \times \dfrac{1 \text{ mole of C}_6\text{H}_{12}\text{O}_6}{2 \text{ moles of C}_2\text{H}_6\text{O}} = 1.35 \text{ moles of C}_6\text{H}_{12}\text{O}_6 \text{ (3SF)}$

b. $0.240 \text{ kg of C}_6\text{H}_{12}\text{O}_6 \times \dfrac{1000 \text{ g}}{1 \text{ kg}} \times \dfrac{1 \text{ mole of C}_6\text{H}_{12}\text{O}_6}{180.0 \text{ g of C}_6\text{H}_{12}\text{O}_6} \times \dfrac{2 \text{ moles of C}_2\text{H}_6\text{O}}{1 \text{ mole of C}_6\text{H}_{12}\text{O}_6}$

$\times \dfrac{46.0 \text{ g of C}_2\text{H}_6\text{O}}{1 \text{ mole of C}_2\text{H}_6\text{O}} = 123 \text{ g of C}_2\text{H}_6\text{O} \text{ (3SF)}$

6.109 $2\text{NH}_3(g) + 5\text{F}_2(g) \rightarrow \text{N}_2\text{F}_4(g) + 6\text{HF}(g)$

a. $4.00 \text{ moles of HF} \times \dfrac{2 \text{ moles of NH}_3}{6 \text{ moles of HF}} = 1.33 \text{ moles of NH}_3 \text{ (3SF)}$

$4.00 \text{ moles of HF} \times \dfrac{5 \text{ moles of F}_2}{6 \text{ moles of HF}} = 3.33 \text{ moles of F}_2 \text{ (3SF)}$

b. $1.50 \text{ moles of NH}_3 \times \dfrac{5 \text{ moles of F}_2}{2 \text{ moles of NH}_3} \times \dfrac{38.0 \text{ g of F}_2}{1 \text{ mole of F}_2} = 143 \text{ g of F}_2 \text{ (3SF)}$

c. $3.40 \text{ g of NH}_3 \times \dfrac{1 \text{ mole of NH}_3}{17.0 \text{ g of NH}_3} \times \dfrac{1 \text{ mole of N}_2\text{F}_4}{2 \text{ moles of NH}_3} \times \dfrac{104.0 \text{ g of N}_2\text{F}_4}{1 \text{ mole of N}_2\text{F}_4} = 10.4 \text{ g of N}_2\text{F}_4 \text{ (3SF)}$

6.111 a. $1.60 \text{ moles of C}_2\text{Cl}_6 \times \dfrac{6 \text{ moles of Cl}_2}{1 \text{ mole of C}_2\text{Cl}_6} \times \dfrac{71.0 \text{ g of Cl}_2}{1 \text{ mole of Cl}_2} = 682 \text{ g of Cl}_2 \text{ (3SF)}$

b. $50.0 \text{ g of C}_2\text{H}_6 \times \dfrac{1 \text{ mole of C}_2\text{H}_6}{30.0 \text{ g of C}_2\text{H}_6} \times \dfrac{6 \text{ moles of HCl}}{1 \text{ mole of C}_2\text{H}_6} \times \dfrac{36.5 \text{ g of HCl}}{1 \text{ mole of HCl}} = 365 \text{ g of HCl (3SF)}$

6.113 $2\text{C}_2\text{H}_2(g) + 5\text{O}_2(g) \rightarrow 4\text{CO}_2(g) + 2\text{H}_2\text{O}(g)$

$22.5 \text{ g of C}_2\text{H}_2 \times \dfrac{1 \text{ mole of C}_2\text{H}_2}{26.0 \text{ g of C}_2\text{H}_2} \times \dfrac{4 \text{ moles of CO}_2}{2 \text{ moles of C}_2\text{H}_2} \times \dfrac{44.0 \text{ g of CO}_2}{1 \text{ mole of CO}_2}$

$= 76.2 \text{ g of CO}_2 \text{ (theoretical)}$

$\dfrac{62.0 \text{ g of CO}_2 \text{ (actual)}}{76.2 \text{ g of CO}_2 \text{ (theoretical)}} \times 100\% = 81.4\% \text{ (percent yield) (3SF)}$

6.115 **a.** $4.0 \text{ moles of } H_2O \times \dfrac{1 \text{ mole of } C_5H_{12}}{6 \text{ moles of } H_2O} \times \dfrac{72.2 \text{ g of } C_5H_{12}}{1 \text{ mole of } C_5H_{12}} = 48 \text{ g of } C_5H_{12} \text{ (2SF)}$

b. $32.0 \text{ g of } O_2 \times \dfrac{1 \text{ mole of } O_2}{32.0 \text{ g of } O_2} \times \dfrac{5 \text{ moles of } CO_2}{8 \text{ moles of } O_2} \times \dfrac{44.0 \text{ g of } CO_2}{1 \text{ mole of } CO_2} = 27.5 \text{ g of } CO_2 \text{ (3SF)}$

c. $44.5 \text{ g of } C_5H_{12} \times \dfrac{1 \text{ mole of } C_5H_{12}}{72.0 \text{ g of } C_5H_{12}} \times \dfrac{5 \text{ moles of } CO_2}{1 \text{ mole of } C_5H_{12}} = 3.09 \text{ moles of } CO_2$

$108 \text{ g of } O_2 \times \dfrac{1 \text{ mole of } O_2}{32.0 \text{ g of } O_2} \times \dfrac{5 \text{ moles of } CO_2}{8 \text{ moles of } O_2} = 2.11 \text{ moles of } CO_2 \text{ (smaller moles of product)}$

$2.11 \text{ moles of } CO_2 \times \dfrac{44.0 \text{ g of } CO_2}{1 \text{ mole of } CO_2} = 92.8 \text{ g of } CO_2 \text{ (3SF)}$

6.117 $12.8 \text{ g of Na} \times \dfrac{1 \text{ mole of Na}}{23.0 \text{ g of Na}} \times \dfrac{2 \text{ moles of NaCl}}{2 \text{ moles of Na}} = 0.557 \text{ mole of NaCl}$

$10.2 \text{ g of } Cl_2 \times \dfrac{1 \text{ mole of } Cl_2}{71.0 \text{ g of } Cl_2} \times \dfrac{2 \text{ moles of NaCl}}{1 \text{ mole of } Cl_2} = 0.287 \text{ mole of NaCl (smaller moles of product)}$

$0.287 \text{ mole of NaCl} \times \dfrac{58.5 \text{ g of NaCl}}{1 \text{ mole of NaCl}} = 16.8 \text{ g of NaCl (3SF)}$

6.119 **a.** $3.00 \text{ g of NO} \times \dfrac{1 \text{ mole of NO}}{30.0 \text{ g of NO}} \times \dfrac{21.6 \text{ kcal}}{2 \text{ moles of NO}} = 1.08 \text{ kcal needed (3SF)}$

b. $2 \text{ NO}(g) \rightarrow N_2(g) + O_2(g) + 21.6 \text{ kcal}$

c. $5.00 \text{ g of NO} \times \dfrac{1 \text{ mole of NO}}{30.0 \text{ g of NO}} \times \dfrac{21.6 \text{ kcal}}{2 \text{ mole of NO}} = 1.80 \text{ kcal released (3SF)}$

6.121 **a.** $3Pb(NO_3)_2(aq) + 2Na_3PO_4(aq) \rightarrow Pb_3(PO_4)_2(s) + 6NaNO_3(aq)$ double replacement
b. $4Ga(s) + 3O_2(g) \rightarrow 2Ga_2O_3(s)$ combination
c. $2NaNO_3(s) \rightarrow 2 \text{ NaNO}_2(s) + O_2(g)$ decomposition
d. $Bi_2O_3(s) + 3C(s) \rightarrow 2 \text{ Bi}(s) + 3CO(g)$ single replacement

6.123 **a.** $\text{Volume} = l \times w \times h = (2.31 \text{ cm}) \times (1.48 \text{ cm}) \times (0.075\ 8 \text{ cm}) = 0.259 \text{ cm}^3$

$0.259 \text{ cm}^3 \times \dfrac{19.3 \text{ g of Au}}{1 \text{ cm}^3} = 5.00 \text{ g of Au (3SF)}$

b. $5.00 \text{ g of Au} \times \dfrac{1 \text{ mole of Au}}{197.0 \text{ g of Au}} \times \dfrac{6.02 \times 10^{23} \text{ Au atoms}}{1 \text{ mole of Au}} = 1.53 \times 10^{22} \text{ Au atoms (3SF)}$

c. $5.61 \text{ g of oxide} - 5.00 \text{ g of Au} = 0.61 \text{ g of O}$

$0.61 \text{ g of O} \times \dfrac{1 \text{ mole of O}}{16.0 \text{ g of O}} = 0.038 \text{ mole of O (2SF)}$

d. $5.00 \text{ g of Au} \times \dfrac{1 \text{ mole of Au}}{197.0 \text{ g of Au}} = 0.254 \text{ mole of Au and so } \dfrac{\text{mole of Au}}{\text{mole of O}} = \dfrac{0.254 \text{ mole of Au}}{0.038 \text{ mole of O}} = \dfrac{2}{3}$
and the oxide is Au_2O_3.

6.125 **a.** $22.0 \text{ g of } C_2H_2 \times \dfrac{1 \text{ mole of } C_2H_2}{26.0 \text{ g of } C_2H_2} \times \dfrac{5 \text{ moles of } O_2}{2 \text{ moles of } C_2H_2} \times \dfrac{6.02 \times 10^{23} \text{ molecules } O_2}{1 \text{ mole of } O_2}$

$= 1.27 \times 10^{24} \text{ molecules of } O_2 \text{ (3SF)}$

b. $22.0 \text{ g of } C_2H_2 \times \dfrac{1 \text{ mole of } C_2H_2}{26.0 \text{ g of } C_2H_2} \times \dfrac{4 \text{ moles of } CO_2}{2 \text{ moles of } C_2H_2} \times \dfrac{44.0 \text{ g of } CO_2}{1 \text{ mole of } CO_2}$

$= 74.5 \text{ g of } CO_2 \text{ (theoretical)}$

c. $\dfrac{64.0 \text{ g (actual)}}{74.5 \text{ g (theoretical)}} \times 100\% = 86.0\% \text{ (percent yield) (3SF)}$

6.127 **a.** $4Al(s) + 3O_2(g) \rightarrow 2Al_2O_3(s)$

b. This is a combination reaction.

c. $4.50 \text{ moles of Al} \times \dfrac{3 \text{ moles of } O_2}{4 \text{ moles of Al}} = 3.38 \text{ moles of } O_2 \text{ (3SF)}$

d. $50.2 \text{ g of Al} \times \dfrac{1 \text{ mole of Al}}{27.0 \text{ g of Al}} \times \dfrac{2 \text{ moles of } Al_2O_3}{4 \text{ moles of Al}} \times \dfrac{102.0 \text{ g of } Al_2O_3}{1 \text{ mole of } Al_2O_3} = 94.8 \text{ g of } Al_2O_3 \text{ (3SF)}$

e. $0.500 \text{ mole of Al} \times \dfrac{2 \text{ moles of } Al_2O_3}{4 \text{ moles of Al}} \times \dfrac{102.0 \text{ g of } Al_2O_3}{1 \text{ mole of } Al_2O_3} = 25.5 \text{ g of } Al_2O_3$

$8.00 \text{ g of } O_2 \times \dfrac{1 \text{ mole of } O_2}{32.0 \text{ g of } O_2} \times \dfrac{2 \text{ moles of } Al_2O_3}{3 \text{ moles of } O_2} \times \dfrac{102.0 \text{ g of } Al_2O_3}{1 \text{ mole of } Al_2O_3}$

$= 17.0 \text{ g of } Al_2O_3 \text{ (smaller amount of product)}$

17.0 g Al_2O_3 produced. (3SF)

f. $45.0 \text{ g of Al} \times \dfrac{1 \text{ mole of Al}}{27.0 \text{ g of Al}} \times \dfrac{2 \text{ moles of } Al_2O_3}{4 \text{ moles of Al}} \times \dfrac{102.0 \text{ g of } Al_2O_3}{1 \text{ mole of } Al_2O_3}$

$= 85.0 \text{ g of } Al_2O_3 \text{ (smaller amount of product)}$

$62.0 \text{ g of } O_2 \times \dfrac{1 \text{ mole of } O_2}{32.0 \text{ g of } O_2} \times \dfrac{2 \text{ moles of } Al_2O_3}{3 \text{ moles of } O_2} \times \dfrac{102.0 \text{ g of } Al_2O_3}{1 \text{ mole of } Al_2O_3} = 132 \text{ g of } Al_2O_3 \text{ (3SF)}$

$85.0 \text{ g of } Al_2O_3 \times \dfrac{70.0 \text{ g}}{100 \text{ g}} = 59.5 \text{ g of } Al_2O_3 \text{ (actual)}$

CI.7 **a.**

Isotope	Number of Protons	Number of Neutrons	Number of Electrons
^{27}Si	14	13	14
^{28}Si	14	14	14
^{29}Si	14	15	14
^{30}Si	14	16	14
^{31}Si	14	17	14

b. $1s^2 2s^2 2p^6 3s^2 3p^2$

c. ^{28}Si $27.99 \times \dfrac{92.23}{100} = 25.82$ amu

   ^{29}Si $28.99 \times \dfrac{4.67}{100} = 1.35$ amu

   ^{30}Si $29.98 \times \dfrac{3.10}{100} = \underline{0.929}$ amu

   Atomic mass of Si $= 28.10$ amu (4SF)

d. $^{27}_{14}Si \rightarrow {}^{27}_{13}Al + {}^{0}_{+1}e$ $^{31}_{14}Si \rightarrow {}^{31}_{15}P + {}^{0}_{-1}e$

e.

$$
\begin{array}{c}
:\ddot{C}l: \\
| \\
:\ddot{C}l - Si - \ddot{C}l: \quad \text{Tetrahedral} \\
| \\
:\ddot{C}l:
\end{array}
$$

f. The decay of 16 μCi to 2.0 μCi will require 3 half lives (16 μCi $\rightarrow$ 8.0 μCi $\rightarrow$ 4.0 μCi $\rightarrow$ 2.0 μCi).

   $3 \text{ half-lives} \times \dfrac{2.6 \text{ h}}{1 \text{ half life}} = 7.8$ h (2SF)

CI.9 **a.** $^{226}_{88}Ra \rightarrow {}^{222}_{86}Rn + {}^{4}_{2}He$

   b. $^{222}_{86}Rn \rightarrow {}^{218}_{84}Po + {}^{4}_{2}He$

   c. First determine how many half-lives have passed: $15.2 \text{ days} \times \dfrac{1 \text{ half-life}}{3.8 \text{ days}} = 4.0$ half-lives
   The number of atoms of radon-222 that remain:

   $24\,000 \text{ atoms} \times \frac{1}{2} \times \frac{1}{2} \times \frac{1}{2} \times \frac{1}{2} = 24\,000 \text{ atoms} \times \frac{1}{16} = 1500$ atoms of radon-222 (2SF)

   d. $7.2 \times 10^4 \text{ L} \times \dfrac{2.5 \text{ pCi}}{1 \text{ L}} \times \dfrac{10^{-12} \text{ Ci}}{1 \text{ pCi}} \times \dfrac{3.7 \times 10^{10} \frac{\text{disintegrations}}{\text{s}}}{1 \text{ Ci}} \times \dfrac{3600 \text{ s}}{1 \text{ h}} \times \dfrac{24 \text{ h}}{1 \text{ day}} =$

   5.8×10^8 alpha particles per day (2SF)

CI.11 **a.** X is a metal; Y is a nonmetal.

   b. Y has the higher electronegativity, since it is a nonmetal.

   c. X^{2+}, Y^-

   d. 1. $X = 1s^2 2s^2 2p^6 3s^2$ $Y = 1s^2 2s^2 2p^6 3s^2 3p^5$
      2. $X^{2+} = 1s^2 2s^2 2p^6$ $Y^- = 1s^2 2s^2 2p^6 3s^2 3p^6$
      3. X^{2+} has the same electron configuration as Ne.
         Y^- has the same electron configuration as Ar.
      4. $MgCl_2$, magnesium chloride

   e. Li is D; Na is A; K is C, and Rb is B.

CI.13 a.

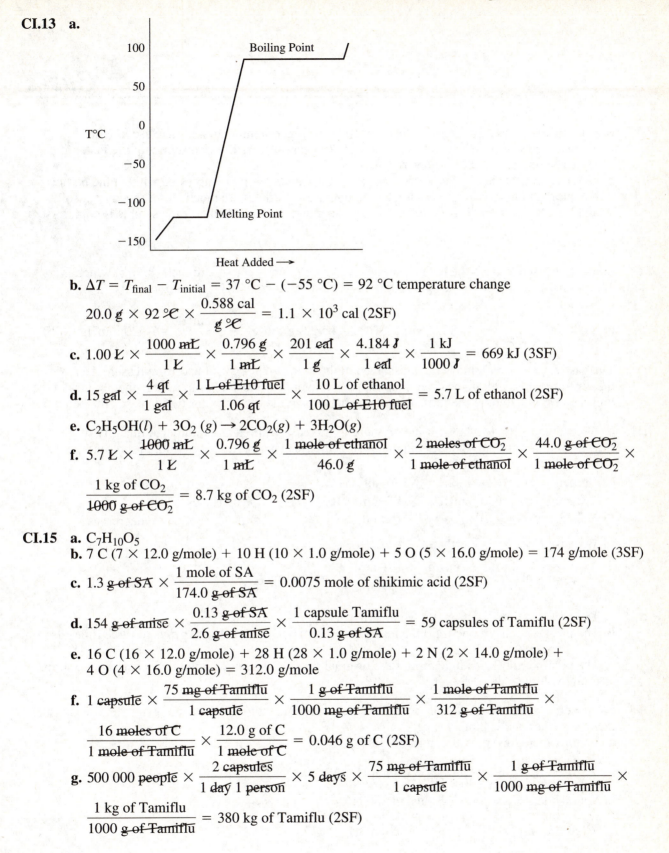

b. $\Delta T = T_{final} - T_{initial} = 37\ °C - (-55\ °C) = 92\ °C$ temperature change

$$20.0\ \cancel{g} \times 92\ \cancel{°C} \times \frac{0.588\ cal}{\cancel{g}\ \cancel{°C}} = 1.1 \times 10^3\ cal\ (2SF)$$

c. $1.00\ \cancel{L} \times \dfrac{1000\ \cancel{mL}}{1\ \cancel{L}} \times \dfrac{0.796\ \cancel{g}}{1\ \cancel{mL}} \times \dfrac{201\ \cancel{cal}}{1\ \cancel{g}} \times \dfrac{4.184\ \cancel{J}}{1\ \cancel{cal}} \times \dfrac{1\ kJ}{1000\ \cancel{J}} = 669\ kJ\ (3SF)$

d. $15\ \cancel{gal} \times \dfrac{4\ \cancel{qt}}{1\ \cancel{gal}} \times \dfrac{1\ \cancel{L\ of\ E10\ fuel}}{1.06\ \cancel{qt}} \times \dfrac{10\ L\ of\ ethanol}{100\ \cancel{L\ of\ E10\ fuel}} = 5.7\ L\ of\ ethanol\ (2SF)$

e. $C_2H_5OH(l) + 3O_2\ (g) \rightarrow 2CO_2(g) + 3H_2O(g)$

f. $5.7\ \cancel{L} \times \dfrac{1000\ \cancel{mL}}{1\ \cancel{L}} \times \dfrac{0.796\ \cancel{g}}{1\ \cancel{mL}} \times \dfrac{1\ \cancel{mole\ of\ ethanol}}{46.0\ \cancel{g}} \times \dfrac{2\ \cancel{moles\ of\ CO_2}}{1\ \cancel{mole\ of\ ethanol}} \times \dfrac{44.0\ \cancel{g\ of\ CO_2}}{1\ \cancel{mole\ of\ CO_2}} \times$

$$\dfrac{1\ kg\ of\ CO_2}{1000\ \cancel{g\ of\ CO_2}} = 8.7\ kg\ of\ CO_2\ (2SF)$$

CI.15 a. $C_7H_{10}O_5$

b. $7\ C\ (7 \times 12.0\ g/mole) + 10\ H\ (10 \times 1.0\ g/mole) + 5\ O\ (5 \times 16.0\ g/mole) = 174\ g/mole\ (3SF)$

c. $1.3\ \cancel{g\ of\ SA} \times \dfrac{1\ mole\ of\ SA}{174.0\ \cancel{g\ of\ SA}} = 0.0075\ mole\ of\ shikimic\ acid\ (2SF)$

d. $154\ \cancel{g\ of\ anise} \times \dfrac{0.13\ \cancel{g\ of\ SA}}{2.6\ \cancel{g\ of\ anise}} \times \dfrac{1\ capsule\ Tamiflu}{0.13\ \cancel{g\ of\ SA}} = 59\ capsules\ of\ Tamiflu\ (2SF)$

e. $16\ C\ (16 \times 12.0\ g/mole) + 28\ H\ (28 \times 1.0\ g/mole) + 2\ N\ (2 \times 14.0\ g/mole) +$
$4\ O\ (4 \times 16.0\ g/mole) = 312.0\ g/mole$

f. $1\ \cancel{capsule} \times \dfrac{75\ \cancel{mg\ of\ Tamiflu}}{1\ \cancel{capsule}} \times \dfrac{1\ \cancel{g\ of\ Tamiflu}}{1000\ \cancel{mg\ of\ Tamiflu}} \times \dfrac{1\ \cancel{mole\ of\ Tamiflu}}{312\ \cancel{g\ of\ Tamiflu}} \times$

$$\dfrac{16\ \cancel{moles\ of\ C}}{1\ \cancel{mole\ of\ Tamiflu}} \times \dfrac{12.0\ g\ of\ C}{1\ \cancel{mole\ of\ C}} = 0.046\ g\ of\ C\ (2SF)$$

g. $500\ 000\ \cancel{people} \times \dfrac{2\ \cancel{capsules}}{1\ \cancel{day}\ 1\ \cancel{person}} \times 5\ \cancel{days} \times \dfrac{75\ \cancel{mg\ of\ Tamiflu}}{1\ \cancel{capsule}} \times \dfrac{1\ \cancel{g\ of\ Tamiflu}}{1000\ \cancel{mg\ of\ Tamiflu}} \times$

$$\dfrac{1\ kg\ of\ Tamiflu}{1000\ \cancel{g\ of\ Tamiflu}} = 380\ kg\ of\ Tamiflu\ (2SF)$$

7.1   **a.** Gaseous particles have greater kinetic energies at higher temperatures. Because kinetic energy is a measure of the energy of motion, the gaseous particles must be moving faster at higher temperatures than at lower values.

   b. Because particles in a gas are very far apart, gases can be easily compressed without the particles bumping into neighboring gas particles. Neighboring particles are much closer together in solids and liquids, and they will "bump" into each other and repel each other if the sample is compressed.

7.3   **a.** temperature   **b.** volume   **c.** amount of gas   **d.** pressure

7.5   Some units used to describe the pressure of a gas are pounds per square inch (lb/in.^{2}, which is also abbreviated as psi), atmospheres (abbreviated atm), torr, mmHg, and kilopascals.

7.7   **a.** $2.00 \, \text{atm} \times \dfrac{760 \, \text{torr}}{1 \, \text{atm}} = 1520 \, \text{torr (3SF)}$ **b.** $2.00 \, \text{atm} \times \dfrac{760 \, \text{mmHg}}{1 \, \text{atm}} = 1520 \, \text{mmHg (3SF)}$

7.9   The gases in the diver's lungs (and dissolved in the blood) will expand because pressure decreases as the diver ascends. Unless the diver exhales, the expanding gases could rupture the membranes in the lung tissues. In addition, the formation of gas bubbles in the bloodstream could cause "the bends."

7.11   **a.** According to Boyle's law, for the pressure to increase while temperature and quantity of gas remains constant, the gas volume must decrease. Thus, cylinder A would represent the final volume.

   b.

Property	Conditions 1	Conditions 2	Know	Predict
Pressure (P)	650 mmHg	1.2 atm (910 mmHg)	P increases	
Volume (V)	220 mL	160 mL		V decreases

   Because $P_1V_1 = P_2V_2$, then $V_2 = P_1V_1/P_2$

   $$V_2 = 220 \, \text{mL} \times \frac{650 \, \text{mmHg}}{1.2 \, \text{atm}} \times \frac{1 \, \text{atm}}{760 \, \text{mmHg}} = 160 \, \text{mL (2SF)}$$

7.13   **a.** The pressure doubles when the volume is halved.

   b. The pressure falls to one-third the initial pressure when the volume expands to three times its initial volume.

   c. The pressure increases to ten times the original pressure when the volume decreases to 1/10 its initial volume.

7.15   From Boyle's law, we know that pressure is inversely related to volume. (For example, the pressure increases when the volume decreases.)

   a. Volume increases; pressure must decrease.

   $$P_2 = 655 \, \text{mmHg} \times \frac{10.0 \, \text{L}}{20.0 \, \text{L}} = 328 \, \text{mmHg (3SF)}$$

   b. Volume decreases; pressure must increase.

   $$P_2 = 655 \, \text{mmHg} \times \frac{10.0 \, \text{L}}{2.50 \, \text{L}} = 2620 \, \text{mmHg (3SF)}$$

   c. The mL units must be converted to L for unit cancellation in the calculation; and because the volume decreases, pressure must increase.

   $$P_2 = 655 \, \text{mmHg} \times \frac{10.0 \, \text{L}}{1500 \, \text{mL}} \times \frac{1000 \, \text{mL}}{1 \, \text{L}} = 4400 \, \text{mmHg (2SF)}$$

7.17 From Boyle's law, we know that pressure is inversely related to volume.
   a. Pressure increases; volume must decrease.

$$V_2 = 50.0 \text{ L} \times \frac{760 \text{ mmHg}}{1500 \text{ mmHg}} = 25 \text{ L (2SF)}$$

   b. The mmHg units must be converted to atm for unit cancellation in the calculation; and because the pressure increases, volume must decrease.

$$P_2 = 760 \text{ mmHg} \times \frac{1 \text{ atm}}{760 \text{ mmHg}} = 1.00 \text{ atm}$$

$$V_2 = 50.0 \text{ L} \times \frac{1.00 \text{ atm}}{2.0 \text{ atm}} = 25 \text{ L (2SF)}$$

   c. The mmHg units must be converted to atm for unit cancellation in the calculation; and because the pressure decreases, volume must increase.

$$P_2 = 760 \text{ mmHg} \times \frac{1 \text{ atm}}{760 \text{ mmHg}} = 1.00 \text{ atm}$$

$$V_2 = 50.0 \text{ L} \times \frac{1.00 \text{ atm}}{0.500 \text{ atm}} = 100. \text{ L (3SF)}$$

7.19 $V_2 = 5.0 \text{ L} \times \dfrac{5.0 \text{ atm}}{1.0 \text{ atm}} = 25 \text{ L (2SF)}$

7.21 **a.** Inspiration begins when the diaphragm flattens, causing the lungs to expand. The increased volume reduces the pressure in the lungs such that air flows into the lungs.
   b. Expiration occurs as the diaphragm relaxes, causing a decrease in the volume of the lungs. The pressure of the air in the lungs increases and air flows out of the lungs.
   c. Inspiration occurs when the pressure in the lungs is less than the pressure of the air in the atmosphere.

7.23 According to Charles's law, there is a direct relationship between temperature and volume. For example, volume increases when temperature increases while the pressure and amount of gas remains constant.
   a. Diagram C describes an increased volume corresponding to an increased temperature.
   b. Diagram A describes a decreased volume corresponding to a decrease in temperature.
   c. Diagram B shows no change in volume, which corresponds to no change in temperature.

7.25 According to Charles's law, a change in a gas's volume is directly proportional to the change in its Kelvin temperature. In all gas law computations, temperatures must be in Kelvin units. (Temperatures in °C are converted to K by the addition of 273.) The initial temperature for all cases is $15 \, °C + 273 = 288 \text{ K}$.

   a. $T_2 = 288 \text{ K} \times \dfrac{5.00 \text{ L}}{2.50 \text{ L}} = 576 \text{ K}$ $576 \text{ K} - 273 = 303 \, °C$ (3SF)

   b. $T_2 = 288 \text{ K} \times \dfrac{1250 \text{ mL}}{2.50 \text{ L}} \times \dfrac{1 \text{ L}}{1000 \text{ mL}} = 144 \text{ K}$ $144 \text{ K} - 273 = -129 \, °C$ (3SF)

   c. $T_2 = 288 \text{ K} \times \dfrac{7.50 \text{ L}}{2.50 \text{ L}} = 864 \text{ K}$ $864 \text{ K} - 273 = 591 \, °C$ (3SF)

   d. $T_2 = 288 \text{ K} \times \dfrac{3550 \text{ mL}}{2.50 \text{ L}} \times \dfrac{1 \text{ L}}{1000 \text{ mL}} = 409 \text{ K}$ $409 \text{ K} - 273 = 136 \, °C$ (3SF)

7.27 According to Charles's law, gas volume is directly proportional to Kelvin temperature when P and n are constant. In all gas law computations, temperatures must be in Kelvin units. (Temperatures in °C are converted to K by the addition of 273.)
   a. When temperature decreases, volume must also decrease.
   $75 \, °C + 273 = 348 \text{ K}$ $55 \, °C + 273 = 328 \text{ K}$

$$V_2 = 2500 \text{ mL} \times \frac{328 \text{ K}}{348 \text{ K}} = 2400 \text{ mL (2SF)}$$

b. When temperature increases, volume must also increase.

$$V_2 = 2500 \text{ mL} \times \frac{680.\ K}{348\ K} = 4900 \text{ mL (2SF)}$$

c. $-25\,°C + 273 = 248$ K

$$V_2 = 2500 \text{ mL} \times \frac{248\ K}{348\ K} = 1800 \text{ mL (2SF)}$$

d. $V_2 = 2500 \text{ mL} \times \frac{240.\ K}{348\ K} = 1700 \text{ mL (2SF)}$

7.29 Because gas pressure increases with an increase in temperature, the gas pressure in an aerosol can may exceed the tolerance of the can when it is heated and cause it to explode.

7.31 According to Gay–Lussac's law, temperature is directly related to pressure. For example, temperature increases when the pressure increases. In all gas law computations, temperatures must be in Kelvin units. (Temperatures in °C are converted to K by the addition of 273.)

a. $25\,°C + 273 = 298$ K

$$T_2 = 298 \text{ K} \times \frac{625 \text{ mmHg}}{745 \text{ mmHg}} = 250.\text{ K (2SF)} \qquad 250.\text{ K} - 273 = -23\,°C \text{ (3SF)}$$

b. $-18\,°C + 273 = 255$ K

$$T_2 = 255 \text{ K} \times \frac{1250 \text{ torr}}{0.950 \text{ atm}} \times \frac{1 \text{ atm}}{760 \text{ torr}} = 441 \text{ K} \qquad 441 \text{ K} - 273 = 168\,°C \text{ (3SF)}$$

7.33 According to Gay–Lussac's law, temperature is directly related to pressure. For example, temperature increases when the pressure increases. In all gas law computations, temperatures must be in Kelvin units. (Temperatures in °C are converted to K by the addition of 273.)

a. $155\,°C + 273 = 428$ K $\qquad 0\,°C + 273 = 273$ K

$$P_2 = 1200 \text{ torr} \times \frac{273\ K}{428\ K} = 770 \text{ torr (2SF)}$$

b. $12\,°C + 273 = 285$ K $\qquad 35\,°C + 273 = 308$ K

$$P_2 = 1.40 \text{ atm} \times \frac{308\ K}{285\ K} = 1.51 \text{ atm (3SF)}$$

7.35 **a.** boiling point **b.** vapor pressure **c.** atmospheric pressure **d.** boiling point

7.37 **a.** Water boils at temperatures less than 100 °C because the atmospheric pressure is less than one atmosphere on top of a mountain. The boiling point is the temperature at which the vapor pressure of a liquid becomes equal to the external (in this case, atmospheric) pressure.
b. The pressure inside a pressure cooker is greater than one atmosphere; therefore, water boils above 100 °C. Foods cook faster at higher temperatures.

7.39 $T_1 = 25\,°C + 273 = 298$ K; $\quad V_1 = 6.50$ L; $\quad P_1 = 845$ mmHg
a. $T_2 = 325$ K; $\quad V_2 = 1.85$ L

$$P_2 = 845 \text{ mmHg} \times \frac{1 \text{ atm}}{760 \text{ mmHg}} \times \frac{6.50\ L}{1.85\ L} \times \frac{325\ K}{298\ K} = 4.26 \text{ atm (3SF)}$$

b. $T_2 = 12\,°C + 273 = 285$ K; $\quad V_2 = 2.25$ L

$$P_2 = 845 \text{ mmHg} \times \frac{1 \text{ atm}}{760 \text{ mmHg}} \times \frac{6.50\ L}{2.25\ L} \times \frac{285\ K}{298\ K} = 3.07 \text{ atm (3SF)}$$

c. $T_2 = 47\,°C + 273 = 320$ K; $\quad V_2 = 12.8$ L

$$P_2 = 845 \text{ mmHg} \times \frac{1 \text{ atm}}{760 \text{ mmHg}} \times \frac{6.50\ L}{12.8\ L} \times \frac{320\ K}{298\ K} = 0.605 \text{ atm (3SF)}$$

7.41 $T_1 = 212\,°C + 273 = 485\,K;\ V_1 = 124\,mL;\ P_1 = 1.80\,atm$
$T_2 = ?;\ V_2 = 138\,mL;\ P_2 = 0.800\,atm$

$$T_2 = 485\,K \times \frac{0.800\ \cancel{atm}}{1.80\ \cancel{atm}} \times \frac{138\ \cancel{mL}}{124\ \cancel{mL}} = 240.\,K \qquad 240.\,K - 273 = -33\,°C\ (2SF)$$

7.43 Addition of more air molecules to a tire or basketball will increase its volume.

7.45 According to Avogadro's law, a change in a gas's volume is directly proportional to the change in the number of moles of gas.

a. $V_2 = 8.00\,L \times \dfrac{\frac{1}{2}(1.50)\ \cancel{moles}}{1.50\ \cancel{moles}} = 4.00\,L\ (3SF)$

b. $n_2 = 25.0\ \cancel{g\ of\ neon} \times \dfrac{1\ mole\ of\ neon}{20.2\ \cancel{g\ of\ neon}} = 1.24\ moles\ of\ Ne\ added$

$1.50\ moles + 1.24\ moles = 2.74\ moles\ of\ Ne$

$8.00\,L \times \dfrac{2.74\ \cancel{moles}}{1.50\ \cancel{moles}} = 14.6\,L\ (3SF)$

c. $1.50\ moles + 3.50\ moles = 5.00\ moles\ of\ gases$

$V_2 = 8.00\,L \times \dfrac{5.00\ \cancel{moles}}{1.50\ \cancel{moles}} = 26.7\,L\ (3SF)$

7.47 At STP, the molar volume of any gas is 22.4 L per mole.

a. $44.8\ \cancel{L} \times \dfrac{1\ mole\ of\ O_2}{22.4\ \cancel{L\ (STP)}} = 2.00\ moles\ of\ O_2\ (3SF)$

b. $4.00\ \cancel{L} \times \dfrac{1\ mole\ of\ CO_2}{22.4\ \cancel{L\ (STP)}} = 0.179\ mole\ of\ CO_2\ (3SF)$

c. $6.40\ \cancel{g\ of\ O_2} \times \dfrac{1\ \cancel{mole\ of\ O_2}}{32.0\ \cancel{g\ of\ O_2}} \times \dfrac{22.4\ L\ (STP)}{1\ \cancel{mole\ of\ O_2}} = 4.48\,L\ (3SF)$

d. $50.0\ \cancel{g\ of\ Ne} \times \dfrac{1\ \cancel{mole\ of\ Ne}}{20.2\ \cancel{g\ of\ Ne}} \times \dfrac{22.4\ \cancel{L\ (STP)}}{1\ \cancel{mole\ of\ Ne}} \times \dfrac{1000\ mL}{1\ \cancel{L}} = 55\,400\ mL\ (3SF)$

7.49 $8.25\ \cancel{g\ of\ Mg} \times \dfrac{1\ \cancel{mole\ of\ Mg}}{24.3\ \cancel{g\ of\ Mg}} \times \dfrac{1\ \cancel{mole\ of\ H_2}}{1\ \cancel{mole\ of\ Mg}} \times \dfrac{22.4\ L\ (STP)}{1\ \cancel{mole\ of\ H_2}} = 7.60\,L\ of\ H_2\ (3SF)$

7.51 $T = 27\,°C + 273 = 300.\,K \qquad PV = nRT$

$$P = \frac{nRT}{V} = \frac{(2.00\ \cancel{moles})(0.0821\ \cancel{L} \cdot atm)(300.\ \cancel{K})}{(10.0\ \cancel{L})(\cancel{mole} \cdot \cancel{K})} = 4.93\,atm\ (3SF)$$

7.53 $T = 22\,°C + 273 = 295\,K \qquad PV = nRT$

$$n = \frac{PV}{RT} = \frac{(845\ \cancel{mmHg})(20.0\ \cancel{L})}{\left(\dfrac{62.4\ \cancel{L} \cdot \cancel{mmHg}}{\cancel{mole} \cdot \cancel{K}}\right)(295\ \cancel{K})} \times \frac{32.0\ g\ of\ O_2}{1\ \cancel{mole\ of\ O_2}} = 29.4\,g\ of\ O_2\ (3SF)$$

7.55 $n = 25.0\ \cancel{g\ of\ N_2} \times \dfrac{1\ mole\ of\ N_2}{28.0\ \cancel{g\ of\ N_2}} = 0.893\ mole\ of\ N_2 \qquad PV = nRT$

$$T = \frac{PV}{nR}\quad \frac{(630.\ \cancel{mmHg})(50.0\ \cancel{L})}{(0.893\ \cancel{mole})\left(\dfrac{62.4\ \cancel{L} \cdot \cancel{mmHg}}{\cancel{mole} \cdot K}\right)} = 565\,K - 273 = 292\,°C\ (3SF)$$

7.57 **a.** $450 \ \text{mL} \times \dfrac{1 \ L}{1000 \ \text{mL}} \times \dfrac{1 \ \text{mole}}{22.4 \ \text{L (STP)}} = 0.020 \ \text{mole}$

$$\dfrac{0.84 \ \text{g}}{0.020 \ \text{mole}} = 42 \ \text{g/mole (2SF)}$$

b. $T = 22 \ °\text{C} + 273 = 295 \ \text{K} \qquad PV = nRT$

$$n = \dfrac{PV}{RT} = \dfrac{(685 \ \text{mmHg})(1.00 \ L)}{\left(\dfrac{62.4 \ L \cdot \text{mmHg}}{\text{mole} \cdot K}\right)(295 \ K)} = 0.0372 \ \text{mole}$$

$$\dfrac{1.48 \ \text{g}}{0.0372 \ \text{mole}} = 39.8 \ \text{g/mole (3SF)}$$

c. $T = 24 \ °\text{C} + 273 = 297 \ \text{K} \qquad PV = nRT$

$$n = \dfrac{PV}{RT} = \dfrac{(0.95 \ \text{atm})(2.30 \ L)}{\left(\dfrac{0.0821 \ L \cdot \text{atm}}{\text{mole} \cdot K}\right)(297 \ K)} = 0.090 \ \text{mole}$$

$$\dfrac{2.96 \ \text{g}}{0.090 \ \text{mole}} = 33 \ \text{g/mole (2SF)}$$

7.59 $55.2 \ \text{g of C}_4\text{H}_{10} \times \dfrac{1 \ \text{mole of C}_4\text{H}_{10}}{58.0 \ \text{g of C}_4\text{H}_{10}} \times \dfrac{13 \ \text{moles of O}_2}{2 \ \text{moles of C}_4\text{H}_{10}} = 6.19 \ \text{moles of O}_2$

$T = 25 \ °\text{C} + 273 = 298 \ \text{K} \qquad PV = nRT$

$$V = \dfrac{nRT}{P} = \dfrac{(6.19 \ \text{mole})(0.0821 \ L \cdot \text{atm})(298 \ K)}{(0.850 \ \text{atm})(\text{mole} \cdot K)} = 178 \ \text{L of O}_2 \ \text{(3SF)}$$

7.61 $50.0 \ \text{g of KNO}_3 \times \dfrac{1 \ \text{mole of KNO}_3}{101.1 \ \text{g of KNO}_3} \times \dfrac{1 \ \text{mole of O}_2}{2 \ \text{moles of KNO}_3} = 0.247 \ \text{mole of O}_2$

$T = 35 \ °\text{C} + 273 = 308 \ \text{K} \qquad PV = nRT$

$$V = \dfrac{nRT}{P} = \dfrac{(0.247 \ \text{mole})(0.0821 \ L \cdot \text{atm})(308 \ K)}{(1.19 \ \text{atm})(\text{mole} \cdot K)} = 5.25 \ \text{L of O}_2 \ \text{(3SF)}$$

7.63 Each gas particle in a gas mixture exerts a pressure as it strikes the walls of the container. The total gas pressure for any gaseous sample is thus a sum of all of the individual pressures. When the portion of the pressure due to a particular type of gaseous particle is discussed, it is only part of the total. Accordingly, these "portions" are referred to as "partial" pressures.

7.65 To obtain the total pressure in a gaseous mixture, add up all of the partial pressures using the same pressure unit.

$P_{\text{total}} = P_{\text{Nitrogen}} + P_{\text{Oxygen}} + P_{\text{Helium}}$

$\qquad = 425 \ \text{torr} + 115 \ \text{torr} + 225 \ \text{torr} = 765 \ \text{torr} \ \text{(3SF)}$

7.67 Because the total pressure in a gaseous mixture is the sum of the partial pressures using the same pressure unit, addition and subtraction is used to obtain the "missing" partial pressure.

$P_{\text{Nitrogen}} = P_{\text{total}} - (P_{\text{Oxygen}} + P_{\text{Helium}})$

$\qquad = 925 \ \text{torr} - (425 \ \text{torr} + 75 \ \text{torr}) = 425 \ \text{torr (3SF)}$

7.69 **a.** If oxygen cannot readily cross from the lungs into the bloodstream, then the partial pressure of oxygen will be lower in the blood of an emphysema patient.

b. An increase in the partial pressure of oxygen in the air supplied to the lungs will result in an increase in the partial pressure of oxygen in the bloodstream (addition of reactant causes the formation of more product). Because an emphysema patient has a lower partial pressure of oxygen in the blood, the use of a portable oxygen tank helps to bring the oxygenation of the patient's blood to a more desirable level.

7.71 **a.** 2 Fewest number of gas particles exerts the lowest pressure.
b. 1 Greatest number of gas particles exerts the highest pressure.

7.73 **a.** A Volume decreases when temperature decreases.
b. C Volume increases when pressure decreases.
c. A Volume decreases when the moles of gas decrease.
d. B Doubling temperature doubles the volume, but losing half the gas particles decreases the volume by half. The two effects cancel, and no change in volume occurs.
e. C Increasing the moles increases the volume to keep T and P constant.

7.75 **a.** The volume of the chest and lungs will decrease when compressed during the Heimlich maneuver.
b. A decrease in volume causes the pressure to increase. A piece of food would be dislodged with a sufficiently high pressure.

7.77 $31\,000 \ \cancel{L} \times \dfrac{1 \ \cancel{\text{mole of } H_2}}{22.4 \ \cancel{\text{L (STP)}}} \times \dfrac{2.0 \text{ g of } H_2}{1 \ \cancel{\text{mole of } H_2}} = 2800 \text{ g of } H_2 \text{ (2SF)}$

7.79 Recall that all temperatures *must* be in kelvins in computations involving gas laws!

$T_1 = 25 \ °C + 273 = 298 \text{ K} \qquad T_2 = 75 \ °C + 273 = 348 \text{ K}$

$P_2 = 10. \text{ atm} \times \dfrac{348 \ \cancel{K}}{298 \ \cancel{K}} = 12 \text{ atm (2SF)}$

7.81 Remember to use Kelvin temperature units in the calculation and convert to Celsius degrees after completing the calculation!

$T_1 = 127 \ °C + 273 = 400. \text{ K}$

$T_2 = 400. \text{ K} \times \dfrac{0.25 \ \cancel{\text{atm}}}{2.00 \ \cancel{\text{atm}}} = 50. \text{ K} \qquad 50. \text{ K} - 273 = -223 \ °C \text{ (3SF)}$

7.83 $T = 18 \ °C + 273 = 291 \text{ K} \qquad PV = nRT$

$n = \dfrac{PV}{RT} = \dfrac{(2500 \ \cancel{\text{mmHg}})(2.00 \ \cancel{L})}{\left(\dfrac{62.4 \ \cancel{L} \cdot \cancel{\text{mmHg}}}{\text{mole} \cdot \cancel{K}}\right)(291 \ \cancel{K})} = 0.28 \text{ mole of } CH_4$

$0.28 \ \cancel{\text{mole of } CH_4} \times \dfrac{16.0 \text{ g of } CH_4}{1 \ \cancel{\text{mole of } CH_4}} = 4.5 \text{ g of } CH_4 \text{ (2SF)}$

7.85 $T = 5 \ °C + 273 = 278 \text{ K} \qquad PV = nRT$

$n = \dfrac{PV}{RT} = \dfrac{(1.2 \ \cancel{\text{atm}})(35.0 \ \cancel{L})}{\left(\dfrac{0.0821 \ \cancel{L} \cdot \cancel{\text{atm}}}{\text{mole} \cdot \cancel{K}}\right)(278 \ \cancel{K})} = 1.8 \text{ moles of } CO_2$

$1.8 \ \cancel{\text{moles } CO_2} \times \dfrac{6.02 \times 10^{23} \text{ molecules of } CO_2}{1 \ \cancel{\text{mole } CO_2}} = 1.1 \times 10^{24} \text{ molecules of } CO_2 \text{ (2SF)}$

7.87 The mole–mole conversion factor is obtained from the reaction and used to convert to moles of gas, and the STP molar volume conversion factor is used to convert moles of gas into liters of gas, as shown below:

$2.00 \ \cancel{\text{moles of } CaCO_3} \times \dfrac{1 \ \cancel{\text{mole of } CO_2}}{1 \ \cancel{\text{mole of } CaCO_3}} \times \dfrac{22.4 \text{ L of } CO_2 \text{ (STP)}}{1 \ \cancel{\text{mole of } CO_2}} = 44.8 \text{ L of } CO_2 \text{ (STP) (3SF)}$

7.89 $T_1 = 24\,°C + 273 = 297\text{ K}$ $T_2 = -95\,°C + 273 = 178\text{ K}$

$$V_2 = 425\text{ mL} \times \frac{745\text{ mmHg}}{0.115\text{ atm}} \times \frac{1\text{ atm}}{760\text{ mmHg}} \times \frac{178\text{ K}}{297\text{ K}} = 2170\text{ mL (3SF)}$$

7.91 $5.4\text{ g of Al} \times \dfrac{1\text{ mole of Al}}{27.0\text{ g of Al}} \times \dfrac{3\text{ moles of O}_2}{4\text{ moles of Al}} \times \dfrac{22.4\text{ L of O}_2\text{ (STP)}}{1\text{ mole of O}_2} = 3.4\text{ L of O}_2\text{ (2SF)}$

7.93 $T = 20.\,°C + 273 = 293\text{ K}$ $PV = nRT$

$$n = \frac{PV}{RT} = \frac{(748\text{ torr})(941\text{ mL})\left(\dfrac{1\text{ L}}{1000\text{ mL}}\right)}{\left(\dfrac{62.4\text{ L}\cdot\text{torr}}{\text{mole}\cdot\text{K}}\right)(293\text{ K})} = 0.0385\text{ mole}$$

$$\frac{1.62\text{ g}}{0.0385\text{ mole}} = 42.1\text{ g/mole (3SF)}$$

7.95 a. $2.5\times10^{23}\text{ NO}_2\text{ molecules} \times \dfrac{1\text{ mole of NO}_2}{6.02 \times 10^{23}\text{ NO}_2\text{ molecules}} \times \dfrac{7\text{ moles of O}_2}{4\text{ moles of NO}_2} \times \dfrac{22.4\text{ L of O}_2\text{ (STP)}}{1\text{ mole of O}_2}$

$= 16\text{ L of O}_2\text{ (2SF)}$

b. $T = 375\,°C + 273 = 648\text{ K}$ $PV = nRT$

$$n = \frac{PV}{RT} = \frac{(725\text{ torr})(5.00\text{ L})}{\left(\dfrac{62.4\text{ L}\cdot\text{torr}}{\text{mole}\cdot\text{K}}\right)(648\text{ K})} = 0.0896\text{ mole of H}_2\text{O}$$

$0.0896\text{ mole of H}_2\text{O} \times \dfrac{4\text{ moles of NH}_3}{6\text{ moles of H}_2\text{O}} \times \dfrac{17.0\text{ g of NH}_3}{1\text{ mole of NH}_3} = 1.02\text{ g of NH}_3\text{ (3SF)}$

7.97 a. $25.0\text{ L of He} \times \dfrac{1\text{ mole of He}}{22.4\text{ L of He (STP)}} \times \dfrac{4.00\text{ g of He}}{1\text{ mole of He}} = 4.46\text{ g of He (3SF)}$

b. $T_1 = 273\text{ K}; P_1 = 1\text{ atm}; V_1 = 25.0\text{ L}$

$T_2 = -35\,°C + 273 = 238\text{ K}; P_2 = ?; V_2 = 2460\text{ L}$

$P_2 = P_1 \times V_1/V_2 \times T_2/T_1$

$$= 1\text{ atm} \times \frac{25.0\text{ L}}{2460\text{ L}} \times \frac{238\text{ K}}{273\text{ K}} = 0.00886\text{ atm} \times \frac{760\text{ mmHg}}{1\text{ atm}} = 6.73\text{ mmHg (3SF)}$$

7.99 Because the partial pressure of nitrogen is to be reported in torr, the atm and mmHg units (for oxygen and argon, respectively) must be converted to torr, as follows:

$0.60\text{ atm} \times \dfrac{760\text{ torr}}{1\text{ atm}} = 460\text{ torr of O}_2$ and $425\text{ mmHg} \times \dfrac{1\text{ torr}}{1\text{ mmHg}} = 425\text{ torr of Ar}$

and $P_{\text{Nitrogen}} = P_{\text{total}} - (P_{\text{Oxygen}} + P_{\text{Argon}})$

$= 1250\text{ torr} - (460\text{ torr} + 425\text{ torr}) = 370\text{ torr (2SF)}$

7.101 $T_1 = 15\,°C + 273 = 288\text{ K}; P_1 = 745\text{ mmHg}; V_1 = 4250\text{ mL}$

$T_2 = ?; P_2 = 1.20\text{ atm} \times \dfrac{760\text{ mmHg}}{1\text{ atm}} = 912\text{ mmHg}; V_2 = 2.50\text{ L} \times \dfrac{1000\text{ mL}}{1\text{ L}} = 2.50 \times 10^3\text{ mL}$

$T_2 = 288\text{ K} \times \dfrac{2500\text{ mL}}{4250\text{ mL}} \times \dfrac{912\text{ mmHg}}{745\text{ mmHg}} = 207\text{ K} - 273 = -66\,°C\text{ (2SF)}$

7.103 $132 \cancel{\text{ g of NaN}_3} \times \dfrac{1 \cancel{\text{ mole of NaN}_3}}{65.0 \cancel{\text{ g of NaN}_3}} \times \dfrac{3 \cancel{\text{ moles of N}_2}}{2 \cancel{\text{ moles of NaN}_3}} \times \dfrac{22.4 \text{ L of N}_2 \text{ (STP)}}{1 \cancel{\text{ mole of N}_2}}$

  $= 68.2 \text{ L of N}_2 \text{ at STP (3SF)}$

7.105 $T = 24\,°\text{C} + 273 = 297 \text{ K}; V = 4.60 \text{ L};$

  $1.00 \cancel{\text{ g of CO}_2} \times \dfrac{1 \text{ mole of CO}_2}{44.0 \cancel{\text{ g of CO}_2}} = 0.0227 \text{ mole of CO}_2$

  $P = \dfrac{nRT}{V} = \dfrac{(0.0227 \cancel{\text{ mole}})(62.4\ \cancel{L}\cdot\text{mmHg})(297\ \cancel{K})}{(4.60\ \cancel{L})(\cancel{\text{mole}}\cdot \cancel{K})} = 91.5 \text{ mmHg (3SF)}$

7.107 $12.0 \cancel{\text{ g of Mg}} \times \dfrac{1 \cancel{\text{ mole of Mg}}}{24.3 \cancel{\text{ g of Mg}}} \times \dfrac{1 \text{ mole of H}_2}{1 \cancel{\text{ mole of Mg}}} = 0.494 \text{ mole of H}_2$

  $T = 24\,°\text{C} + 273 = 297 \text{ K} \qquad PV = nRT$

  $V = \dfrac{nRT}{P} = \dfrac{(0.494 \cancel{\text{ mole}})(62.4\ \text{L}\cdot\cancel{\text{mmHg}})(297\ \cancel{K})}{(835\ \cancel{\text{mmHg}})(\cancel{\text{mole}}\cdot \cancel{K})} = 11.0 \text{ L of H}_2 \text{ (3SF)}$

7.109 $T = 23\,°\text{C} + 273 = 296 \text{ K} \qquad PV = nRT$

  $n = \dfrac{PV}{RT} = \dfrac{(734\ \cancel{\text{mmHg}})(415\ \cancel{\text{mL}})\left(\dfrac{1\ \cancel{L}}{1000\ \cancel{\text{mL}}}\right)}{\left(\dfrac{62.4\ \cancel{L}\cdot\cancel{\text{mmHg}}}{\text{mole}\cdot \cancel{K}}\right)(296\ \cancel{K})} = 0.0165 \text{ mole of H}_2$

  $0.0165 \cancel{\text{ mole of H}_2} \times \dfrac{2 \cancel{\text{ moles of Al}}}{3 \cancel{\text{ moles of H}_2}} \times \dfrac{27.0 \text{ g of Al}}{1 \cancel{\text{ mole of Al}}} = 0.297 \text{ g of Al (3SF)}$

7.111 a. 2000: $780 \cancel{\text{ Tg of CO}_2} \times \dfrac{10^{12} \cancel{\text{ g of CO}_2}}{1 \cancel{\text{ Tg of CO}_2}} \times \dfrac{1 \text{ kg of CO}_2}{1000 \cancel{\text{ g of CO}_2}} = 7.8 \times 10^{11} \text{ kg of CO}_2 \text{ (2SF)}$

  2020: $990 \cancel{\text{ Tg of CO}_2} \times \dfrac{10^{12} \cancel{\text{ g of CO}_2}}{1 \cancel{\text{ Tg of CO}_2}} \times \dfrac{1 \text{ kg of CO}_2}{1000 \cancel{\text{ g of CO}_2}} = 9.9 \times 10^{11} \text{ kg of CO}_2 \text{ (2SF)}$

b. 2000: $780 \cancel{\text{ Tg of CO}_2} \times \dfrac{10^{12} \cancel{\text{ g of CO}_2}}{1 \cancel{\text{ Tg of CO}_2}} \times \dfrac{1 \text{ mole of CO}_2}{44.0 \cancel{\text{ g of CO}_2}} = 1.8 \times 0^{13} \text{ moles of CO}_2 \text{ (2SF)}$

  2020: $990 \cancel{\text{ Tg of CO}_2} \times \dfrac{10^{12} \cancel{\text{ g of CO}_2}}{1 \cancel{\text{ Tg of CO}_2}} \times \dfrac{1 \text{ mole of CO}_2}{44.0 \cancel{\text{ g of CO}_2}} = 2.3 \times 10^{13} \text{ moles of CO}_2 \text{ (2SF)}$

c. increase is $990 \text{ Tg} - 780 \text{ g} = 210 \text{ Tg}$

  $210 \cancel{\text{ Tg of CO}_2} \times \dfrac{10^{12} \cancel{\text{ g of CO}_2}}{1 \cancel{\text{ Tg of CO}_2}} \times \dfrac{1 \text{ Mg of CO}_2}{10^6 \cancel{\text{ g of CO}_2}} = 2.1 \times 10^8 \text{ Mg of CO}_2 \text{ increase (2SF)}$

8.1 The component present in the smaller amount is the solute; the larger amount is the solvent.
   a. sodium chloride, solute; water, solvent
   b. water, solute; ethanol, solvent
   c. oxygen, solute; nitrogen, solvent

8.3 The K^+ and I^- ions at the surface of the solid are pulled into solution by the polar water molecules, where the hydration process surrounds separate ions with water molecules.

8.5 **a.** Potassium chloride, an ionic solute, would be soluble in water (a polar solvent).
   b. Iodine, a nonpolar solute, would be soluble in carbon tetrachloride, CCl_4 (a nonpolar solvent).
   c. Sucrose, a polar solute, would be soluble in water, which is a polar solvent.
   d. Gasoline, a nonpolar solute, would be soluble in carbon tetrachloride, CCl_4, which is a nonpolar solvent.

8.7 The salt KF completely dissociates into ions when it dissolves in water. The weak acid HF exists as mostly molecules along with some ions when it dissolves in water.

8.9 Strong electrolytes dissociate into ions.

   a. $KCl(s) \xrightarrow{H_2O} K^+(aq) + Cl^-(aq)$ **b.** $CaCl_2(s) \xrightarrow{H_2O} Ca^{2+}(aq) + 2Cl^-(aq)$

   c. $K_3PO_4(s) \xrightarrow{H_2O} 3K^+(aq) + PO_4^-(aq)$ **d.** $Fe(NO_3)_3(s) \xrightarrow{H_2O} Fe^{3+}(aq) + 3NO_3^-(aq)$

8.11 **a.** In solution, a weak electrolyte exists mostly as molecules with a few ions.
   b. Sodium bromide is a strong electrolyte and forms only ions in solution.
   c. A nonelectrolyte does not dissociate and forms only molecules in solution.

8.13 **a.** Strong electrolyte because only ions are present in the K_2SO_4 solution.
   b. Weak electrolyte because both ions and molecules are present in the NH_4OH solution.
   c. Nonelectrolyte because only molecules are present in the $C_6H_{12}O_6$ solution.

8.15 **a.** $1 \text{ mole of } K^+ \times \dfrac{1 \text{ Eq of } K^+}{1 \text{ mole of } K^+} = 1 \text{ Eq of } K^+$

   b. $2 \text{ moles of } OH^- \times \dfrac{1 \text{ Eq of } OH^-}{1 \text{ mole of } OH^-} = 2 \text{ Eq of } OH^-$

   c. $1 \text{ mole of } Ca^{2+} \times \dfrac{2 \text{ Eq of } Ca^{2+}}{1 \text{ mole of } Ca^{2+}} = 2 \text{ Eq of } Ca^{2+}$

   d. $3 \text{ moles of } CO_3^{2-} \times \dfrac{2 \text{ Eq of } CO_3^{2-}}{1 \text{ mole of } CO_3^{2-}} = 6 \text{ Eq of } CO_3^{2-}$

8.17 $1.00 \text{ L} \times \dfrac{154 \text{ mEq}}{1 \text{ L}} \times \dfrac{1 \text{ Eq}}{1000 \text{ mEq}} \times \dfrac{1 \text{ mole of } Na^+}{1 \text{ Eq}} = 0.154 \text{ mole of } Na^+ \text{ (3SF)}$

   $1.00 \text{ L} \times \dfrac{154 \text{ mEq}}{1 \text{ L}} \times \dfrac{1 \text{ Eq}}{1000 \text{ mEq}} \times \dfrac{1 \text{ mole of } Cl^-}{1 \text{ Eq}} = 0.154 \text{ mole of } Cl^- \text{ (3SF)}$

8.19 The total equivalents of anions must be equal to the equivalents of cations in any solution.

mEq of anions = 40. mEq of Cl^-/L + 15 mEq of HPO_4^{2-}/L = 55 mEq/L of anions

mEq of Na^+ = mEq of anions = 55 mEq of Na^+/L

8.21 **a.** The solution must be saturated because no additional solute dissolves.
b. The solution was unsaturated because the sugar cube dissolves completely.

8.23 **a.** It is unsaturated because 34.0 g of KCl is the maximum that dissolves in 100 g of H_2O at 20 °C.
b. Adding 11.0 g of $NaNO_3$ in 25 g of H_2O is 44 g of $NaNO_3$ in 100 g of H_2O. At 20 °C, 88.0 g of Na_2CO_3 can dissolve, so the solution is unsaturated.
c. Adding 400.0 g of sugar to 125 g of H_2O is 320 g in 100 g of H_2O. At 20 °C, only 203.9 g sugar can dissolve, which is less than 320 g. The sugar solution is saturated, and excess undissolved sugar is present.

8.25 **a.** $\dfrac{34 \text{ g of KCl}}{100 \text{ g of } H_2O} \times 200. \text{ g of } H_2O = 68 \text{ g of KCl}$ (This will dissolve at 20 °C.) (2SF)

At 20 °C, 68. g of KCl can dissolve in 200 g of H_2O.
b. Since 80. g of KCl dissolves at 50 °C and 68 g is in solution at 20 °C, the mass of solid is 80. g − 68 g = 12 g of KCl. (2SF)

8.27 **a.** In general, the solubility of solid solutes increases as temperature is increased.
b. The solubility of a gaseous solute (CO_2) decreases as the temperature is increased.
c. The solubility of a gaseous solute is lowered as temperature increases. When the can of warm soda is opened, more CO_2 is released, producing more spray.

8.29 **a.** Li^+ salts are soluble.
b. The Cl^- salt containing Ag^+ is insoluble.
c. Salts containing CO_3^{2-} are usually insoluble.
d. Salts containing K^+ ions are soluble.
e. Salts containing NO_3^- ions are soluble.

8.31 **a.** No solid forms; salts containing K^+ and Na^+ are soluble.
b. Solid silver sulfide forms:

$2AgNO_3(aq) + K_2S(aq) \rightarrow Ag_2S(s) + 2KNO_3(aq)$

$2Ag^+(aq) + 2NO_3^-(aq) + 2K^+(aq) + S^{2-}(aq) \rightarrow Ag_2S(s) + 2NO_3^-(aq) + 2K^+(aq)$

$2Ag^+(aq) + S^{2-}(aq) \rightarrow Ag_2S(s)$

c. Solid calcium sulfate forms:

$CaCl_2(aq) + Na_2SO_4(aq) \rightarrow CaSO_4(s) + 2NaCl(aq)$

$Ca^{2+}(aq) + 2Cl^-(aq) + 2Na^+(aq) + SO_4^{2-}(aq) \rightarrow CaSO_4(s) + 2Cl^-(aq) + 2Na^+(aq)$

$Ca^{2+}(aq) + SO_4^{2-}(aq) \rightarrow CaSO_4(s)$

d. Solid copper phosphate forms:

$3CuCl_2(aq) + 2Li_3PO_4(aq) \rightarrow Cu_3(PO_4)_2(s) + 6LiCl(aq)$

$3Cu^{2+}(aq) + 6Cl^-(aq) + 6Li^+(aq) + 2PO_4^{3-}(aq) \rightarrow Cu_3(PO_4)_2(s) + 6Cl^-(aq) + 6Li^+(aq)$

$3Cu^{2+}(aq) + 2PO_4^{2-}(aq) \rightarrow Cu_3(PO_4)_2(s)$

8.33 A 5% (m/m) glucose solution contains 5 g of glucose in 100 g of solution (5 g of glucose + 95 g of water), while a 5% (m/v) glucose solution contains 5 g of glucose in 100 mL of solution.

8.35 **a.** $\dfrac{25 \text{ g of KCl}}{(25 + 125) \text{ g of solution}} \times 100\% = \dfrac{25 \text{ g of KCl}}{150 \text{ g of solution}} \times 100\% = 17\% \text{ (m/m) KCl (2SF)}$

b. $\dfrac{12 \text{ g of sugar}}{225 \text{ g of solution}} \times 100\% = 5.3\% \text{ (m/m) sugar (2SF)}$

8.37 $\dfrac{\text{mass (in grams) solute}}{\text{volume (in mL) solution}} \times 100\% = \% \text{ mass/volume}$

a. $\dfrac{75 \text{ g of Na}_2\text{SO}_4}{250 \text{ mL of solution}} \times 100\% = 30.\% \text{ (m/v) Na}_2\text{SO}_4\text{(2SF)}$

b. $\dfrac{39 \text{ g of sucrose}}{355 \text{ mL of solution}} \times 100\% = 11\% \text{ (m/v) sucrose (2SF)}$

8.39 **a.** $50.0 \text{ mL of solution} \times \dfrac{5.0 \text{ g of KCl}}{100 \text{ mL of solution}} = 2.5 \text{ g of KCl (2SF)}$

b. $1250 \text{ mL of solution} \times \dfrac{4.0 \text{ g of NH}_4\text{Cl}}{100 \text{ mL of solution}} = 50. \text{ g of NH}_4\text{Cl (2SF)}$

8.41 $355 \text{ mL of solution} \times \dfrac{22.5 \text{ mL of alcohol}}{100 \text{ mL of solution}} = 79.9 \text{ mL of alcohol (3SF)}$

8.43 **a.** $1 \text{ L} \times \dfrac{100 \text{ mL of solution}}{1 \text{ L}} \times \dfrac{20. \text{ g of mannitol}}{100. \text{ mL of solution}} = 20. \text{ g of mannitol (2SF)}$

b. $15 \text{ L} \times \dfrac{100 \text{ mL of solution}}{1 \text{ L}} \times \dfrac{20. \text{ g of mannitol}}{100. \text{ mL of solution}} = 300 \text{ g of mannitol (2SF)}$

8.45 $100 \text{ g of glucose} \times \dfrac{100. \text{ mL of solution}}{5 \text{ g of glucose}} \times \dfrac{1 \text{ L}}{1000 \text{ mL}} = 2 \text{ L of solution (1SF)}$

8.47 molarity = moles of solute/L of solution

a. $\dfrac{2.0 \text{ moles of glucose}}{4.0 \text{ L of solution}} = 0.50 \text{ M glucose (2SF)}$

b. $\dfrac{4.0 \text{ g of KOH}}{2.0 \text{ L of solution}} \times \dfrac{1 \text{ mole of KOH}}{56.1 \text{ g of KOH}} = 0.036 \text{ M KOH (2SF)}$

c. $\dfrac{5.85 \text{ g of NaCl}}{400. \text{ mL of solution}} \times \dfrac{1 \text{ mole of NaCl}}{58.5 \text{ g of NaCl}} \times \dfrac{1000 \text{ mL of solution}}{1 \text{ L of solution}} = 0.250 \text{ M NaCl (3SF)}$

8.49 **a.** $1.0 \text{ L of solution} \times \dfrac{3.0 \text{ moles of NaCl}}{1 \text{ L of solution}} = 3.0 \text{ moles of NaCl (2SF)}$

b. $0.40 \text{ L of solution} \times \dfrac{1.0 \text{ mole of KBr}}{1 \text{ L of solution}} = 0.40 \text{ mole of KBr (2SF)}$

c. $125 \text{ mL of solution} \times \dfrac{2.0 \text{ moles of MgCl}_2}{1 \text{ L of solution}} \times \dfrac{1 \text{ L of solution}}{1000 \text{ mL of solution}} = 0.25 \text{ mole of MgCl}_2 \text{ (2SF)}$

8.51 **a.** $2.0 \text{ L} \times \dfrac{1.5 \text{ moles of NaOH}}{1 \text{ L}} \times \dfrac{40.0 \text{ g of NaOH}}{1 \text{ mole of NaOH}} = 120 \text{ g of NaOH (2SF)}$

b. $4.0 \text{ L} \times \dfrac{0.20 \text{ mole of KCl}}{1 \text{ L}} \times \dfrac{74.6 \text{ g of KCl}}{1 \text{ mole of KCl}} = 60. \text{ g of KCl (2SF)}$

c. $25.0 \text{ mL of solution} \times \dfrac{6.0 \text{ moles of HCl}}{1 \text{ L of solution}} \times \dfrac{1 \text{ L of solution}}{1000 \text{ mL of solution}} \times \dfrac{36.5 \text{ g of HCl}}{1 \text{ mole of HCl}}$

$= 5.5 \text{ g of HCl (2SF)}$

8.53 **a.** $3.0 \text{ moles of NaOH} \times \dfrac{1 \text{ L of solution}}{2 \text{ moles of NaOH}} = 1.5 \text{ L of solution (2SF)}$

b. $15 \text{ moles of NaCl} \times \dfrac{1 \text{ L of solution}}{1.5 \text{ moles of NaCl}} = 10. \text{ L of solution (2SF)}$

c. $0.0500 \text{ mole of Ca(NO}_3)_2 \times \dfrac{1 \text{ L of solution}}{0.800 \text{ mole of Ca(NO}_3)_2} \times \dfrac{1000 \text{ mL of solution}}{1 \text{ L of solution}}$

$= 62.5 \text{ mL of solution (3SF)}$

8.55 The concentration of a diluted solution can be calculated using the following relationship:

$$\% \text{ (m/v) of dilute solution} = \dfrac{\text{grams of solute}}{\text{volume of dilute solution}} \times 100\%$$

$$\text{or molarity of dilute solution} = \dfrac{\text{moles of solute}}{\text{volume of dilute solution in L}}$$

a. From the initial solution:

$$2.0 \text{ L of solution} \times \dfrac{6.0 \text{ moles of HCl}}{1 \text{ L of solution}} = 12 \text{ moles of HCl (solute)}$$

$$\text{Molarity of the dilute solution} = \dfrac{12 \text{ moles of HCl}}{6.0 \text{ L of solution}} = 2.0 \text{ M HCl (2SF)}$$

b. $\dfrac{12 \text{ moles NaOH}}{1 \text{ L of solution}} \times 0.50 \text{ L of solution} = 6.0 \text{ moles of NaOH (solute)}$

$$\text{Final molarity is } \dfrac{6.0 \text{ moles of NaOH}}{3.0 \text{ L of solution}} = 2.0 \text{ M NaOH (solute)}$$

c. $10.0 \text{ mL of solution} \times \dfrac{25 \text{ g of KOH}}{100 \text{ mL of solution}} = 2.5 \text{ g of KOH (solute)}$

$$\text{Final \% (m/v) is } \dfrac{2.5 \text{ g of KOH}}{100.0 \text{ mL of solution}} \times 100\% = 2.5\% \text{ (m/v) KOH (2SF)}$$

d. $50.0 \text{ mL of solution} \times \dfrac{15 \text{ g of H}_2\text{SO}_4}{100 \text{ mL of solution}} = 7.5 \text{ g of H}_2\text{SO}_4 \text{ (solute)}$

$$\text{Final \% (m/v) is } \dfrac{7.5 \text{ g of H}_2\text{SO}_4}{250 \text{ mL of solution}} \times 100\% = 3.0\% \text{ (m/v) H}_2\text{SO}_4 \text{ (2SF)}$$

8.57 The final volume of a diluted solution can be found by using the following relationship: $C_1 V_1 = C_2 V_2$, where C_1 is the concentration (M or %) of the initial (concentrated) and C_2 is the concentration (M or %) of final (dilute) solution and V_1 is the volume of the initial (concentrated) solution. Solving for V_2 gives the volume of the dilute solution.

a. $V_2 = \dfrac{M_1}{M_2} V_1 = \dfrac{6.0 \text{ moles/L}}{0.20 \text{ mole/L}} \times 0.0200 \text{ L} = 0.60 \text{ L (2SF)}$

b. $V_2 = \dfrac{\%_1}{\%_2} V_1 = \dfrac{10.0\%}{2.0\%} \times 50.0 \text{ mL} = 250 \text{ mL (2SF)}$

c. $V_2 = \dfrac{M_1}{M_2} V_1 = \dfrac{6.0 \text{ moles/L}}{0.50 \text{ mole/L}} \times 0.500 \text{ L} = 6.0 \text{ L (2SF)}$

d. $V_2 = \dfrac{\%_1}{\%_2} V_1 = \dfrac{12\%}{5.0\%} \times 75 \text{ mL} = 180 \text{ mL (2SF)}$

8.59 **a.** $50.0 \; \text{mL of solution} \times \dfrac{1 \; \text{L of solution}}{1000 \; \text{mL of solution}} \times \dfrac{1.50 \; \text{moles of KCl}}{1 \; \text{L of solution}} = 0.0750 \; \text{mole of KCl}$

$0.0750 \; \text{mole of KCl} \times \dfrac{1 \; \text{mole of PbCl}_2}{2 \; \text{moles of KCl}} \times \dfrac{278.2 \; \text{g of PbCl}_2}{1 \; \text{mole of PbCl}_2} = 10.4 \; \text{g of PbCl}_2 \; (3\text{SF})$

b. $50.0 \; \text{mL of solution} \times \dfrac{1 \; \text{L of solution}}{1000 \; \text{mL of solution}} \times \dfrac{1.50 \; \text{moles of KCl}}{1 \; \text{L of solution}} = 0.0750 \; \text{mole of KCl}$

$0.0750 \; \text{mole of KCl} \times \dfrac{1 \; \text{mole of Pb(NO}_3)_2}{2 \; \text{moles of KCl}} \times \dfrac{1 \; \text{L of solution}}{2.00 \; \text{moles of Pb(NO}_3)_2} = 0.0188 \; \text{L of solution}$

$0.0188 \; \text{L} \times \dfrac{1000 \; \text{mL}}{1 \; \text{L}} = 18.8 \; \text{mL of solution} \; (3\text{SF})$

8.61 **a.** $15.0 \; \text{g of Mg} \times \dfrac{1 \; \text{mole of Mg}}{24.3 \; \text{g of Mg}} = 0.617 \; \text{mole of Mg}$

$0.617 \; \text{mole of Mg} \times \dfrac{2 \; \text{moles HCl}}{1 \; \text{mole of Mg}} \times \dfrac{1 \; \text{L of solution}}{6.00 \; \text{moles of HCl}} = 0.206 \; \text{L of solution}$

$0.206 \; \text{L} \times \dfrac{1000 \; \text{mL}}{1 \; \text{L}} = 206 \; \text{mL of HCl solution} \; (3\text{SF})$

b. $0.500 \; \text{L of solution} \times \dfrac{2.00 \; \text{moles of HCl}}{1 \; \text{L of solution}} \times \dfrac{1 \; \text{mole of H}_2}{2 \; \text{moles of HCl}} = 0.500 \; \text{mole of H}_2 \; \text{gas} \; (3\text{SF})$

8.63 **a.** A solution cannot be separated by a semipermeable membrane.
b. A suspension settles as time passes.

8.65 **a.** Since each NaCl unit dissociates into two particles, the number of moles of NaCl is half of the number of moles of particles desired or 0.060 mole of NaCl.
b. Since each K_3PO_4 unit dissociates into four particles, the number of moles K_3PO_4 is one quarter of the number of moles of particles desired or 0.030 moles of K_3PO_4.

8.67 **a.** The 10% (m/v) starch solution has a higher osmotic pressure than pure water.
b. The water will initially flow into the starch solution to dilute the solute concentration.
c. The volume of the starch solution will increase due to inflow of water.

8.69 Water flows out of the solution with the higher solvent concentration (which corresponds to a lower solute concentration) to the solution with a lower solvent concentration (which corresponds to a higher solute concentration).
a. The volume of compartment B will rise because water flows into compartment B, which contains the 10% (m/v) starch solution.
b. The volume of compartment B will rise because water flows into compartment B, which contains the 8% (m/v) albumin solution.
c. The volume of compartment B will rise because water flows into compartment B, which contains the 10% (m/v) sucrose solution.

8.71 A red blood cell has an osmotic pressure of a 5% (m/v) glucose solution or a 0.9% (m/v) NaCl solution. In a hypotonic solution (lower osmotic pressure), solvent flows from the hypotonic solution into the red blood cell. When a red blood cell is placed in a hypertonic solution (higher osmotic pressure), solvent (water) flows from the red blood cell to the hypertonic solution. Isotonic solutions have the same osmotic pressure, and a red blood cell in an isotonic solution will not change volume because the flow of solvent into and out of the cell is equal.
a. Distilled water is a hypotonic solution when compared with a red blood cell's contents.
b. A 1% (m/v) glucose solution is a hypotonic solution.
c. A 0.90% (m/v) NaCl solution is isotonic with a red blood cell's contents.
d. A 5.0% (m/v) glucose solution is an isotonic solution.

8.73 Colloids cannot pass through the semipermeable dialysis membrane; water and solutions freely pass through semipermeable membranes.
   a. Sodium and chloride ions will both pass through the membrane into the distilled water.
   b. The amino acid alanine can pass through a dialysis membrane; the colloid starch will not.
   c. Sodium and chloride ions will both be present in the water surrounding the dialysis bag; the colloid starch will not.
   d. Urea will diffuse through the dialysis bag into the water.

8.75 **a.** 3 (no dissociation)   **b.** 1 (some dissociation, a few ions)   **c.** 2 (all ionized)

8.77 The skin of the cucumber acts like a semipermeable membrane. A "brine" salt water solution has a high concentration of Na^+Cl^-, which is hypertonic to the pickle. Therefore, water flows from the cucumber into the hypertonic salt solution that surrounds it. The loss of water causes the cucumber to become a wrinkled pickle.

8.79 **a.** 2 To halve the % concentration, the volume would double.
   b. 3 To go to one-fourth the % concentration, the volume would be four times the initial.

8.81 **a.** 3 Silver chloride will precipitate when the two solutions are mixed.
   b. $NaCl(aq) + AgNO_3(aq) \rightarrow NaNO_3(aq) + AgCl(s)$

$$Na^+(aq) + Cl^-(aq) + Ag^+(aq) + NO_3^-(aq) \rightarrow AgCl(s) + Na^+(aq) + NO_3^-(aq)$$

   c. $Ag^+(aq) + Cl^-(aq) \rightarrow AgCl(s)$

8.83 **a.** 2 Water will flow into the B (8%) side.
   b. 1 Water will continue to flow equally in both directions; no change in volumes.
   c. 3 Water will flow into the A (5%) side.
   d. 2 Water will flow into the B (1%) side.

8.85 Iodine is a nonpolar molecule and needs a nonpolar solvent such as hexane. Iodine does not dissolve in water because water is a polar solvent.

8.87 $80.0 \text{ g of NaCl} \times \dfrac{100 \text{ g of water}}{36.0 \text{ g of NaCl}} = 222 \text{ g of water (3SF)}$

8.89 **a.** Unsaturated solution; 200 g of H_2O can dissolve up to 68 g of KNO_3.
   b. Saturated solution; this is equal to 34 g of KNO_3 in 100 g of H_2O.
   c. Saturated solution; this is equal to 45 g of KNO_3 in 100 g of H_2O, exceeding the 34 g of KNO_3 maximum that can dissolve in 100 g of H_2O at 20 °C.

8.91 $\dfrac{15.5 \text{ g of } Na_2SO_4}{15.5 \text{ g of } Na_2SO_4 + 75.5 \text{ g of water}} \times 100\% = 17.0\% \text{ (m/m) } Na_2SO_4 \text{ (3SF)}$

8.93 **a.** $24 \text{ h} \times \dfrac{750 \text{ mL of solution}}{12 \text{ h}} \times \dfrac{4 \text{ g of amino acids}}{100 \text{ mL of solution}} = 60 \text{ g of amino acids (1SF)}$

$24 \text{ h} \times \dfrac{750 \text{ mL of solution}}{12 \text{ h}} \times \dfrac{25 \text{ g of glucose}}{100 \text{ mL of solution}} = 380 \text{ g of glucose (2SF)}$

$24 \text{ h} \times \dfrac{500 \text{ mL of solution}}{12 \text{ h}} \times \dfrac{10 \text{ g of lipid}}{100 \text{ mL of solution}} = 100 \text{ g of lipid (1SF)}$

   b. $60 \text{ g of amino acid (protein)} \times \dfrac{4 \text{ kcal}}{1 \text{ g of protein}} = 240 \text{ kcal (1SF)}$

$380 \text{ g of glucose (carbohydrate)} \times \dfrac{4 \text{ kcal}}{1 \text{ g of carbohydrate}} = 1520 \text{ kcal (2SF)}$

$100 \text{ g of lipid (fat)} \times \dfrac{9 \text{ kcal}}{1 \text{ g of fat}} = 900 \text{ kcal (1SF)}$

For a total of 240 kcal + 1520 kcal + 900 kcal = (2660 kcal) = 2700 kcal per day (2SF)

8.95 $4.5 \text{ mL of propyl alcohol} \times \dfrac{100 \text{ mL of solution}}{12 \text{ mL of propyl alcohol}} = 38 \text{ mL of solution (2SF)}$

8.97 $0.250 \text{ L of solution} \times \dfrac{2.00 \text{ moles of KCl}}{1 \text{ L of solution}} \times \dfrac{74.6 \text{ g of KCl}}{1 \text{ mole of KCl}} = 37.3 \text{ g of KCl (3SF)}$

To make a 2.00-M KCl solution, weigh out 37.3 g KCl (0.500 mole) and place in a volumetric flask. Add enough water to dissolve the KCl and give a final volume of 0.250 L.

8.99 Mass of solution: 70.0 g of solute + 130.0 g of solvent = 200.0 g of solution

a. $\dfrac{70.0 \text{ g of } HNO_3}{(70.0 \text{ g} + 130.0 \text{ g})} \times 100\% = \dfrac{70.0 \text{ g of } HNO_3}{200.0 \text{ g of solution}} \times 100\% = 35.0\% \text{ (m/m) } HNO_3 \text{ (3SF)}$

b. $200.0 \text{ g of solution} \times \dfrac{1 \text{ mL of solution}}{1.21 \text{ g of solution}} = 165 \text{ mL of solution (3SF)}$

c. $\dfrac{70.0 \text{ g of } HNO_3}{165 \text{ mL of solution}} \times 100\% = 42.4\% \text{ (m/v) } HNO_3 \text{ (3SF)}$

d. $\dfrac{70.0 \text{ g of } HNO_3}{165 \text{ mL of solution}} \times \dfrac{1 \text{ mole of } HNO_3}{63.0 \text{ g of } HNO_3} \times \dfrac{1000 \text{ mL of solution}}{1 \text{ L of solution}} = 6.73 \text{ M } HNO_3 \text{ (3SF)}$

8.101 a. $2.5 \text{ L of solution} \times \dfrac{3.0 \text{ moles of } Al(NO_3)_3}{1 \text{ L of solution}} \times \dfrac{213.0 \text{ g of } Al(NO_3)_3}{1 \text{ mole of } Al(NO_3)_3} = 1600 \text{ g of } Al(NO_3)_3 \text{ (2SF)}$

b. $75 \text{ mL of solution} \times \dfrac{1 \text{ L of solution}}{1000 \text{ mL of solution}} \times \dfrac{0.50 \text{ mole of } C_6H_{12}O_6}{1 \text{ L of solution}} \times \dfrac{180.0 \text{ g of } C_6H_{12}O_6}{1 \text{ mole of } C_6H_{12}O_6}$

$= 6.8 \text{ g of } C_6H_{12}O_6 \text{ (2SF)}$

8.103 When solutions of $NaNO_3$ and KCl are mixed, no insoluble product forms because all of the possible combinations of salts are soluble. When KCl and $Pb(NO_3)_2$ solutions are mixed, the insoluble salt $PbCl_2$ forms.

8.105 a. $Ag^+(aq) + Cl^-(aq) \rightarrow AgCl(s)$
b. none
c. $Ba^{2+}(aq) + SO_4^{2-}(aq) \rightarrow BaSO_4(s)$

8.107 $M_1V_1 = M_2V_2$

a. $M_2 = \dfrac{M_1V_1}{V_2} = \dfrac{(0.200 \text{ M})(25.0 \text{ mL})}{50.0 \text{ mL}} = 0.100 \text{ M NaBr (3SF)}$

b. $M_2 = \dfrac{M_1V_1}{V_2} = \dfrac{(1.20 \text{ M})(15.0 \text{ mL})}{40.0 \text{ mL}} = 0.450 \text{ M } K_2SO_4 \text{ (3SF)}$

c. $M_2 = \dfrac{M_1V_1}{V_2} = \dfrac{(6.00 \text{ M})(75.0 \text{ mL})}{255 \text{ mL}} = 1.76 \text{ M NaOH (3SF)}$

8.109 a. $M_1V_1 = M_2V_2 \quad V_2 = \dfrac{M_1V_1}{M_2} = \dfrac{(5.00 \text{ M})(25.0 \text{ mL})}{2.50 \text{ M}} = 50.0 \text{ mL of HCl solution (3SF)}$

b. $M_1V_1 = M_2V_2 \quad V_2 = \dfrac{M_1V_1}{M_2} = \dfrac{(5.00 \text{ M})(25.0 \text{ mL})}{1.00 \text{ M}} = 125 \text{ mL of HCl solution (3SF)}$

c. $M_1V_1 = M_2V_2 \quad V_2 = \dfrac{M_1V_1}{M_2} = \dfrac{(5.00 \text{ M})(25.0 \text{ mL})}{0.500 \text{ M}} = 250. \text{ mL of HCl solution (3SF)}$

8.111 $60.0 \; \cancel{\text{mL of antacid}} \times \dfrac{1 \; \cancel{\text{L of antacid}}}{1000 \; \cancel{\text{mL of antacid}}} \times \dfrac{1.00 \; \cancel{\text{mole of Al(OH)}_3}}{1 \; \cancel{\text{L of antacid}}} \times \dfrac{3 \; \cancel{\text{moles of HCl}}}{1 \; \cancel{\text{mole of Al(OH)}_3}}$

$\times \dfrac{1000 \; \text{mL of HCl}}{6.00 \; \cancel{\text{moles of HCl}}} = 30.0 \; \text{mL of HCl solution (3SF)}$

8.113 A solution with a high salt (solute) concentration will dry flowers because water (solvent) flows out of the flowers' cells and into the salt solution to dilute the salt concentration.

8.115 Drinking seawater, which is hypertonic, will cause water to flow out of the body cells and dehydrate the body's cells.

8.117 $80.0 \; \cancel{\text{mL of solution}} \times \dfrac{1 \; \cancel{\text{L of solution}}}{1000 \; \cancel{\text{mL of solution}}} \times \dfrac{4.00 \; \text{moles of HNO}_3}{1 \; \cancel{\text{L of solution}}} = 0.320 \; \text{mole of HNO}_3$

$0.320 \; \cancel{\text{mole of HNO}_3} \times \dfrac{2 \; \cancel{\text{moles of NO}}}{8 \; \cancel{\text{moles of HNO}_3}} \times \dfrac{30.0 \; \text{g of NO}}{1 \; \cancel{\text{mole of NO}}} = 2.40 \; \text{g of NO (3SF)}$

8.119 **a.** Na^+ salts are soluble.
b. The halide salts containing Pb^{2+} are insoluble.
c. K^+ salts are soluble.
d. Salts containing NH_4^+ ions are soluble.
e. Salts containing CO_3^{2-} are usually insoluble.
f. The salt containing PO_4^{3-} and Fe^{3+} is insoluble.

8.121 **a.** Mass of NaCl is $25.50 \; \text{g} - 24.10 \; \text{g} = 1.40 \; \text{g of NaCl}$
   Mass of solution is $36.15 \; \text{g} - 24.10 \; \text{g} = 12.05 \; \text{g of solution}$

   $\dfrac{1.40 \; \text{g of NaCl}}{12.05 \; \text{g of solution}} \times 100\% = 11.6\% \; \text{(m/m) NaCl (3SF)}$

   b. $1.40 \; \cancel{\text{g of NaCl}} \times \dfrac{1 \; \text{mole of NaCl}}{58.5 \; \cancel{\text{g of NaCl}}} = 0.0239 \; \text{mole of NaCl}$

   $\dfrac{0.0239 \; \text{mole of NaCl}}{10.0 \; \cancel{\text{mL of solution}}} \times \dfrac{1000 \; \cancel{\text{mL of solution}}}{1 \; \text{L of solution}} = 2.39 \; \text{M NaCl (3SF)}$

   c. $M_1 V_1 = M_2 V_2 \quad M_2 = \dfrac{M_1 V_1}{V_2} = \dfrac{(2.39 \; \text{M})(10.0 \; \cancel{\text{mL}})}{60.0 \; \cancel{\text{mL}}} = 0.398 \; \text{M NaCl (3SF)}$

8.123 Mass of solution: $22.0 \; \text{g of solute} + 118.0 \; \text{g of solvent} = 140.0 \; \text{g of solution}$
   a. $\dfrac{22.0 \; \text{g of NaOH}}{140.0 \; \text{g of solution}} \times 100\% = 15.7\% \; \text{(m/m) NaOH (3SF)}$

   b. $140.0 \; \cancel{\text{g of solution}} \times \dfrac{1 \; \text{mL of solution}}{1.15 \; \cancel{\text{g of solution}}} = 122 \; \text{mL of solution (3SF)}$

   c. $\dfrac{22.0 \; \cancel{\text{g NaOH}}}{122 \; \cancel{\text{mL of solution}}} \times \dfrac{1 \; \text{mole of NaOH}}{40.0 \; \cancel{\text{g of NaOH}}} \times \dfrac{1000 \; \cancel{\text{mL of solution}}}{1 \; \text{L of solution}} = \dfrac{4.51 \; \text{moles of NaOH}}{\text{L of solution}}$
   $= 4.51 \; \text{M NaOH (3SF)}$

8.125 $75.0 \; \cancel{\text{mL of solution}} \times \dfrac{1 \; \cancel{\text{L of solution}}}{1000 \; \cancel{\text{mL of solution}}} \times \dfrac{1.50 \; \cancel{\text{moles of NaBr}}}{1 \; \cancel{\text{L of solution}}} \times \dfrac{102.9 \; \text{g of NaBr}}{1 \; \cancel{\text{mole of NaBr}}}$
   $= 11.6 \; \text{g of NaBr (3SF)}$

9.1 **a.** The rate of a reaction relates the speed at which reactants are transformed into products.
   b. Because fewer reactants will have the energy necessary to proceed to products (the activation energy) at refrigerator temperature than at room temperature, the rate of formation of mold will be slower at a cooler temperature in a refrigerator.

9.3 Adding Br_2 increases the concentration of reactants, which increases the number of collisions that take place between the reactants.

9.5 **a.** Adding more reactant increases the reaction rate.
   b. Increasing the temperature increases the number of collisions with the energy of activation, which increases the rate of reaction.
   c. Adding a catalyst increases the reaction rate.
   d. Removing a reactant decreases the reaction rate.

9.7 If a reaction takes place in both a forward and reverse direction, it is called a reversible reaction.

9.9 **a.** Broken glass cannot be put back together; it is not reversible.
   b. In this physical process, heat melts the solid form of water, while removing heat can change liquid water back to solid. It is reversible.
   c. A pan is warmed when heated and cooled when heat is removed; it is reversible.

9.11 In the expression for K_c, the products are divided by the reactants, with each concentration raised to a power that equals the coefficient in the equation:

a. $K_c = \dfrac{[CS_2][H_2]^4}{[CH_4][H_2S]^2}$ **b.** $K_c = \dfrac{[N_2][O_2]}{[NO]^2}$ **c.** $K_c = \dfrac{[CS_2][O_2]^4}{[SO_3]^2[CO_2]}$

9.13 **a.** only one state (gas) is present; homogeneous
   b. solid and gaseous states; heterogeneous
   c. only one state (gas) is present; homogeneous
   d. gas and liquid states; heterogeneous

9.15 **a.** $K_c = \dfrac{[O_2]^3}{[O_3]^2}$ **b.** $K_c = [CO_2][H_2O]$

c. $K_c = \dfrac{[H_2]^3[CO]}{[CH_4][H_2O]}$ **d.** $K_c = \dfrac{[Cl_2]^2}{[HCl]^4[O_2]}$

9.17 $K_c = \dfrac{[NO_2]^2}{[N_2O_4]} = \dfrac{[0.21]^2}{[0.030]} = 1.5 \ (2SF)$

9.19 $K_c = \dfrac{[CH_4][H_2O]}{[CO][H_2]^3} = \dfrac{[1.8][2.0]}{[0.51][0.30]^3} = 260 \ (2SF)$

9.21 **a.** A large K_c indicates that the equilibrium mixture contains mostly products.
   b. A K_c of about 1 indicates that the equilibrium mixture contains significant amounts of both reactants and products.
   c. A small K_c indicates that the equilibrium mixture contains mostly reactants.

9.23 $K_c = \dfrac{[HI]^2}{[H_2][I_2]}$

Rearrange K_c to solve for $[H_2]$ and substitute concentrations to calculate $[H_2]$.

$[H_2] = \dfrac{[HI]^2}{K_c[I_2]} = \dfrac{[0.030]^2}{[54][0.015]} = 1.1 \times 10^{-3}$ M (2SF)

9.25 $K_c = \dfrac{[NO]^2[Br_2]}{[NOBr]^2}$

Rearrange K_c to solve for $[NOBr]$.

$[NOBr]^2 = \dfrac{[NO]^2[Br_2]}{K_c} = \dfrac{[2.0]^2[1.0]}{2.0} = 2.0$ Take the square root of both sides of the equation.

$[NOBr] = \sqrt{2.0} = 1.4$ M (2SF)

9.27 **a.** When more reactant is added to an equilibrium mixture, the product/reactant ratio is initially less than K_c.
   b. According to Le Châtelier's principle, equilibrium is established once again when the forward reaction shifts to products to make the product/reactant ratio equal the K_c.

9.29 **a.** Adding more reactant shifts equilibrium to form more products.
   b. Adding more product shifts equilibrium to form more reactants.
   c. Adding heat, a reactant, shifts equilibrium to form more products.
   d. Decreasing volume favors the side of the reaction with fewer moles of gas, so there is a shift to form more products.
   e. A catalyst does not shift an equilibrium.

9.31 **a.** Adding more reactant shifts equilibrium to form more products.
   b. Adding heat, a reactant, shifts equilibrium to form more products.
   c. Removing product shifts equilibrium to form more products.
   d. A catalyst does not shift an equilibrium.
   e. Removing reactant shifts equilibrium to form more reactants.

9.33 **a.** $MgCO_3(s) \rightleftharpoons Mg^{2+}(aq) + CO_3^{2-}(aq)$; $K_{sp} = [Mg^{2+}][CO_3^{2-}]$

   b. $PbI_2(s) \rightleftharpoons Pb^{2+}(aq) + 2I^-(aq)$; $K_{sp} = [Pb^{2+}][I^-]^2$

   c. $Ag_3PO_4(s) \rightleftharpoons 3Ag^+(aq) + PO_4^{3-}(aq)$; $K_{sp} = [Ag^+]^3[PO_4^{3-}]$

9.35 $BaSO_4(s) \rightleftharpoons Ba^{2+}(aq) + SO_4^{2-}(aq)$; $K_{sp} = [Ba^{2+}][SO_4^{2-}] = (1 \times 10^{-5})(1 \times 10^{-5})$
   $= K_{sp} = 1 \times 10^{-10}$ (1SF)

9.37 $Ag_2CO_3(s) \rightleftharpoons 2Ag^+(aq) + CO_3^{2-}(aq)$; $K_{sp} = [Ag^+]^2[CO_3^{2-}] = (2.6 \times 10^{-4})^2(1.3 \times 10^{-4})$
   $= K_{sp} = 8.8 \times 10^{-12}$ (2SF)

9.39 $CuI(s) \rightleftharpoons Cu^+(aq) + I^-(aq)$; $K_{sp} = [Cu^+][I^-]$

Show the molarity of the ions as S in the equation with the known value of K_{sp}.

$K_{sp} = [S][S] = 1 \times 10^{-12}$ Solve for the solubility S.

$S \times S = S^2 = 1 \times 10^{-12}$ Take the square root of both sides of the equation.

$S = \sqrt{1 \times 10^{-12}} = 1 \times 10^{-6}$ mole/L; $[Cu^+] = 1 \times 10^{-6}$ M; $[I^-] = 1 \times 10^{-6}$ M (1SF)

9.41 There are mostly reactants and a few products, which gives a small equilibrium constant.

9.43 **a.** There are more products, which means that heat must be reduced; T_2 is lower than T_1.
b. Because the equilibrium mixture at T_2 has more products, the K_c for T_2 is larger than the K_c for the equilibrium mixture at T_1.

9.45 **a.** Adding heat, a product, shifts equilibrium toward reactants.
b. Decreasing volume favors products with fewer moles of gas.
c. Adding a catalyst does not shift equilibrium.
d. Adding a reactant shifts equilibrium toward products.

9.47 Convert the powers of the concentrations in the K_{sp} expression to give the stoichiometry.
$$Fe(OH)_3(s) \rightleftharpoons Fe^{3+}(aq) + 3OH^-(aq)$$

9.49 **a.** $K_c = \dfrac{[CO_2][H_2O]^2}{[CH_4][O_2]^2}$ **b.** $K_c = \dfrac{[N_2]^2[H_2O]^6}{[NH_3]^4[O_2]^3}$ **c.** $K_c = \dfrac{[CH_4]}{[H_2]^2}$

9.51 **a.** An equilibrium mixture with a large K_c consists of mostly products.
b. An equilibrium mixture with a K_c of about 1 consists of significant quantities of both products and reactants.
c. An equilibrium mixture with a small K_c consists of mostly reactants.

9.53 The numerator in the K_c expression gives the products in the equation, and the denominator gives the reactants.
a. $SO_2Cl_2(g) \rightleftharpoons SO_2(g) + Cl_2(g)$ **b.** $Br_2(g) + Cl_2(g) \rightleftharpoons 2BrCl(g)$
c. $CO(g) + 3H_2(g) \rightleftharpoons CH_4(g) + H_2O(g)$ **d.** $2O_2(g) + 2NH_3(g) \rightleftharpoons N_2O(g) + 3H_2O(g)$

9.55 **a.** $K_c = \dfrac{[N_2][H_2]^3}{[NH_3]^2}$ **b.** $K_c = \dfrac{[3.0][0.50]^3}{[0.20]^2} = 9.4$ (2SF)

9.57 $K_c = \dfrac{[N_2O_4]}{[NO_2]^2}$ Rearranging K_c: $[N_2O_4] = K_c[NO_2]^2$

$[N_2O_4] = 5.0[0.50]^2 = 1.3$ M (2SF)

9.59 **a.** Adding a reactant shifts equilibrium to form more products.
b. Adding a product shifts equilibrium to form more reactants.
c. Adding a reactant shifts equilibrium to form more products.
d. Adding a product shifts equilibrium to form more reactants.

9.61 Decreasing the volume of an equilibrium mixture shifts the equilibrium to the side of the reaction that has the fewer number of moles of gas. No shift occurs when there are an equal number of moles of gas on both sides of the equation.
a. Three moles of gas on the reactant side and two moles of gas on the product side shifts equilibrium to form more products.
b. Two moles of gas on the reactant side and three moles of gas on the product side shifts equilibrium to form more reactants.
c. Six moles of gas on reactant side and zero moles of gas on the product side shifts equilibrium to form more products.
d. Four moles of gas on the reactant side and five moles of gas on the product side shifts equilibrium to form more reactants.

9.63 **a.** A small K_c indicates that the equilibrium mixture contains mostly reactants.
b. A large K_c indicates that the equilibrium mixture contains mostly products.

9.65 **a.** $CuCO_3(s) \rightleftarrows Cu^{2+}(aq) + CO_3^{2-}(aq)$; $K_{sp} = [Cu^{2+}][CO_3^{2-}]$

  b. $PbF_2(s) \rightleftarrows Pb^{2+}(aq) + 2F^-(aq)$; $K_{sp} = [Pb^{2+}][F^-]^2$

  c. $Fe(OH)_3(s) \rightleftarrows Fe^{3+}(aq) + 3OH^-(aq)$; $K_{sp} = [Fe^{3+}][OH^-]^3$

9.67 $FeS(s) \rightleftarrows Fe^{2+}(aq) + S^{2-}(aq)$; $K_{sp} = [Fe^{2+}][S^{2-}]$

$K_{sp} = (7.7 \times 10^{-10})(7.7 \times 10^{-10}) = 5.9 \times 10^{-19}$ (2SF)

9.69 $Mn(OH)_2(s) \rightleftarrows Mn^{2+}(aq) + 2OH^-(aq)$; $K_{sp} = [Mn^{2+}][OH^-]^2$

$K_{sp} = (3.7 \times 10^{-5})(7.4 \times 10^{-5})^2 = 2.0 \times 10^{-13}$ (2SF)

9.71 $CdS(s) \rightleftarrows Cd^{2+}(aq) + S^{2-}(aq)$; $K_{sp} = [Cd^{2+}][S^{2-}]$

Show the molarity of the ions as S in the equation with the known value of K_{sp}.

$K_{sp} = [S][S] = 1.0 \times 10^{-24}$ Solve for the solubility S.

$S \times S = S^2 = 1.0 \times 10^{-24}$ Take the square root of both sides of the equation.

$S = \sqrt{1.0 \times 10^{-24}} = 1.0 \times 10^{-12}$ mole/L; $[Cd^{2+}] = 1.0 \times 10^{-12}$ M; $[S^{2-}] = 1.0 \times 10^{-12}$ M (2SF)

9.73 **a.** $\dfrac{[PCl_3][Cl_2]}{[PCl_5]} = \dfrac{[0.050\ M][0.050\ M]}{[0.10\ M]} = 0.025$ (2SF), which is not equal to K_c (0.042).

  This mixture is not at equilibrium.

  b. Since 0.025 is less than K_c, the new equilibrium mixture must have more PCl_5 and less Cl_2 and PCl_3; the reaction will proceed in the forward direction.

9.75 **a.** $K_c = \dfrac{[PCl_3][Cl_2]}{[PCl_5]}$

  b. Since PCl_3 and Cl_2 are formed in a 1:1 ratio, 0.16 mole of Cl_2 is formed and 0.16 mole of PCl_5 is reacted, leaving $0.60 - 0.16 = 0.44$ mole of PCl_5. At equilibrium, the concentrations are $[PCl_3] = [Cl_2] = 0.16$ M, $[PCl_5] = 0.44$ M (2SF)

  c. $K_c = \dfrac{[PCl_3][Cl_2]}{[PCl_5]} = \dfrac{[0.16][0.16]}{[0.44]} = 0.058$ (2SF)

  d. When Cl_2 is added to the equilibrium mixture, the shift will be toward the reactant and $[PCl_5]$ will increase.

9.77 **a.** $K_c = \dfrac{[CO]^2}{[CO_2]} = \dfrac{[0.030]^2}{[0.060]} = 0.015$ (2SF)

  b. If more CO_2 is added, the equilibrium will shift toward the products.

  c. If the container volume is decreased, the equilibrium will shift to the side with the least number of moles of gas, which is the reactant side.

9.79 $Mg(OH)_2(s) \rightleftarrows Mg^{2+}(aq) + 2OH^-(aq)$; $K_{sp} = [Mg^{2+}][OH^-]^2$

$\dfrac{9.7 \times 10^{-3}\ \text{g of Mg(OH)}_2}{1\ \text{L of solution}} \times \dfrac{1\ \text{mole of Mg(OH)}_2}{58.3\ \text{g of Mg(OH)}_2} = 1.7 \times 10^{-4}\ \text{M Mg(OH)}_2$

$\dfrac{1.7 \times 10^{-4}\ \text{mole of Mg(OH)}_2}{1\ \text{L of solution}} \times \dfrac{1\ \text{mole of Mg}^{2+}}{1\ \text{mole of Mg(OH)}_2} = 1.7 \times 10^{-4}\ \text{M Mg}^{2+} = [Mg^{2+}]$

$\dfrac{1.7 \times 10^{-4}\ \text{mole of Mg(OH)}_2}{1\ \text{L of solution}} \times \dfrac{2\ \text{moles of OH}^-}{1\ \text{mole of Mg(OH)}_2} = 3.4 \times 10^{-4}\ \text{M OH}^- = [OH^-]$

$K_{sp} = (1.7 \times 10^{-4})(3.4 \times 10^{-4})^2 = 2.0 \times 10^{-11}$ (2SF)

79

10

Acids and Bases

10.1   **a.** Acids taste sour.   **b.** Acids neutralize bases.
c. Acids produce H^+ ions in water.   **d.** Potassium hydroxide is the name of a base.

10.3   The names of non–oxy acids begin with *hydro–*, followed by the name of the anion. The names of oxyacids use the element root with *–ic acid*. Acids with one oxygen less than the common *–ic acid* name are named as *–ous acids*. Bases are named as ionic compounds containing hydroxide anions.
a. hydrochloric acid   **b.** calcium hydroxide   **c.** carbonic acid
d. nitric acid   **e.** sulfurous acid   **f.** iron(II) hydroxide

10.5   **a.** $Mg(OH)_2$ **b.** HF   **c.** H_3PO_4
d. LiOH   **e.** $Cu(OH)_2$

10.7   The acid donates a proton (H^+), whereas the base accepts a proton.
a. acid (proton donor), HI   proton acceptor (base), H_2O
b. acid (proton donor), H_2O proton acceptor (base), F^-

10.9   To form the conjugate base, remove a proton (H^+) from the acid.
a. F^-, fluoride ion   **b.** OH^-, hydroxide ion
c. HCO_3^-, bicarbonate ion or hydrogen carbonate ion   **d.** SO_4^{2-}, sulfate ion

10.11   To form the conjugate acid, add a proton (H^+) to the base.
a. HCO_3^-, bicarbonate ion or hydrogen carbonate ion   **b.** H_3O^+, hydronium ion
c. H_3PO_4, phosphoric acid   **d.** HBr, hydrobromic acid

10.13   The conjugate acid is a proton donor, and the conjugate base is a proton acceptor.
a. acid H_2CO_3; conjugate base HCO_3^-; base H_2O; conjugate acid H_3O^+
b. acid NH_4^+; conjugate base NH_3; base H_2O; conjugate acid H_3O^+
c. acid HCN; conjugate base CN^-; base NO_2^-; conjugate acid HNO_2

10.15   A strong acid is a good proton donor, whereas its conjugate base is a poor proton acceptor.

10.17   Use Table 10.3 to answer.
a. HBr   **b.** HSO_4^- **c.** H_2CO_3

10.19   Use Table 10.3 to answer.
a. HSO_4^- **b.** HNO_2 **c.** HCO_3^-

10.21   **a.** From Table 10.3, we see that H_2O is a weaker base than HCO_3^- and that H_2CO_3 is a weaker acid than H_3O^+. Thus, the reactants are favored.
b. From Table 10.3, we see that NH_4^+ is a weaker acid than H_3O^+ and H_2O is a weaker base than NH_3. Thus, the reactants are favored.
c. From Table 10.3, we see that NH_4^+ is a weaker acid than HCl and that Cl^- is a weaker base than NH_3. Thus, the products are favored.

10.23   The reactants are favored because NH_4^+ is a weaker acid than HSO_4^-.

$$NH_4^+(aq) + SO_4^{2-}(aq) \rightleftharpoons NH_3(aq) + HSO_4^-(aq)$$

10.25   The smaller the K_a, the weaker the acid. The weaker acid has the stronger conjugate base.
a. H_2SO_3, which has a larger K_a than HS^-, is a stronger acid.
b. The conjugate base is formed by removing a proton from the acid, HSO_3^-.
c. The stronger acid, H_2SO_3, has a weaker conjugate base, HSO_3^-.

d. The weaker acid, HS^-, has a stronger conjugate base, S^{2-}.

e. H_2SO_3, the stronger acid, produces more ions.

10.27 $H_3PO_4(aq) + H_2O(l) \rightleftharpoons H_3O^+(aq) + H_2PO_4^-(aq)$

The K_a is the ratio of the [products] divided by the [reactants], with [H_2O] considered constant and part of the K_a.

$$K_a = \frac{[H_3O^+][H_2PO_4^-]}{[H_3PO_4]}$$

10.29 In pure water, a small fraction of the water molecules break apart to form H^+ and OH^-. The H^+ combines with H_2O to form H_3O^+. Every time a H^+ is formed, a OH^- is also formed. Therefore, the concentration of the two must be equal in pure water.

10.31 In an acidic solution, [H_3O^+] is greater than [OH^-], which means that [H_3O^+] is greater than 1×10^{-7} M and the [OH^-] is less than 1×10^{-7} M.

10.33 A neutral solution has [OH^-] = [H_3O^+] = 1.0×10^{-7} M. If [OH^-] is greater than 1×10^{-7} M, the solution is basic; if [H_3O^+] is greater than 1×10^{-7} M, the solution is acidic.
a. Acidic; [H_3O^+] is greater than 1×10^{-7} M.
b. Basic; [H_3O^+] is less than 1×10^{-7} M.
c. Basic; [OH^-] is greater than 1×10^{-7} M.
d. Acidic; [OH^-] is less than 1×10^{-7} M.

10.35 The [H_3O^+] multiplied by the [OH^-] is equal to K_w, which is 1.0×10^{-14}. When [OH^-] is known, the [H_3O^+] can be calculated. Rearranging the K_w gives [H_3O^+] = K_w/[OH^-].
a. [H_3O^+] = 1.0×10^{-5} M (2SF)   **b.** [H_3O^+] = 1.0×10^{-8} M (2SF)
c. [H_3O^+] = 5.0×10^{-10} M (2SF)   **d.** [H_3O^+] = 2.5×10^{-2} M (2SF)

10.37 The value of the [H_3O^+] multiplied by the value of the [OH^-] is always equal to K_w, which is 1×10^{-14}. When [H_3O^+] is known, the [OH^-] can be calculated. Rearranging the K_w gives [OH^-] = K_w/[H_3O^+].
a. [OH^-] = 1.0×10^{-11} M (2SF)   **b.** [OH^-] = 2.0×10^{-9} M (2SF)
c. [OH^-] = 5.6×10^{-3} M (2SF)   **d.** [OH^-] = 2.5×10^{-2} M (2SF)

10.39 In neutral solutions, [H_3O^+] = 1.0×10^{-7} M. pH = $-\log[1.0 \times 10^{-7}]$ = 7.00. The pH value contains two *decimal places*, which represent the two significant figures in the coefficient 1.0.

10.41 An acidic solution has a pH less than 7. A neutral solution has a pH equal to 7. A basic solution has a pH greater than 7.
a. basic   **b.** acidic   **c.** basic
d. acidic   **e.** acidic   **f.** basic

10.43 pH = $-\log[H_3O^+]$
The value of [H_3O^+][OH^-] = K_w, which is 1.0×10^{-14}. If [H_3O^+] needs to be calculated from [OH^-], then rearranging the K_w for [H_3O^+] gives [H_3O^+] = $\dfrac{1.0 \times 10^{-14}}{[OH^-]}$

a. pH = $-\log[1.0 \times 10^{-4}]$ = 4.00 (2 places to right of decimal point − 3SF)
b. pH = $-\log[3.0 \times 10^{-9}]$ = 8.52 (2 places to right of decimal point − 3SF)
c. [H_3O^+] = $\dfrac{1.0 \times 10^{-14}}{[1.0 \times 10^{-5}]}$ = 1.0×10^{-9} M   pH = $-\log[1.0 \times 10^{-9}]$ = 9.00 (2 places to right of decimal point − 3SF)
d. [H_3O^+] = $\dfrac{1.0 \times 10^{-14}}{[2.5 \times 10^{-11}]}$ = 4.0×10^{-4} M   pH = $-\log[4.0 \times 10^{-4}]$ = 3.40 (2 places to right of decimal point − 3SF)

e. $pH = -\log[6.7 \times 10^{-8}] = 7.17$ (2 places to right of decimal point $-$ 3SF)

f. $[H_3O^+] = \dfrac{1.0 \times 10^{-14}}{[8.2 \times 10^{-4}]} = 1.2 \times 10^{-11}$ M $\quad pH = -\log[1.2 \times 10^{-11}] = 10.92$ (2 places to right of decimal point $-$ 3SF)

10.45 On a calculator, pH is calculated by entering $-log$, followed by the coefficient *EE (EXP)* key and the power of 10 followed by the change sign *(+/−)* key. On some calculators, the concentration is entered first (coefficient *EXP*–power) followed by *log* and +/− key.

$$[H_3O^+] = \dfrac{1.0 \times 10^{-14}}{[OH^-]}; \; [OH^-] = \dfrac{1.0 \times 10^{-14}}{[H_3O^+]} \; \text{and} \quad pH = -\log[H_3O^+]$$

$[H_3O^+]$	$[OH^-]$	pH	Acidic, Basic, or Neutral?
1.0×10^{-8} M	1.0×10^{-6} M	8.00	Basic
1.0×10^{-3} M	1.0×10^{-11} M	3.00	Acidic
2.8×10^{-5} M	3.6×10^{-10} M	4.55	Acidic
2.4×10^{-5} M	4.2×10^{-10} M	4.62	Basic

$[H_3O^+]$ and $[OH^-]$ all have 2SF; all pH values have 2 places to the right of the decimal point $-$ 3SF

10.47 Acids react with active metals to form H_2 and a salt of the metal. The reaction of acids with carbonates yields CO_2, H_2O, and a salt of the metal. In a neutralization reaction, an acid and a base react to form a salt and H_2O.
a. $ZnCO_3(s) + 2HBr(aq) \rightarrow ZnBr_2(aq) + CO_2(g) + H_2O(l)$
b. $Zn(s) + 2HCl(aq) \rightarrow ZnCl_2(aq) + H_2(g)$
c. $HCl(aq) + NaHCO_3(s) \rightarrow NaCl(aq) + H_2O(l) + CO_2(g)$
d. $H_2SO_4(aq) + Mg(OH)_2(s) \rightarrow MgSO_4(aq) + 2H_2O(l)$

10.49 In balancing a neutralization equation, the number of H^+ and OH^- must be equalized by placing coefficients in front of the formulas for the acid and base.
a. $2HCl(aq) + Mg(OH)_2(s) \rightarrow MgCl_2(aq) + 2H_2O(l)$
b. $H_3PO_4(aq) + 3LiOH(aq) \rightarrow Li_3PO_4(aq) + 3H_2O(l)$

10.51 The products of a neutralization are water and a salt. In balancing a neutralization equation, the number of H^+ and OH^- must be equalized by placing coefficients in front of the formulas for the acid and base.
a. $H_2SO_4(aq) + 2NaOH(aq) \rightarrow Na_2SO_4(aq) + 2H_2O(l)$
b. $3HCl(aq) + Fe(OH)_3(s) \rightarrow FeCl_3(aq) + 3H_2O(l)$
c. $H_2CO_3(aq) + Mg(OH)_2(s) \rightarrow MgCO_3(aq) + 2H_2O(l)$

10.53 In the equation, one mole of HCl reacts with one mole of NaOH.
Moles of NaOH:

$$28.6 \text{ mL} \times \dfrac{1 \text{ L}}{1000 \text{ mL}} = 0.0286 \text{ L} \times \dfrac{0.145 \text{ mole of NaOH}}{1 \text{ L}} = 0.004\,15 \text{ mole of NaOH}$$

$$0.004\,15 \text{ mole of NaOH} \times \dfrac{1 \text{ mole of HCl}}{1 \text{ mole of NaOH}} = 0.004\,15 \text{ mole of HCl}$$

Molarity of HCl:

$$5.00 \text{ mL} \times \dfrac{1 \text{ L}}{1000 \text{ mL}} = 0.005\,00 \text{ L} \quad \dfrac{0.004\,15 \text{ mole of HCl}}{0.005\,00 \text{ L}} = 0.829 \text{ M HCl (3SF)}$$

10.55 In the equation, one mole of H_2SO_4 reacts with two moles of KOH.

Moles of KOH: $38.2 \; \text{mL} \times \dfrac{1 \; \text{L}}{1000 \; \text{mL}} = 0.0382 \; \text{L} \times \dfrac{0.163 \; \text{mole of KOH}}{1 \; \text{L}} = 0.006 \; 23 \; \text{mole of KOH}$

Moles of H_2SO_4: $0.006 \; 23 \; \text{mole of KOH} \times \dfrac{1 \; \text{mole of } H_2SO_4}{2 \; \text{moles of KOH}} = 0.003 \; 12 \; \text{mole of } H_2SO_4$

Volume of H_2SO_4: $25.0 \; \text{mL} \times \dfrac{1 \; \text{L}}{1000 \; \text{mL}} = 0.0250 \; \text{L}$

Molarity of H_2SO_4: $\dfrac{0.00 \; 312 \; \text{mole of } H_2SO_4}{0.0250 \; \text{L}} = 0.125 \; \text{M } H_2SO_4 \; (3SF)$

10.57 In the equation, one mole of H_3PO_4 reacts with three moles of NaOH.

Moles of NaOH: $16.4 \; \text{mL} \times \dfrac{1 \; \text{L}}{1000 \; \text{mL}} = 0.0164 \; \text{L} \times \dfrac{0.204 \; \text{mole of NaOH}}{1 \; \text{L}} = 0.003 \; 35 \; \text{mole of NaOH}$

Moles of H_3PO_4: $0.003 \; 35 \; \text{mole of NaOH} \times \dfrac{1 \; \text{mole of } H_3PO_4}{3 \; \text{moles of NaOH}} = 0.001 \; 12 \; \text{mole of } H_3PO_4$

Volume of H_3PO_4: $50.0 \; \text{mL} \times \dfrac{1 \; \text{L}}{1000 \; \text{mL}} = 0.0500 \; \text{L}$

Molarity of H_3PO_4: $\dfrac{0.001 \; 12 \; \text{mole of } H_3PO_4}{0.0500 \; \text{L}} = 0.0223 \; \text{M } H_3PO_4 \; (3SF)$

10.59 When a salt contains an anion from a weak acid, the anion of a weak acid removes a proton from H_2O to make a basic solution.

10.61 A solution of a salt with an anion from a strong acid and a cation from a weak base will form an acidic solution. A salt with an anion from a weak acid and a cation from a strong base will form a basic solution. Solutions of salts with ions of strong acids and strong bases are neutral.
   a. Neutral: Mg^{2+} is the cation of a strong base; Cl^- is the anion of a strong acid.
   b. Acidic: $NH_4^+(aq) + H_2O(l) \rightleftarrows NH_3(aq) + H_3O^+(aq)$ NO_3^- is the anion of a strong acid and won't affect pH; NH_4^+, the cation of the weak base NH_3, donates a proton to water to make the solution acidic.
   c. Basic: $CO_3^{2-}(aq) + H_2O(l) \rightleftarrows HCO_3^-(aq) + OH^-(aq)$ Na^+, the cation of a strong base won't affect pH; CO_3^{2-}, the anion of a weak acid, removes a proton from water to make the solution basic.
   d. Basic: $S^{2-}(aq) + H_2O(l) \rightleftarrows HS^-(aq) + OH^-(aq)$ K^+, the cation of a strong base won't affect pH; S^{2-}, the anion of a weak acid, removes a proton from water to make the solution basic.

10.63 A buffer system contains a weak acid and its salt or a weak base and its salt.
   a. This is not a buffer system because it only contains the strong base NaOH and the neutral salt NaCl.
   b. This is a buffer system; it contains the weak acid H_2CO_3, and its salt, $NaHCO_3$.
   c. This is a buffer system; it contains HF, a weak acid, and its salt, KF.
   d. This is not a buffer system because it contains the neutral salts KCl and NaCl.

10.65 **a.** A buffer system keeps the pH of a solution constant.
   b. The buffer needs to contain species that neutralize both acids and bases. As the neutralization occurs, there is a shift in the equilibrium between the acid and the conjugate base in solution.
   c. When H_3O^+ is added to the buffer, the F^- from NaF, the salt of the weak acid, reacts with the acid to neutralize it.
   $F^-(aq) + H_3O^+(aq) \rightarrow HF(aq) + H_2O(l)$
   d. When OH^- is added to the buffer solution, HF (weak acid) reacts to neutralize the OH^-.
   $HF(aq) + OH^-(aq) \rightarrow F^-(aq) + H_2O(l)$

10.67 $HNO_2(aq) + H_2O(l) \rightleftharpoons H_3O^+(aq) + NO_2^-(aq)$

Rearrange the K_a for $[H_3O^+]$ and use it to calculate the pH.

$$[H_3O^+] = K_a \times \frac{[HNO_2]}{[NO_2^-]} = 4.5 \times 10^{-4} \times \frac{[0.10\ \cancel{M}]}{[0.10\ \cancel{M}]} = 4.5 \times 10^{-4}\,M$$

$pH = -\log[4.5 \times 10^{-4}] = 3.35$ (2 places to the right of the decimal point)

10.69 Rearrange the K_a for $[H_3O^+]$ and use it to calculate the pH.

$$[H_3O^+] = 7.2 \times 10^{-4} \times \frac{[0.10\ \cancel{M}]}{[0.10\ \cancel{M}]} = 7.2 \times 10^{-4}\,M \quad pH = -\log[7.2 \times 10^{-4}] = 3.14$$

$$[H_3O^+] = 7.2 \times 10^{-4} \times \frac{[0.060\ \cancel{M}]}{[0.120\ \cancel{M}]} = 3.6 \times 10^{-4}\,M \quad pH = -\log[3.6 \times 10^{-4}] = 3.44$$

The solution with 0.10 M HF is more acidic. (2 places to the right of the decimal point)

10.71 **A.** This diagram represents a weak acid; only a few HX molecules separate into H_3O^+ and X^- ions.
B. This diagram represents a strong acid; all of the HX molecules separate H_3O^+ and X^- ions.
C. This diagram represents a weak acid; only a few HX molecules separate H_3O^+ and X^- ions.

10.73 **a.** Hyperventilation will lower the CO_2 level in the blood, which lowers the H_2CO_3 concentration, which decreases the H_3O^+ and increases the blood pH.
b. Breathing into a bag will increase the CO_2 level, increase the H_2CO_3, increase H_3O^+, and lower the blood pH.

10.75 **a.** Base, lithium hydroxide   **b.** Salt, calcium nitrate
c. Acid, hydrobromic acid   **d.** Base, barium hydroxide
e. Acid, carbonic acid   **f.** Acid, chlorous acid

10.77 An acidic solution has a pH less than 7. A neutral solution has a pH equal to 7. A basic solution has a pH greater than 7.
a. acidic   **b.** basic   **c.** acidic   **d.** acidic   **e.** basic

10.79 **a.** $Mg(OH)_2$ is a fairly strong base because all the base that dissolves is dissociated in aqueous solution.
b. $Mg(OH)_2(s) + 2HCl(aq) \rightarrow 2H_2O(l) + MgCl_2(aq)$

10.81 **a.** HF   **b.** H_3O^+ **c.** HNO_2 **d.** HCO_3^-

10.83 $[H_3O^+] = \dfrac{1.0 \times 10^{-14}}{[OH^-]}$ and $pH = -\log[H_3O^+]$

a. $pH = -\log[2.0 \times 10^{-8}] = 7.70$ (2 places to right of decimal point $-$ 3SF)
b. $pH = -\log[5.0 \times 10^{-2}] = 1.30$ (2 places to right of decimal point $-$ 3SF)
c. $[H_3O^+] = \dfrac{1.0 \times 10^{-14}}{[3.5 \times 10^{-4}]} = 2.9 \times 10^{-11}\,M \quad pH = -\log[2.9 \times 10^{-11}] = 10.54$ (2 places to right of decimal point $-$ 4SF)
d. $[H_3O^+] = \dfrac{1.0 \times 10^{-14}}{[0.0054]} = 1.9 \times 10^{-12}\,M \quad pH = -\log[1.9 \times 10^{-12}] = 11.73$ (2 places to right of decimal point $-$ 4SF)

10.85 An acidic solution has a pH less than 7. A neutral solution has a pH equal to 7. A basic solution has a pH greater than 7.
a. basic   **b.** acidic   **c.** basic   **d.** basic

10.87 If the pH is given, the $[H_3O^+]$ can be found by using the relationship $[H_3O^+] = 10^{-pH}$. The $[OH^-]$ can be found by rearranging $K_w = [H_3O^+][OH^-] = 1 \times 10^{-14}$.

a. pH = 3.00; $[H_3O^+] = 10^{-3.00} = 1.0 \times 10^{-3}$ M (2SF); $[OH^-] = 1.0 \times 10^{-11}$ M (2SF)

b. $[H_3O^+] = 10^{-6.48} = 6.48 +/- 2nd$ *function 10^x* (or *inv log*) $= 3.3 \times 10^{-7}$ M (2SF)

$$[OH^-] = \frac{1.0 \times 10^{-14}}{3.3 \times 10^{-7}} = 3.0 \times 10^{-8} \text{ M (2SF)}$$

c. $[H_3O^+] = 10^{-8.85} = 8.85 +/- 2nd$ *function 10^x* (or *inv log*) $= 1.4 \times 10^{-9}$ M (2SF);
$[OH^-] = 7.1 \times 10^{-6}$ M (2SF)

d. $[H_3O^+] = 10^{-11.00} = 11.00 +/- 2nd$ *function 10^x* (or *inv log*) $= 1.0 \times 10^{-11}$ M (2SF);
$[OH^-] = 1.0 \times 10^{-3}$ M (2SF)

e. $[H_3O^+] = 10^{-9.20} = 9.20 +/- 2nd$ *function 10^x* (or *inv log*) $= 6.3 \times 10^{-10}$ M (2SF);
$[OH^-] = 1.6 \times 10^{-5}$ M (2SF)

10.89 **a.** Solution A, with a pH of 4.5, is more acidic.
b. In A, the $[H_3O^+] = 10^{-4.5} = 3 \times 10^{-5}$ M; in B, the $[H_3O^+] = 10^{-6.7} = 2 \times 10^{-7}$ M (1SF).
c. In A, the $[OH^-] = 3 \times 10^{-10}$ M; in B, the $[OH^-] = 5 \times 10^{-8}$ M (1SF).

10.91 The concentration of OH^- can be calculated from the moles of NaOH and volume of the solution.

$$0.225 \text{ g of NaOH} \times \frac{1 \text{ mole of NaOH}}{40.0 \text{ g of NaOH}} = 0.005\,63 \text{ mole of NaOH}$$

$$\frac{0.005\,63 \text{ mole of NaOH}}{0.250 \text{ L}} = 0.0225 \text{ M NaOH (3SF)}$$

10.93 $2.5 \text{ g of HCl} \times \dfrac{1 \text{ mole of HCl}}{36.5 \text{ g of HCl}} = 0.068 \text{ mole of HCl}$

$$\frac{0.068 \text{ mole of HCl}}{0.425 \text{ L}} = 0.16 \text{ M HCl (2SF)}$$

Since HCl is a strong acid, the $[H_3O^+]$ is also 0.16 M.
pH $= -\log[1.6 \times 10^{-1} \text{ M}] = 0.80$ (2SF)

10.95 **a.** One mole of HCl reacts with one mole of NaOH.

Moles of HCl: $25.0 \text{ mL} \times \dfrac{1 \text{ L}}{1000 \text{ mL}} = 0.0250 \text{ L} \times \dfrac{0.288 \text{ mole of HCl}}{1 \text{ L}} = 0.007\,20 \text{ mole of HCl}$

$0.007\,20 \text{ mole of HCl} \times \dfrac{1 \text{ mole of NaOH}}{1 \text{ mole of HCl}} = 0.007\,20 \text{ mole of NaOH}$

Volume of NaOH: $0.00720 \text{ mole} \times \dfrac{1 \text{ L}}{0.150 \text{ mole}} \times \dfrac{1000 \text{ mL}}{1 \text{ L}} = 48.0 \text{ mL (3SF)}$

b. One mole H_2SO_4 reacts with two moles NaOH.
Moles of H_2SO_4:

$10.0 \text{ mL} \times \dfrac{1 \text{ L}}{1000 \text{ mL}} = 0.0100 \text{ L} \times \dfrac{0.560 \text{ mole}}{1 \text{ L}} = 0.005\,60 \text{ mole of } H_2SO_4$

$0.005\,60 \text{ mole of } H_2SO_4 \times \dfrac{2 \text{ moles of NaOH}}{1 \text{ mole of } H_2SO_4} = 0.0112 \text{ mole of NaOH}$

Volume of NaOH: $0.0112 \text{ mole} \times \dfrac{1 \text{ L}}{0.150 \text{ mole}} \times \dfrac{1000 \text{ mL}}{1 \text{ L}} = 74.7 \text{ mL (3SF)}$

10.97 One mole of H_2SO_4 reacts with two moles of NaOH.

Moles of NaOH: $45.6 \text{ mL} \times \dfrac{1 \text{ L}}{1000 \text{ mL}} = 0.0456 \text{ L} \times \dfrac{0.205 \text{ mole}}{1 \text{ L}} = 0.009\,35 \text{ mole of NaOH}$

Moles of H_2SO_4: $0.009\ 35$ ~~mole NaOH~~ $\times \dfrac{1 \text{ mole } H_2SO_4}{2 \text{ moles NaOH}} = 0.004\ 68$ mole of H_2SO_4

Molarity of H_2SO_4:

20.0 ~~mL~~ $\times \dfrac{1 \text{ L}}{1000 \text{ mL}} = 0.0200$ L; $\qquad \dfrac{0.004\ 68 \text{ mole of } H_2SO_4}{0.0200 \text{ L}} = 0.234$ M H_2SO_4 (3SF)

10.99 **a.** The solution will be basic. K^+ is the cation of a strong base; no effect on pH. The anion, F^-, reacts with water to form the weak acid, HF and OH^-.

$F^-(aq) + H_2O(l) \rightleftharpoons HF(aq) + OH^-(aq)$

b. The solution will be basic. Na^+ is the cation of a strong acid; no effect on pH. CN^-, the anion, reacts with water to form the weak acid, HCN, and OH^-.

$CN^-(aq) + H_2O(l) \rightleftharpoons HCN(aq) + OH^-(aq)$

c. The solution will be acidic. NH_4^+ is the cation of a weak base, NH_4OH. The anion, NO_3^-, is from a strong acid and does not change the pH.

d. The solution will be neutral. The cation, Na^+, is from a strong base and the anion, Br^-, is from a strong acid. None of the ions of the salt will change the pH.

10.101 In a buffer, the anion accepts H^+ and the cation provides H^+.
  a. Add acid: $H_2PO_4^-(aq) + H_3O^+(aq) \rightarrow H_3PO_4(aq) + H_2O(l)$
  b. Add base: $H_3PO_4(aq) + OH^-(aq) \rightarrow H_2PO_4^-(aq) + H_2O(l)$
  c. $[H_3O^+] = 7.5 \times 10^{-3} \times \dfrac{[0.10 \text{ M}]}{[0.10 \text{ M}]} = 7.5 \times 10^{-3}$ M pH $= -\log[7.5 \times 10^{-3}] = 2.12$

  (2 places to the right of the decimal point $- $ 3SF)

  d. $[H_3O^+] = 7.5 \times 10^{-3} \times \dfrac{[0.50 \text{ M}]}{[0.20 \text{ M}]} = 1.9 \times 10^{-2}$ M pH $= -\log[1.9 \times 10^{-2}] = 1.72$

  (2 places to the right of the decimal point $- $ 3SF)

10.103 To form the conjugate acid, add a proton (H^+) to the base. To form the conjugate base, remove a proton (H^+) from the acid.

Acid	Conjugate base
H_2O	OH^-
HCN	CN^-
HNO_2	NO_2^-
H_3PO_4	$H_2PO_4^-$

10.105 **a.** To form the conjugate base, remove a proton (H^+) from the acid.
    1. HS^- 2. $H_2PO_4^-$ 3. CO_3^{2-}

  b. 1. $\dfrac{[H_3O^+][HS^-]}{[H_2S]}$ 2. $\dfrac{[H_3O^+][H_2PO_4^-]}{[H_3PO_4]}$ 3. $\dfrac{[CO_3^{2-}][H_3O^+]}{[HCO_3^-]}$

  c. HCO_3^- (see Table 10.3)
  d. H_3PO_4 (see Table 10.3)

10.107 **a.** $ZnCO_3(s) + H_2SO_4(aq) \rightarrow ZnSO_4(aq) + CO_2(g) + H_2O(l)$
  b. $2Al(s) + 6HNO_3(aq) \rightarrow 2Al(NO_3)_3(aq) + 3H_2(g)$
  c. $2H_3PO_4(aq) + 3Ca(OH)_2(s) \rightarrow Ca_3(PO_4)_2(aq) + 6H_2O(l)$
  d. $KHCO_3(s) + HNO_3(aq) \rightarrow KNO_3(aq) + CO_2(g) + H_2O(l)$

10.109 $KOH(aq) \rightarrow K^+(aq) + OH^-(aq)$

$[OH^-] = 0.050 \text{ M} = 5.0 \times 10^{-2} \text{ M}$

a. $[H_3O^+] = \dfrac{1.0 \times 10^{-14}}{[5.0 \times 10^{-2}]} = 2.0 \times 10^{-13} \text{ M (2SF)}$

b. $pH = -\log[2.0 \times 10^{-13}] = 12.70$ (2 places to the right of the decimal point)

c. $3KOH(aq) + H_3PO_4(aq) \rightarrow K_3PO_4(aq) + 3H_2O(l)$

d. Moles of H_2SO_4: $40.0 \text{ mL} \times \dfrac{1 \text{ L}}{1000 \text{ mL}} = 0.0400 \text{ L} \times \dfrac{0.035 \text{ mole}}{1 \text{ L}} = 0.0014 \text{ mole of } H_2SO_4$

$0.0014 \text{ mole of } H_2SO_4 \times \dfrac{2 \text{ moles of KOH}}{1 \text{ mole of } H_2SO_4} \times \dfrac{1000 \text{ mL of KOH}}{0.050 \text{ mole of KOH}} = 56 \text{ mL of KOH (2SF)}$

10.111 a. The $[H_3O^+]$ can be found by using the relationship $[H_3O^+] = 10^{-pH}$

$[H_3O^+] = 10^{-4.2} = 6 \times 10^{-5} \text{ M}$; $[OH^-] = 2 \times 10^{-10} \text{ M (1SF)}$

b. $[H_3O^+] = 3 \times 10^{-7} \text{ M}$; $[OH^-] = 3 \times 10^{-8} \text{ M (1SF)}$

c. $1.0 \text{ kL} \times \dfrac{1000 \text{ L}}{1 \text{ kL}} \times \dfrac{6 \times 10^{-5} \text{ mole of HA}}{1 \text{ L}} \times \dfrac{1 \text{ mole of } CaCO_3}{2 \text{ moles of HA}} \times \dfrac{100.1 \text{ g of } CaCO_3}{1 \text{ mole of } CaCO_3}$

$= 3 \text{ g of } CaCO_3 \text{ (1SF)}$

CI.17 **a.**

$$\begin{array}{c} \text{H} \\ | \\ \text{H}-\text{C}-\text{H} \\ | \\ \text{H} \end{array} \qquad CH_4$$

b. $7.0 \times 10^6 \, \text{gal} \times \dfrac{4 \, \text{qt}}{1 \, \text{gal}} \times \dfrac{1000 \, \text{mL}}{1.06 \, \text{qt}} \times \dfrac{0.45 \, \text{g}}{1 \, \text{mL}} \times \dfrac{1 \, \text{kg}}{1000 \, \text{g}} = 1.2 \times 10^7 \, \text{kg of LNG (2SF)}$

c. $7.0 \times 10^6 \, \text{gal} \times \dfrac{4 \, \text{qt}}{1 \, \text{gal}} \times \dfrac{1000 \, \text{mL}}{1.06 \, \text{qt}} \times \dfrac{0.45 \, \text{g}}{1 \, \text{mL}} \times \dfrac{1 \, \text{mole of } CH_4}{16.0 \, \text{g}} \times \dfrac{22.4 \, \text{L (STP) of } CH_4}{1 \, \text{mole of } CH_4} =$

$1.7 \times 10^{10} \, \text{L (STP) of LNG} (CH_4) \, (2SF)$

d. $CH_4(g) + 2O_2(g) \rightarrow CO_2(g) + 2H_2O(g)$

e. $7.0 \times 10^6 \, \text{gal} \times \dfrac{4 \, \text{qt}}{1 \, \text{gal}} \times \dfrac{1000 \, \text{mL}}{1.06 \, \text{qt}} \times \dfrac{0.45 \, \text{g}}{1 \, \text{mL}} \times \dfrac{1 \, \text{mole of } CH_4}{16.0 \, \text{g}} \times \dfrac{2 \, \text{moles of } O_2}{1 \, \text{mole of } CH_4} \times$

$\dfrac{32.0 \, \text{g of } O_2}{1 \, \text{mole of } O_2} \times \dfrac{1 \, \text{kg of } O_2}{1000 \, \text{g of } O_2} = 4.8 \times 10^7 \, \text{kg of } O_2 \, (2SF)$

f. $7.0 \times 10^6 \, \text{gal} \times \dfrac{4 \, \text{qt}}{1 \, \text{gal}} \times \dfrac{1000 \, \text{mL}}{1.06 \, \text{qt}} \times \dfrac{0.45 \, \text{g}}{1 \, \text{mL}} \times \dfrac{1 \, \text{mole of } CH_4}{16.0 \, \text{g}} \times \dfrac{883 \, \text{kJ}}{1 \, \text{mole of } CH_4} =$

$6.6 \times 10^{11} \, \text{kJ (2SF)}$

CI.19 **a.** $0.121 \, \text{g of Mg} \times \dfrac{1 \, \text{mole of Mg}}{24.31 \, \text{g of Mg}} = 0.00498 \, \text{mole of Mg}$

$50.0 \, \text{mL} \times \dfrac{1 \, \text{L}}{1000 \, \text{mL}} \times \dfrac{1.00 \, \text{mole of HCl}}{1 \, \text{L}} = 0.0500 \, \text{mole of HCl}$

$0.0500 \, \text{mole of HCl} \times \dfrac{1 \, \text{mole of } H_2}{2 \, \text{moles of HCl}} = 0.0250 \, \text{mole of } H_2$

$0.00498 \, \text{mole of Mg} \times \dfrac{1 \, \text{mole of } H_2}{1 \, \text{mole of Mg}} = 0.004 \, 98 \, \text{mole of } H_2 \quad \text{(smaller amount of product)}$

Mg is the limiting reactant.

b. $33.0 \, °C + 273 = 306 \, K$

$$V = \frac{nRT}{P} = \frac{(0.00498 \, \text{mole})\left(\dfrac{62.4 \, \text{mmHg} \cdot L}{\text{mole} \cdot K}\right)(306 \, K)}{750. \, \text{mmHg}} = 0.127 \, \text{L of } H_2 \, (2SF)$$

c. $50.0 \, \text{mL} \times \dfrac{1.00 \, \text{g}}{1 \, \text{mL}} = 50.0 \, \text{g}$

$\Delta T = T_{\text{final}} - T_{\text{initial}} = 33.0 \, °C - 22.0 \, °C = 11.0 \, °C = \text{temperature change}$

$50.0 \, \text{g} \times \dfrac{4.184 \, \text{J}}{\text{g} \, °C} \times 11.0 \, °C = 2300 \, \text{J} = 2.30 \times 10^3 \, \text{J (3SF)}$

d. $\dfrac{2.30 \times 10^3 \, \text{J}}{0.121 \, \text{g}} = 1.90 \times 10^4 \, \dfrac{\text{J}}{\text{g}} \, \text{of Mg (3SF)}$

$\dfrac{1.90 \times 10^4 \, \text{J}}{1 \, \text{g of Mg}} \times \dfrac{1 \, \text{kJ}}{1000 \, \text{J}} \times \dfrac{24.31 \, \text{g of Mg}}{1 \, \text{mole of Mg}} = 462 \, \text{kJ/mole of Mg (3SF)}$

CI.21 **a.** $2.0 \, \text{g of } H_2 \times \dfrac{1 \, \text{mole of } H_2}{2.02 \, \text{g of } H_2} = \dfrac{1.0 \, \text{mole of } H_2}{10.0 \, \text{L}} = 0.10 \, M \, H_2$

$10. \, \text{g of } S_2 \times \dfrac{1 \, \text{mole of } S_2}{64.1 \, \text{g of } S_2} = \dfrac{0.16 \, \text{mole of } S_2}{10.0 \, \text{L}} = 0.016 \, M \, S_2$

$$68 \; \cancel{\text{g of H}_2\text{S}} \times \frac{1 \text{ mole of H}_2\text{S}}{34.1 \; \cancel{\text{g of H}_2\text{S}}} = \frac{2.0 \text{ moles of H}_2\text{S}}{10.0 \text{ L}} = 0.20 \text{ M H}_2\text{S}$$

$$K_c = \frac{[\text{H}_2\text{S}]^2}{[\text{H}_2]^2[\text{S}_2]} = \frac{[0.20]^2}{[0.01]^2[0.016]} = 250 \; (2\text{SF})$$

b. If H_2 is added, the equilibrium will shift to the right towards products.

c. If the volume decreases from 10.0 L to 5.00 L, equilibrium shifts to the right towards the products (fewer moles of gas). The H_2S concentration will increase.

d. $[\text{H}_2] = \dfrac{0.30 \text{ mole}}{5.00 \text{ L}} = 0.060 \text{ M}$ $[\text{H}_2\text{S}] = \dfrac{2.5 \text{ moles}}{5.00 \text{ L}} = 0.50 \text{ M}$

$$K_c = \frac{[\text{H}_2\text{S}]^2}{[\text{H}_2]^2[\text{S}_2]} \quad \text{Rearranging the } K_c \text{ to solve for } [\text{S}_2]$$

$$[\text{S}_2] = \frac{[\text{H}_2\text{S}]^2}{[\text{H}_2]^2 K_c} = \frac{[0.50]^2}{[0.060]^2[250]} = 0.28 \text{ M S}_2 \; (2\text{SF})$$

e. Because the reaction is exothermic (heat is a product), an increase in temperature (heat) will shift the equilibrium toward the reactants and decrease the value of K_c.

CI.23 **a.** $2\text{M}(s) + 6\text{HCl}(aq) \rightarrow 2\text{MCl}_3(aq) + 3\text{H}_2(g)$

b. $34.8 \; \cancel{\text{mL}} \times \dfrac{0.520 \; \cancel{\text{mole of HCl}}}{\cancel{1000 \text{ mL}}} \times \dfrac{3 \; \cancel{\text{moles of H}_2}}{6 \; \cancel{\text{moles of HCl}}} \times \dfrac{22.4 \; \cancel{\text{L (STP) of H}_2}}{1 \; \cancel{\text{mole of H}_2}} \times \dfrac{\cancel{1000} \text{ mL of H}_2}{1 \; \cancel{\text{L of H}_2}} =$

203 mL of H_2 (3SF)

c. $34.8 \; \cancel{\text{mL}} \times \dfrac{0.520 \; \cancel{\text{mole of HCl}}}{1000 \; \cancel{\text{mL}}} \times \dfrac{2 \text{ moles of M}}{6 \; \cancel{\text{moles of HCl}}} = 6.03 \times 10^{-3} \text{ mole of M} \; (2\text{SF})$

d. $\dfrac{0.420 \text{ g of M}}{0.00603 \text{ mole of M}} = 69.6 \text{ g/mole of M} \; (3\text{SF})$

e. Gallium(Ga) has an atomic mass of 69.7.

f. $2\text{Ga}(s) + 6\text{HCl}(aq) \rightarrow 2\text{GaCl}_3(aq) + 3\text{H}_2(g)$

11
Introduction to Organic Chemistry: Alkanes

11.1 Organic compounds contain C and H and sometimes O, N, or a halogen atom. Inorganic compounds usually contain elements other than C and H.
    a. inorganic   **b.** organic   **c.** organic
    d. inorganic   **e.** inorganic   **f.** organic

11.3   **a.** Inorganic compounds are usually soluble in water.
    b. Organic compounds have lower boiling points than most inorganic compounds.
    c. Organic compounds often burn in air.
    d. Inorganic compounds are more likely to have high melting points.

11.5   **a.** ethane   **b.** ethane   **c.** NaBr   **d.** NaBr

11.7 VSEPR theory predicts that the four bonds in CH_4 will be as far apart as possible, which means that the hydrogen atoms are at the corners of a tetrahedron.

11.9   **a.** In expanded structural formulas, each C—H and each C—C bond is drawn separately.

$$
\begin{array}{ccccc}
 & H & H & H & \\
 & | & | & | & \\
H- & C & -C & -C & -H \\
 & | & | & | & \\
 & H & H & H &
\end{array}
$$

    b. A condensed structural formula groups hydrogen atoms with each carbon atom.
       $CH_3-CH_2-CH_2-CH_2-CH_2-CH_3$
    c. A line-bond formula shows only the bonds connecting the carbon atoms.

11.11   **a.** Pentane has a carbon chain of five (5) carbon atoms.
    b. Heptane has a carbon chain of seven (7) carbon atoms.
    c. Hexane has a carbon chain of six (6) carbon atoms.
    d. Cyclobutane has the geometric figure with four (4) carbons.

11.13   **a.** CH_4 **b.** CH_3-CH_3 **c.** $CH_3-CH_2-CH_2-CH_2-CH_3$ **d.** △

11.15 Two structures are isomers if they have the same chemical formula, but the atoms are bonded in a different order to each other.
    a. same molecule   **b.** isomers of C_5H_{12} **c.** isomers of C_6H_{14}

11.17   **a.** 2-methylbutane   **b.** 2,2-dimethylpropane
    c. 2,3-dimethylpentane   **d.** 4-ethyl-2,2-dimethylhexane

11.19   **a.** A ring of five carbon atoms with one chlorine atom is chlorocyclopentane; no numbering is needed for a single substituent.
    b. A ring of six carbon atoms with one methyl group is methylcyclohexane; no numbering is needed for a single substituent.
    c. 1-bromo-3-methylcyclobutane
    d. 1-bromo-2-chlorocyclopentane

11.21 Draw the main chain with the number of carbon atoms in the ending. For example, butane has a main chain of four carbon atoms, and hexane has a main chain of six carbon atoms. Attach substituents on the carbon atoms indicated. For example, in 3-methylpentane, a CH_3— group is bonded to carbon 3 of a five-carbon chain.

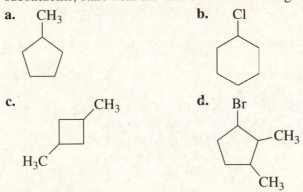

a. CH_3—$\overset{\overset{\displaystyle CH_3}{|}}{CH}$—$CH_2$—$CH_3$

b. CH_3—CH_2—$\overset{\overset{\displaystyle CH_3}{|}}{\underset{\underset{\displaystyle CH_3}{|}}{C}}$—$CH_2$—$CH_3$

c. CH_3—$\overset{\overset{\displaystyle CH_3}{|}}{CH}$—$\overset{\overset{\displaystyle CH_3}{|}}{CH}$—$CH_2$—$\overset{\overset{\displaystyle CH_3}{|}}{CH}$—$CH_3$

d. CH_3—$\overset{\overset{\displaystyle CH_3}{|}}{CH}$—$\overset{\overset{\displaystyle CH_2{-}CH_3}{|}}{CH}$—$CH_2$—$\overset{\overset{\displaystyle CH_3}{|}}{CH}$—$CH_2$—$CH_2$—$CH_3$

11.23 Draw the cyclic structure first, and then attach the substituents. When there are two or more substituents, start with the first on a carbon assigned number 1 and continue around the ring.

a. CH_3

b. Cl

c. CH_3 / H_3C

d. Br / CH_3 / CH_3

11.25 In the IUPAC system, the halogen substituent is named with the prefix *halo-* on the main chain of the carbon atom.
a. bromoethane **b.** 1-fluoropropane
c. 2-chloropropane **d.** trichloromethane

11.27

a. CH_3—$\overset{\overset{\displaystyle Cl}{|}}{CH}$—$CH_3$

b. CH_3—$\overset{\overset{\displaystyle Br}{|}}{CH}$—$\overset{\overset{\displaystyle Cl}{|}}{CH}$—$CH_3$

c. CH_3Br

d. CBr_4

11.29 **a.** CH_3—CH_2—CH_2—CH_2—CH_2—CH_2—CH_3
b. liquid **c.** insoluble in water **d.** float

11.31 Longer carbon chains have higher boiling points. The boiling points of branched alkanes are usually lower than the same number of carbon atoms in a continuous chain. Cycloalkanes have higher boiling points than continuous-chain alkanes.
a. Heptane has a longer carbon chain and a greater molar mass.
b. Cyclopropane is a cycloalkane.
c. The continuous chain hexane has a higher boiling point than its branched-chain isomer.

11.33 In combustion, a hydrocarbon reacts with oxygen to yield CO_2 and H_2O.
a. $2C_2H_6 + 7O_2 \rightarrow 4CO_2 + 6H_2O$ **b.** $2C_3H_6 + 9O_2 \rightarrow 6CO_2 + 6H_2O$
c. $2C_8H_{18} + 25O_2 \rightarrow 16CO_2 + 18H_2O$ **d.** $C_6H_{12} + 9O_2 \rightarrow 6CO_2 + 6H_2O$

11.35 **a.** Alcohols contain a hydroxyl group (—OH).
  b. Alkenes have carbon-carbon double bonds.
  c. Aldehydes contain a C=O bonded to at least one H atom.
  d. Esters contain a carboxyl group attached to an alkyl group.

11.37 **a.** Ethers have an —O— group.
  b. Alcohols have an —OH group.
  c. Ketones have a C=O group between alkyl groups.
  d. Carboxylic acids have a —COOH group.
  e. Amines contain an N atom bonded to at least one carbon atom.

11.39 **a.** aromatic, ether, alcohol, ketone
  b. aromatic, ether, alkene, ester

11.41 aromatic, ether, amide

11.43 **a.** Organic compounds have covalent bonds; inorganic compounds have ionic as well as polar covalent bonds, and a few have nonpolar covalent bonds.
  b. Most organic compounds are insoluble in water; many inorganic compounds are soluble in water.
  c. Most organic compounds have low melting points; inorganic compounds have high melting points.
  d. Most organic compounds are usually flammable; inorganic compounds are not flammable.

11.45 **a.** Butane; organic compounds have low melting points.
  b. Butane; organic compounds burn vigorously in air.
  c. Potassium chloride; inorganic compounds have high melting points.
  d. Potassium chloride; inorganic compounds (ionic) produce ions in water.
  e. Butane; organic compounds are more likely to be gases at room temperature.

11.47 **a.** amine **b.** ketone **c.** ester **d.** alcohol

11.49 **a.** methyl **b.** propyl **c.** chloro

11.51 **a.** methylcyclopentane **b.** 1,2-dibromo-3-chloropropane
  c. 2,3-dimethylhexane **d.** 3-chloro-3-ethylpentane

11.53

a. $CH_3-CH_2-\underset{\underset{CH_3}{|}}{CH}-CH_2-CH_2-CH_3$

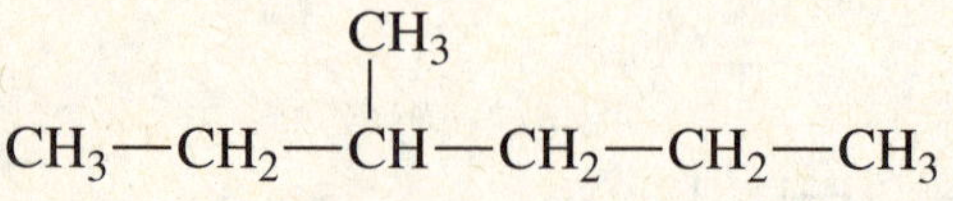

b.

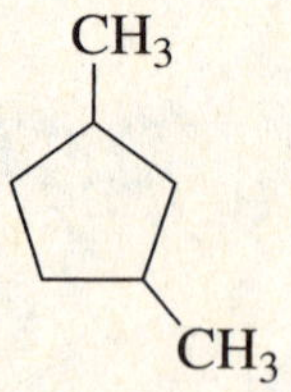

c. $Cl-CH_2-CH_2-\underset{\underset{Cl}{|}}{\overset{\overset{CH_3}{|}}{C}}-CH_2-CH_2-CH_2-CH_3$

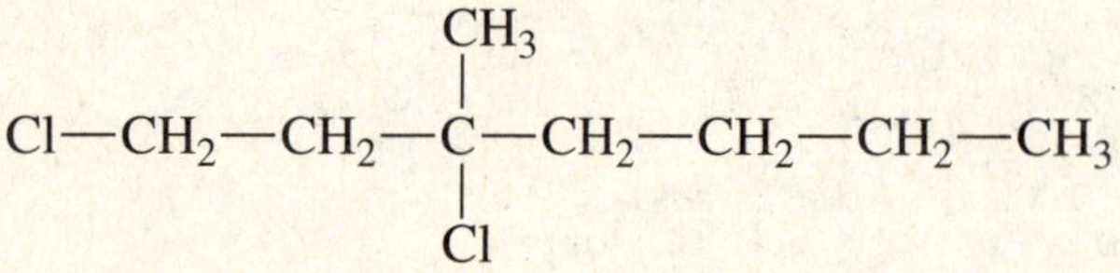

d.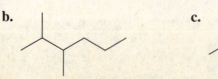

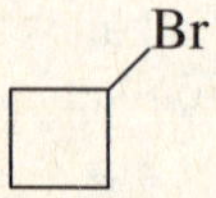

11.55 A line-bond formula shows only the bonds connecting the carbon atoms. The number of bonds to hydrogen atoms is understood.

a.   **b.**   **c.** Br

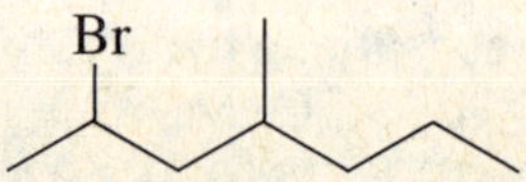

11.57 **a.** Heptane has a longer carbon chain and a greater molar mass.
b. Cyclopentane is a cycloalkane with a rigid structure that stacks closely requiring higher boiling points than the corresponding alkane.
c. Hexane is an unbranched carbon chain that is less compact, which allows more contact between molecules, and requires higher boiling points.

11.59 **a.** $C_3H_8 + 5O_2 \rightarrow 3CO_2 + 4H_2O$ **b.** $C_5H_{12} + 8O_2 \rightarrow 5CO_2 + 6H_2O$
c. $C_4H_8 + 6O_2 \rightarrow 4CO_2 + 4H_2O$ **d.** $2C_8H_{18} + 25O_2 \rightarrow 16CO_2 + 18H_2O$

11.61 **a.** alcohol   **b.** alkene   **c.** aldehyde
d. alkane   **e.** carboxylic acid   **f.** amine

11.63 Condensed structural formula:
$$CH_3-\underset{\underset{CH_3}{|}}{\overset{\overset{CH_3}{|}}{C}}-CH_2-\underset{\underset{CH_3}{|}}{CH}-CH_3$$

Molecular formula: C_8H_{18}
Combustion reaction: $2C_8H_{18} + 25O_2 \rightarrow 16CO_2 + 18H_2O$

11.65 **a.** $C_5H_{12} + 8O_2 \rightarrow 5CO_2 + 6H_2O$
b. 72.0 g/mole (3SF)
c. $1 \text{ gal} \times \dfrac{3.78 \text{ L}}{1 \text{ gal}} \times \dfrac{1000 \text{ mL}}{1 \text{ L}} \times \dfrac{0.63 \text{ g}}{1 \text{ mL}} \times \dfrac{1 \text{ mole of } C_5H_{12}}{72.0 \text{ g}} \times \dfrac{845 \text{ kcal}}{1 \text{ mole}} = 2.8 \times 10^4 \text{ kcal (2SF)}$
d. $1 \text{ gal} \times \dfrac{3.78 \text{ L}}{1 \text{ gal}} \times \dfrac{1000 \text{ mL}}{1 \text{ L}} \times \dfrac{0.63 \text{ g}}{1 \text{ mL}} \times \dfrac{1 \text{ mole of } C_5H_{12}}{72.0 \text{ g}} \times \dfrac{5 \text{ moles of } CO_2}{1 \text{ mole of } C_5H_{12}} \times \dfrac{22.4 \text{ L (STP)}}{1 \text{ mole}}$
$= 3700 \text{ L (2SF)}$

11.67
$$CH_3-\underset{\underset{CH_3}{|}}{CH}-\underset{\underset{CH_3}{|}}{CH}-CH_3 \qquad CH_3-\underset{\underset{CH_3}{|}}{\overset{\overset{CH_3}{|}}{C}}-CH_2-CH_3$$

11.69 **a.** $CH_3-CH_2-CH_3$
b. $C_3H_8 + 5O_2 \rightarrow 3CO_2 + 4H_2O$
c. $12.0 \text{ L of } C_3H_8 \times \dfrac{1 \text{ mole of } C_3H_8}{22.4 \text{ L of } C_3H_8 \text{ (STP)}} \times \dfrac{5 \text{ moles of } O_2}{1 \text{ mole of } C_3H_8} \times \dfrac{32.0 \text{ g of } O_2}{1 \text{ mole of } O_2} = 85.7 \text{ g of } O_2 \text{ (3SF)}$
d. $12.0 \text{ L of } C_3H_8 \times \dfrac{1 \text{ mole of } C_3H_8}{22.4 \text{ L of } C_3H_8 \text{ (STP)}} \times \dfrac{3 \text{ moles of } CO_2}{1 \text{ mole of } C_3H_8} \times \dfrac{44.0 \text{ g of } CO_2}{1 \text{ mole of } CO_2} = 70.7 \text{ g of } CO_2$
(3SF)

11.71 **a.** $C_3H_8 + 5O_2 \rightarrow 3CO_2 + 4H_2O$
b. $5.0 \text{ lb of } C_3H_8 \times \dfrac{454 \text{ g of } C_3H_8}{1 \text{ lb of } C_3H_8} \times \dfrac{1 \text{ mole of } C_3H_8}{44.0 \text{ g of } C_3H_8} \times \dfrac{3 \text{ moles of } CO_2}{1 \text{ mole of } C_3H_8}$

$\times \dfrac{44.0 \text{ g of } CO_2}{1 \text{ mole of } CO_2} \times \dfrac{1 \text{ kg of } CO_2}{1000 \text{ g of } CO_2} = 6.8 \text{ kg of } CO_2 \text{ (2SF)}$

12

Alkenes, Alkynes, and Aromatic Compounds

12.1   **a.** An alkene has a double bond.
   b. An alkyne has a triple bond.
   c. An alkene has a double bond.
   d. A cycloalkene has a double bond in a ring.

12.3   **a.** The two-carbon compound with a double bond is ethene.
   b. This has a three-carbon chain with a methyl substituent. The name is 2-methylpropene.
   c. This has a five-carbon chain with a bromo substituent. The name is 4-bromo-2-pentyne.
   d. This is a four-carbon cyclic structure with a double bond. The name is cyclobutene.
   e. This is a five-carbon cyclic structure with a double bond and an ethyl group. You must count the two carbons of the double bond as 1 and 2. The name is 4-ethylcyclopentene.
   f. Count the chain from the end nearest the double bond: 4-ethyl-2-hexene.

12.5   **a.** Propene is the three-carbon alkene. $H_2C{=}CH{-}CH_3$
   b. 1-pentene is the five-carbon compound with a double bond between carbon 1 and carbon 2.
   $H_2C{=}CH{-}CH_2{-}CH_2{-}CH_3$
   c. 2-methyl-1-butene has a four-carbon chain with a double bond between carbon 1 and carbon 2 and a methyl attached to carbon 2.
$$CH_3$$
$$|$$
$$H_2C{=}C{-}CH_2{-}CH_3$$
   d. 3-methylcyclohexene is a six-carbon cyclic compound with a double bond between carbon 1 and carbon 2 and a methyl group attached to carbon 3.

   e. 2-chloro-3-hexyne is a six-carbon compound with a triple bond between carbon 3 and 4 and a chlorine atom bonded to carbon 2.
$$Cl$$
$$|$$
$$CH_3{-}CH{-}C{\equiv}C{-}CH_2{-}CH_3$$
   f. 1-butyne is a four-carbon compound with a triple bond between carbon 1 and carbon 2.
   $HC{\equiv}C{-}CH_2{-}CH_3$
   g. 5-bromo-1-pentene is a five-carbon compound with a double bond between carbon 1 and carbon 2 and a bromo substituent on carbon 5.
$$Br$$
$$|$$
$$H_2C{=}CH{-}CH_2{-}CH_2{-}CH_2$$

12.7   **a.** This compound cannot have cis–trans isomers since there are two identical hydrogen atoms attached to the first carbon.
   b. This compound can have cis–trans isomers since there are different groups attached to each carbon atom in the double bond.
   c. This compound cannot have cis–trans isomers since there are two of the same groups attached to each carbon.

12.9   **a.** *cis*-2-butene; this is a four-carbon compound with a double bond between carbon 2 and carbon 3. Both methyl groups are on the same side of the double bond; it is cis.

b. *trans*-3-octene; this compound has eight carbons with a double bond between carbon 3 and carbon 4. The alkyl groups are on opposite sides of the double bond; it is trans.

c. *cis*-3-heptene; this is a seven-carbon compound with a double bond between carbon 3 and carbon 4. Both alkyl groups are on the same side of the double bond; it is cis.

12.11   **a.** *trans*-1-chloro-2-butene has a four-carbon chain with a double bond between carbon 2 and carbon 3. The trans isomer has two large groups on opposite sides of the double bond.

$$CH_3 \diagdown_{} {}_{\diagup} H$$
$$C=C$$
$$H \diagup \diagdown CH_2-Cl$$

b. *cis*-2-pentene has a five-carbon chain with a double bond between carbon 2 and carbon 3. The cis isomer has alkyl groups on the same side of the double bond.

$$CH_3 \diagdown_{} {}_{\diagup} CH_2-CH_3$$
$$C=C$$
$$H \diagup \diagdown H$$

c. *trans*-3-heptene has a seven-carbon chain with a double bond between carbon 3 and carbon 4. The trans isomer has the alkyl groups on opposite sides of the double bond.

$$CH_3-CH_2 \diagdown_{} {}_{\diagup} H$$
$$C=C$$
$$H \diagup \diagdown CH_2-CH_2-CH_3$$

12.13   **a.** $CH_3-CH_2-CH_2-CH_2-CH_3$ pentane

b. $\underset{\underset{CH_3}{|}}{\overset{\overset{Cl}{|}}{Cl-CH_2-C-CH_2-CH_3}}$ 1,2-dichloro-2-methylbutane

c. The product is a four-carbon cycloalkane with bromine atoms attached to carbon 1 and carbon 2. The name is 1,2-dibromocyclobutane.

d. When H_2 is added to a cycloalkene, the product is a cycloalkane. Cyclopentene would form cyclopentane.

$$\text{⬠} + H_2 \xrightarrow{Pt} \text{⬠}$$

Cyclopentene   Cyclopentane

e. When Cl_2 is added to an alkene, the product is a dichloroalkane. The product is a four-carbon chain with chlorine atoms attached to carbon 2 and carbon 3 and a methyl group attached to carbon 2. The name of the product is 2,3-dichloro-2-methylbutane.

$$\underset{}{\overset{\overset{CH_3}{|}}{CH_3-C=CH-CH_3}} + Cl_2 \longrightarrow \underset{\underset{Cl Cl}{| |}}{\overset{\overset{CH_3}{|}}{CH_3-C-CH-CH_3}}$$

2-Methyl-2-butene   2,3-Dichloro-2-methylbutane

f. $CH_3-CH_2-CH_2-CH_2-CH_3$ pentane

12.15 **a.** When HBr is added to an alkene, the product is a bromoalkane. In this case, we do not need to use Markovnikov's rule, since 2-butene is symmetrical.

$$\underset{\displaystyle CH_3-CH_2-\overset{\displaystyle \overset{Br}{|}}{C}H-CH_3}{}$$

b. When H_2O is added to a cycloalkene, the product is a cyclic alcohol. In this case, we do not need to use Markovnikov's rule.

c. When HCl is added to an alkene, the product is a chloroalkane. We need to use Markovnikov's rule, which says that hydrogen adds to the carbon with the greater number of hydrogens; in this case, that is carbon 1.

$$\underset{\displaystyle CH_3-\overset{\displaystyle \overset{Cl}{|}}{C}H-CH_2-CH_3}{}$$

d. When HI is added to an alkene, the product is an iodoalkane. In this case, we do not need to use Markovnikov's rule.

$$CH_3-\overset{\displaystyle \overset{CH_3}{|}}{C}H-\overset{\displaystyle \overset{I}{|}}{\underset{\displaystyle \underset{CH_3}{|}}{C}}-CH_3$$

e. When HBr is added to an alkene, the product is a bromoalkane. We need to use Markovnikov's rule, which says that hydrogen adds to the carbon with the greater number of hydrogens; in this case, that is carbon 2.

$$CH_3-CH_2-\overset{\displaystyle \overset{Br}{|}}{\underset{\displaystyle \underset{CH_3}{|}}{C}}-CH_2-CH_3$$

f. Using Markovnikov's rule, the H— from HOH goes to the carbon 2 in the cyclohexane ring, which has more hydrogen atoms. The —OH then goes to carbon 1.

12.17 **a.** Hydrogenation of an alkene gives the saturated compound, the alkane.

$$CH_2{=}\overset{\displaystyle \overset{CH_3}{|}}{C}-CH_3 + H_2 \xrightarrow{\text{Pt}} CH_3-\overset{\displaystyle \overset{CH_3}{|}}{C}H-CH_3$$

b. The addition of HCl to a cycloalkene gives a chlorocycloalkane.

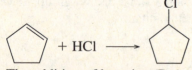

c. The addition of bromine (Br_2) to an alkene gives a dibromoalkane.

$$CH_3-CH{=}CH-CH_2-CH_3 + Br_2 \longrightarrow CH_3-\overset{\displaystyle \overset{Br}{|}}{C}H-\overset{\displaystyle \overset{Br}{|}}{C}H-CH_2-CH_3$$

d. Hydration (the addition of H_2O) of an alkene gives an alcohol. In this case, we use Markovnikov's rule and attach hydrogen to carbon 1.

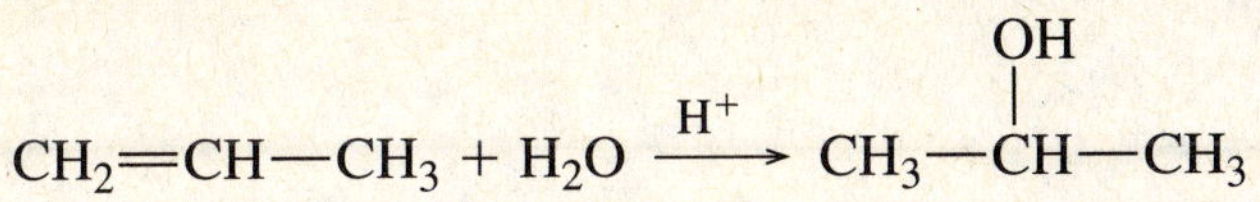

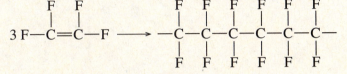

$$CH_2{=}CH{-}CH_3 + H_2O \xrightarrow{H^+} CH_3{-}\underset{\underset{OH}{|}}{CH}{-}CH_3$$

e. 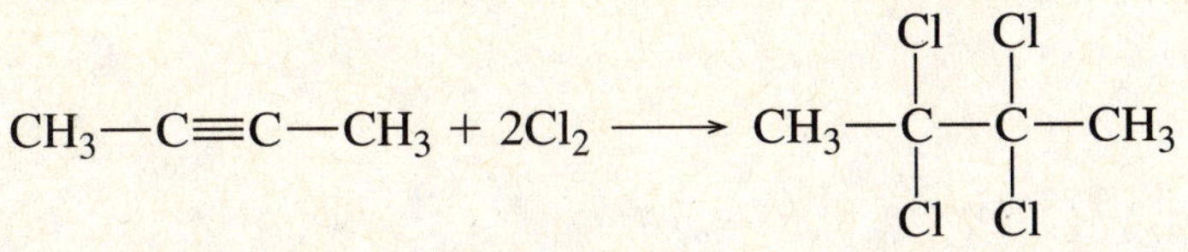 $CH_3{-}C{\equiv}C{-}CH_3 + 2Cl_2 \longrightarrow CH_3{-}\overset{\overset{Cl}{|}}{\underset{\underset{Cl}{|}}{C}}{-}\overset{\overset{Cl}{|}}{\underset{\underset{Cl}{|}}{C}}{-}CH_3$

12.19 A polymer is a long-chain molecule consisting of many repeating smaller units. These smaller units are called monomers.

12.21 Teflon is a polymer of the monomer tetrafluoroethene.

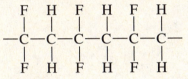

$$3\ F{-}C{=}C{-}F \longrightarrow {-}C{-}C{-}C{-}C{-}C{-}C{-}$$

12.23 1,1-difluoroethene is the two-carbon alkene with two fluorine atoms attached to carbon 1.

$${-}C{-}C{-}C{-}C{-}C{-}C{-}$$

12.25 Cyclohexane, C_6H_{12}, is a cycloalkane in which six carbon atoms are linked by single bonds in a ring. In benzene, C_6H_6, an aromatic system links the six carbon atoms in a ring.

12.27 The six-carbon ring with alternating single and double bonds is benzene. If the groups are in the 1,2 position, this is ortho (*o*); 1,3 is meta (*m*), and 1,4 is para (*p*).
a. 1-chloro-2-methylbenzene; 2-chlorotoluene; *o*-chlorotoluene;
b. ethylbenzene
c. 1,3,5-trichlorobenzene
d. *m*-xylene; 1,3-dimethylbenzene; *m*-dimethylbenzene; 3-methyltoluene; *m*-methyltoluene
e. 1-bromo-3-chloro-5-methylbenzene; 3-bromo-5-chlorotoluene
f. isopropylbenzene

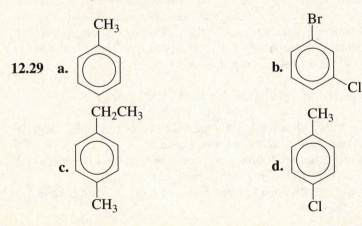

12.29 a.

b. The prefix *m* means that the two halogen atoms are in the 1 and 3 position.

c.

d. The prefix *p* means that the two groups are in the 1 and 4 position.

12.31 Benzene undergoes substitution reactions because a substitution reaction allows benzene to retain the stability of the aromatic system.

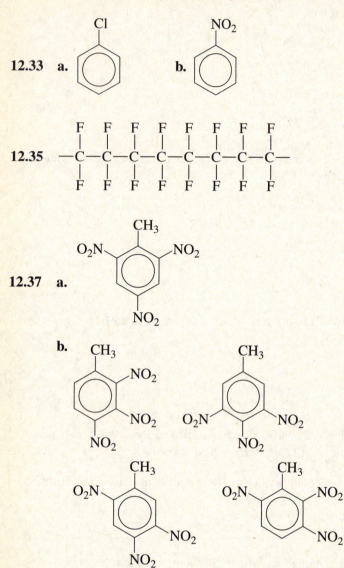

12.33 a. Cl on benzene ring   **b.** NO₂ on benzene ring

12.35

12.37 a.

b.

12.39 Propane is the three-carbon alkane with the formula C_3H_8. All the carbon–carbon bonds in propane are single bonds. Cyclopropane is the three-carbon cycloalkane with the formula C_3H_6. All of the carbon–carbon bonds in cyclopropane are single bonds. Propene is the three-carbon compound that has a carbon–carbon double bond. The formula of propene is C_3H_6. Propyne is the three-carbon compound with a carbon–carbon triple bond. The formula of propyne is C_3H_4.

12.41 a. This compound has a chlorine atom attached to a cyclopentane; the IUPAC name is chlorocyclopentane.
   b. This compound has a five-carbon chain with a chlorine atom attached to carbon 2 and a methyl group attached to carbon 4. The IUPAC name is 2-chloro-4-methylpentane.
   c. This compound contains a five-carbon chain with a double bond between carbon 1 and carbon 2 and a methyl group attached to carbon 2. The IUPAC name is 2-methyl-1-pentene.
   d. This compound contains a five-carbon chain with a triple bond between carbon 2 and carbon 3. The IUPAC name is 2-pentyne.

12.43 **a.**

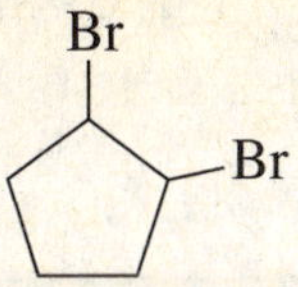

b. $CH_3-C \equiv C-CH_2-CH_3$

c.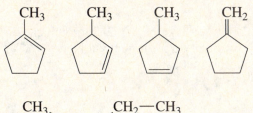

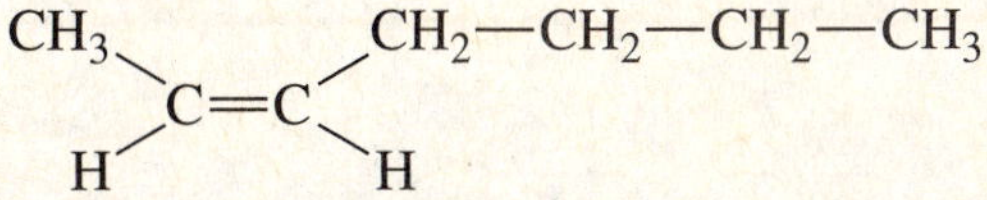

d. 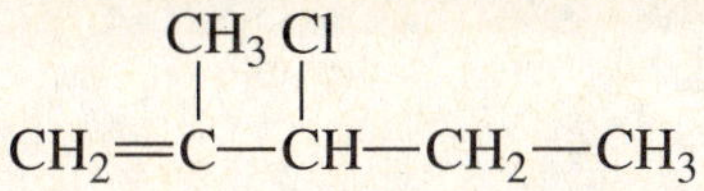 $CH_2 = \overset{\overset{\displaystyle CH_3}{|}}{C} - \overset{\overset{\displaystyle Cl}{|}}{CH} - CH_2 - CH_3$

12.45 **a.** These structures represent a pair of structural isomers. In one isomer, the chlorine is attached to one of the carbons in the double bond; in the other isomer, the carbon bonded to the chlorine is not part of the double bond.

b. These structures are cis–trans isomers. In the cis isomer, the two methyl groups are on the same side of the double bond. In the trans isomer, the methyl groups are on opposite sides of the double bond.

12.47 The structure of methylcyclopentane

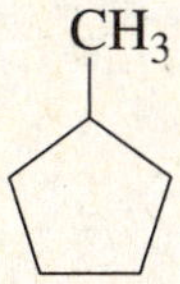

It can be formed by the hydrogenation of four cycloalkenes.

12.49 **a.**

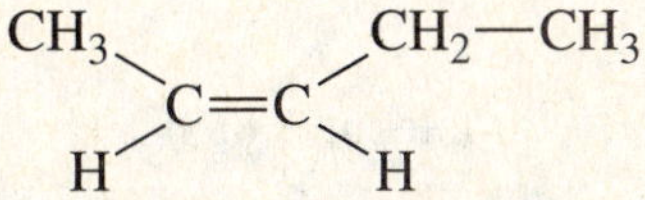

cis-2-pentene; both alkyl groups are on the same side of the double bond.

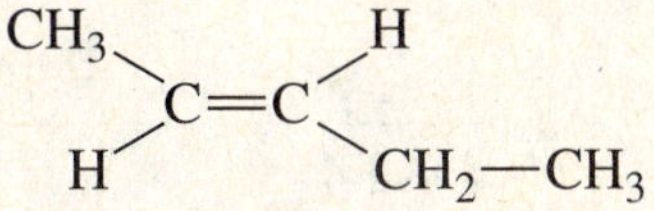

trans-2-pentene; both alkyl groups are on opposite sides of the double bond.

b.

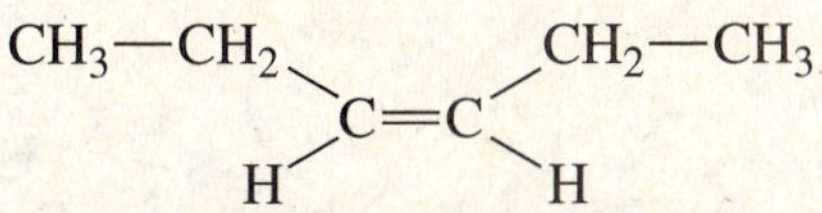

cis-3-hexene; both alkyl groups are on the same side of the double bond.

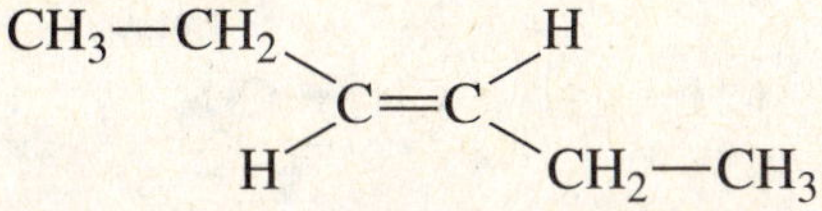

trans-3-hexene; both alkyl groups are on opposite sides of the double bond.

12.51 The multiple bonds are converted to single bonds and two H atoms are added for each bond converted.

a. 3-methylpentane   **b.** cyclohexane   **c.** pentane

12.53 **a.**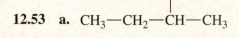

b.

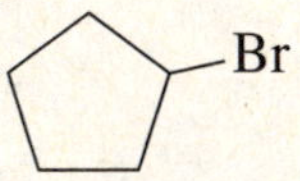

c. 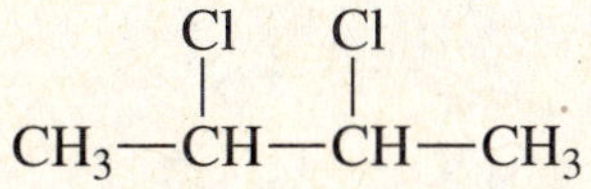 $CH_3 - \overset{\overset{\displaystyle Cl}{|}}{CH} - \overset{\overset{\displaystyle Cl}{|}}{CH} - CH_3$

12.55 **a.** The reaction of H_2 in the presence of a Ni catalyst changes alkenes into alkanes. The reactant must be cyclohexene.

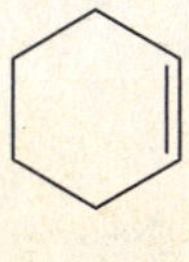

b. Br$_2$ adds to alkenes to give a dibromoalkane. Since there are bromine atoms on carbon 2 and carbon 3, the double bond in the reactant must have been between carbons 2 and 3.

$$CH_3—CH=CH—CH_2—CH_3$$

12.57 Styrene is H$_2$C=CH and acrylonitrile is H$_2$C=CH $\overset{|}{C}\equiv N$. A section of the copolymer of styrene and acrylonitrile would be

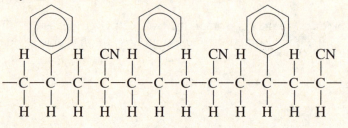

12.59 Each of these reactions is a substitution reaction, except for the last reaction.
    a. chlorobenzene   **b.** *o*-bromotoluene, *m*-bromotoluene, *p*-bromotoluene
    c. benzenesulfonic acid   **d.** no products

12.61   **a.** methylbenzene; toluene
      b. 1-chloro-2-methylbenzene; *o*-chlorotoluene (1,2 position is ortho, *o*); 2-chlorotoluene
      c. 1-ethyl-4-methylbenzene; *p*-ethyltoluene (1,4 position is para, *p*); *p*-ethyltoluene
      d. 1,3-diethylbenzene; *m*-diethylbenzene (1,3 position is meta, *m*)

12.63 Bombykol C$_{16}$H$_{30}$O = 238.4 g/mole

$$50 \ \text{ng} \times \frac{1 \ \text{g}}{10^9 \ \text{ng}} \times \frac{1 \ \text{mole}}{238.4 \ \text{g}} \times \frac{6.02 \times 10^{23} \ \text{molecules}}{1 \ \text{mole}} = 1 \times 10^{14} \ \text{molecules (1SF)}$$

12.65   CH$_3$—CH=CH—CH$_2$—CH$_3$ *cis*-2-pentene or *trans*-2-pentene

      H$_2$C—CH—CH$_2$—CH$_2$—CH$_3$ 1-pentene

      CH$_2$=C($\overset{\text{CH}_3}{|}$)—CH$_2$—CH$_3$ 2-methyl-1-butene

      CH$_3$—C($\overset{\text{CH}_3}{|}$)=CH—CH$_3$ 2-methyl-2-butene

      CH$_3$—CH($\overset{\text{CH}_3}{|}$)—CH—CH$_2$ 3-methyl-1-butene

13

Alcohols, Phenols, Thiols, and Ethers

13.1 The carbon bonded to the hydroxyl group (—OH) is attached to one alkyl group in a primary (1°) alcohol, except for methanol; to two alkyl groups in a secondary alcohol (2°); and to three alkyl groups in a tertiary alcohol (3°).
a. primary alcohol (1°) **b.** primary alcohol (1°)
c. tertiary alcohol (3°) **d.** secondary alcohol (2°)

13.3 **a.** This compound has a two-carbon chain (ethane). The final *–e* is dropped, and *–ol* added to indicate an alcohol. The IUPAC name is ethanol.
b. This compound has a four-carbon chain with a hydroxyl attached to carbon 2. The IUPAC name is 2-butanol.
c. This compound has a five-carbon chain with a hydroxyl attached to carbon 2. The IUPAC name is 2-pentanol.
d. This compound is a six-carbon cycloalkane with a hydroxyl attached to carbon 1 of the ring and a methyl group attached to carbon 4. Since the hydroxyl is always attached to carbon 1, the number 1 is omitted in the name. The IUPAC name is 4-methylcyclohexanol.

13.5 **a.** 1-propanol has a three-carbon chain with a hydroxyl attached to carbon 1.
$$CH_3—CH_2—CH_2—OH$$
b. Methyl alcohol has a hydroxyl attached to a one-carbon alkane: $CH_3—OH$.
c. 3-pentanol has a five-carbon chain with a hydroxyl attached to carbon 3.

$$\begin{array}{c} \quad\quad\quad OH \\ \quad\quad\quad | \\ CH_3—CH_2—CH—CH_2—CH_3 \end{array}$$

d. 2-methyl-2-butanol has a four-carbon chain with a methyl and hydroxyl attached to carbon 2.

$$\begin{array}{c} \quad OH \\ \quad | \\ CH_3—C—CH_2—CH_3 \\ \quad | \\ \quad CH_3 \end{array}$$

e. Cyclohexanol has a six-carbon cycloalkane with a hydroxyl attached.

13.7 A benzene ring with a hydroxyl group is called *phenol.* Substituents are numbered from the carbon bonded to the hydroxyl group as carbon 1. Common names use the prefixes ortho, meta, and para.
a. phenol
b. 2-bromophenol, ortho-bromophenol (groups on the 1 and 2 positions are ortho), *o*-bromophenol
c. 3,5-dichlorophenol
d. 3-bromophenol, meta-bromophenol (groups on the 1 and 3 positions are meta), *m*-bromophenol

13.9 **a.** The *m* (meta) indicates that the two groups are in the 1,3 arrangement.

b. The *p* (para) indicates that the two groups are in the 1,4 arrangement.

c. Two chlorine atoms are attached to the aromatic system, one on carbon 2 and the other on carbon 5, with the hydroxyl attached to carbon 1.

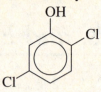

d. The *o* (ortho) indicates that the two groups are in the 1,2 arrangement.

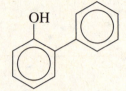

13.11 **a.** This is a one-carbon alkane with a thiol (—SH) group. The IUPAC name is methanethiol.
b. This thiol has a three-carbon alkane, with the thiol group attached to carbon 2. The IUPAC name is 2-propanethiol.
c. This compound has a four-carbon alkane with methyl groups attached to carbon 2 and carbon 3 and the thiol attached to carbon 1. The IUPAC name is 2,3-dimethyl-1-butanethiol.
d. This compound has a thiol attached to a cyclobutane. The IUPAC name is cyclobutanethiol.

13.13 **a.** methoxyethane, ethyl methyl ether
b. methoxycyclohexane, cyclohexyl methyl ether
c. ethoxycyclobutane, cyclobutyl ethyl ether
d. 1-methoxypropane, methyl propyl ether

13.15 **a.** Ethyl propyl ether has a two-carbon group and a three-carbon group attached to oxygen by single bonds. $CH_3—CH_2—O—CH_2—CH_2—CH_3$
b. Cyclopropyl ethyl ether has a two-carbon group and a three-carbon cycloalkyl group attached to oxygen by single bonds.

$CH_3—CH_2—O—\triangleleft$

c. Methoxycyclopentane has a one-carbon group and a five-carbon cycloalkyl group attached to oxygen by single bonds.

d. 1-ethoxy-2-methylbutane has a four-carbon chain with a methyl attached to carbon 2 and an ethoxy attached to carbon 1.

$$CH_3—CH_2—O—CH_2—\overset{\overset{\displaystyle CH_3}{|}}{CH}—CH_2—CH_3$$

e. 2,3-dimethoxypentane has a five-carbon chain with two methoxy groups attached, one to carbon 2 and the other to carbon 3.

$$CH_3—\overset{\overset{\displaystyle O—CH_3}{|}}{CH}—\underset{\underset{\displaystyle O—CH_3}{|}}{CH}—CH_2—CH_3$$

13.17 **a.** Isomers ($C_5H_{12}O$) have the same formula but different arrangements of atoms.
b. Different compounds have different molecular formulas ($C_4H_{10}O$ and C_4H_8O).
c. Isomers ($C_5H_{12}O$) have the same formula but different arrangements of atoms.

13.19 The heterocyclic ethers with five atoms including one oxygen are named *furan*; six atoms including one oxygen are *pyrans*. A six-atom cyclic ether with two oxygen atoms is *dioxane*.
    a. tetrahydrofuran   **b.** 3-methylfuran   **c.** 5-methyl-1,3-dioxane

13.21   **a.** Methanol; hydrogen bonding of alcohols gives higher boiling points than alkanes.
    b. 1-butanol; alcohols hydrogen bond, but ethers cannot.
    c. 1-butanol; hydrogen bonding of alcohols gives higher boiling points than alkanes.

13.23   **a.** Yes; alcohols with one to four carbon atoms hydrogen bond with water.
    b. Yes; the water can hydrogen bond to the O in an ether.
    c. No; a carbon chain longer than four carbon atoms diminishes the effect of the —OH group.
    d. Yes; the —OH in phenol ionizes in water, which makes it slightly soluble.

13.25 Dehydration is the removal of an —OH and an —H from adjacent carbon atoms.

  a. CH_3—CH_2—CH=CH_2 **b.**

  c. There are two possible products, A and B. B will be the major product, since the hydrogen is removed from the carbon that has the smaller number of hydrogens.

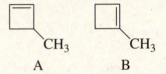

    A   B

  d. There are two possible products, A and B. B will be the major product, since the hydrogen is removed from the carbon that has the smaller number of hydrogens.
    CH_3—CH_2—CH_2—CH=CH_2 CH_3—CH_2—CH=CH—CH_3
        A   B

13.27 An ether is formed when the components of H_2O are eliminated from two alcohols; the alkyl portion of one alcohol combines with the alkoxy portion of the other alcohol.
  a. CH_3—O—CH_3 **b.** CH_3—CH_2—CH_2—O—CH_2—CH_2—CH_3

13.29 Alcohols can produce alkenes and ethers by the loss of water (dehydration).
  a. CH_3—CH_2—OH
  b. Since this ether has two different alkyl groups, it must be formed from two different alcohols.
    CH_3—OH + CH_3—CH_2—OH
  c.   OH

13.31   **a.** A primary alcohol oxidizes to an aldehyde and then to a carboxylic acid:

$$CH_3-CH_2-CH_2-CH_2-\overset{\overset{\displaystyle O}{\|}}{C}-H \text{ then } CH_3-CH_2-CH_2-CH_2-\overset{\overset{\displaystyle O}{\|}}{C}-OH$$

  b. A secondary alcohol oxidizes to a ketone: $CH_3-CH_2-\overset{\overset{\displaystyle O}{\|}}{C}-CH_3$
  c. A secondary alcohol oxidizes to a ketone: O

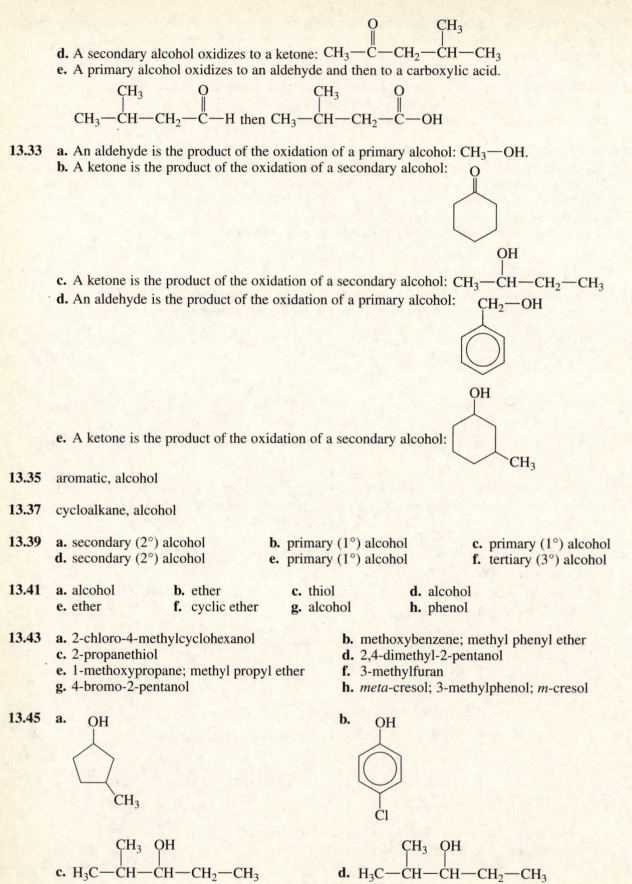

d. A secondary alcohol oxidizes to a ketone: $CH_3-\overset{\displaystyle O}{\overset{\|}{C}}-CH_2-\overset{\displaystyle CH_3}{\underset{|}{C}H}-CH_3$

e. A primary alcohol oxidizes to an aldehyde and then to a carboxylic acid.

$CH_3-\overset{\displaystyle CH_3}{\underset{|}{C}H}-CH_2-\overset{\displaystyle O}{\overset{\|}{C}}-H$ then $CH_3-\overset{\displaystyle CH_3}{\underset{|}{C}H}-CH_2-\overset{\displaystyle O}{\overset{\|}{C}}-OH$

13.33 a. An aldehyde is the product of the oxidation of a primary alcohol: CH_3-OH.
  b. A ketone is the product of the oxidation of a secondary alcohol:

  c. A ketone is the product of the oxidation of a secondary alcohol: $CH_3-\overset{\displaystyle OH}{\underset{|}{C}H}-CH_2-CH_3$
  d. An aldehyde is the product of the oxidation of a primary alcohol: CH_2-OH

  e. A ketone is the product of the oxidation of a secondary alcohol:

13.35 aromatic, alcohol

13.37 cycloalkane, alcohol

13.39 a. secondary (2°) alcohol   **b.** primary (1°) alcohol   **c.** primary (1°) alcohol
  d. secondary (2°) alcohol   **e.** primary (1°) alcohol   **f.** tertiary (3°) alcohol

13.41 a. alcohol   **b.** ether   **c.** thiol   **d.** alcohol
  e. ether   **f.** cyclic ether   **g.** alcohol   **h.** phenol

13.43 a. 2-chloro-4-methylcyclohexanol   **b.** methoxybenzene; methyl phenyl ether
  c. 2-propanethiol   **d.** 2,4-dimethyl-2-pentanol
  e. 1-methoxypropane; methyl propyl ether   **f.** 3-methylfuran
  g. 4-bromo-2-pentanol   **h.** *meta*-cresol; 3-methylphenol; *m*-cresol

13.45 a.   **b.**

  c. $H_3C-\overset{\displaystyle CH_3}{\underset{|}{C}H}-\overset{\displaystyle OH}{\underset{|}{C}H}-CH_2-CH_3$ **d.** $H_3C-\overset{\displaystyle CH_3}{\underset{|}{C}H}-\overset{\displaystyle OH}{\underset{|}{C}H}-CH_2-CH_3$

$$\underset{\overset{|}{SH}}{e.\ CH_3-CH_2-CH-CH_2-CH_3}$$

f. 〔benzene ring〕$-O-CH_2-CH_3$

$$\underset{\overset{|}{SH}}{g.\ CH_3-CH_2-CH-CH_2-CH_3}$$

13.47 Write the carbon chain first, and place the —OH on the carbon atoms in the chain to give different structural formulas. Shorten the chain by one carbon, and attach a methyl group and —OH group to give different compounds.

$$CH_3-CH_2-CH_2-CH_2-OH$$

$$\underset{\overset{|}{OH}}{CH_3-CH-CH_2-CH_3}$$

$$\underset{\overset{|}{CH_3}}{CH_2-CH-CH_2-OH}$$

$$\underset{\overset{|}{CH_3}}{\overset{\overset{OH}{|}}{CH_2-C-CH_3}}$$

13.49 **a.** 1-propanol; hydrogen bonding **b.** 1-propanol; hydrogen bonding
c. 1-butanol; larger molar mass

13.51 **a.** soluble; hydrogen bonding **b.** soluble; hydrogen bonding
c. insoluble; long-carbon chain diminishes effect of polar —OH on hydrogen bonding

13.53 **a.** $CH_3-CH=CH_2$ **b.** $CH_3-CH_2-\overset{\overset{O}{\|}}{C}-H$

c. $CH_3-CH=CH-CH_3$ **d.** $CH_3-CH_2-\overset{\overset{O}{\|}}{C}-CH_3$

e. $CH_3-CH_2-CH_2-O-CH_2-CH_2-CH_3$

f. 〔cyclohexene ring〕 **g.** 〔cyclohexanone ring with =O〕

13.55 **a.** $CH_3-CH_2-CH_2-OH \xrightarrow{H^+,\ heat} CH_2-CH=CH_2 + HCl \longrightarrow CH_3-\underset{\overset{|}{Cl}}{CH}-CH_3$

b. $CH_3-\underset{\overset{|}{CH_3}}{\overset{\overset{OH}{|}}{C}}-CH_3 \xrightarrow{H^+,\ heat} CH_3-\underset{\overset{|}{CH_3}}{C}=CH_2 + H_2 \xrightarrow{Pt} CH_3-\underset{\overset{|}{CH_3}}{CH}-CH_3$

c. $CH_3-CH_2-CH_2-OH \xrightarrow{H^+,\ heat} CH_3-CH=CH_2 + H_2O \xrightarrow{H^+} CH_3-\underset{\overset{|}{OH}}{CH}-CH_3$

$\xrightarrow{[O]} CH_3-\overset{\overset{O}{\|}}{C}-CH_3$

13.57 Testosterone contains cycloalkane, cycloalkene, alcohol, and ketone functional groups.

13.59 4-hexyl-1,3-benzenediol tells us that there is a six-carbon group attached to carbon 4 of a benzene ring and hydroxyls attached to carbons 1 and 3.

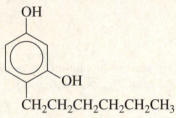

CH₂CH₂CH₂CH₂CH₂CH₃

13.61 **a.** 2,5-dichlorophenol is a benzene ring with a hydroxyl on carbon 1 and chlorine atoms on carbons 2 and 5.

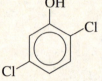

b. 3-methyl-1-butanethiol is a four-carbon chain with a methyl group on carbon 3 and a thiol group on carbon 1. *trans*-2-butene-1-thiol is similar in structure to 3-methyl-1-butanethiol except that there is a double bond between carbon 2 and carbon 3, and the carbon chains on the double bond are on opposite sides of the double bond.

$$CH_3-\underset{\underset{CH_3}{|}}{CH}-CH_2-CH_2-SH \qquad \underset{H}{\overset{CH_3}{\diagdown}}C=C\underset{CH_2-SH}{\overset{H}{\diagup}}$$

c. Pentachlorophenol is a benzene ring with one hydroxyl group and five chloro groups.

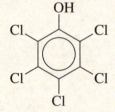

13.63 Since the reactant is a primary alcohol, the product is an aldehyde:

$$CH_3-\underset{\underset{CH_3}{|}}{CH}-\overset{\overset{O}{\|}}{C}-H \qquad \text{2-methylpropanal}$$

13.65 CH₃—CH₂—CH₂—CH₂—CH₂—OH   1-pentanol

$$CH_3-\underset{\underset{OH}{|}}{CH}-CH_2-CH_2-CH_3 \qquad \text{2-pentanol}$$

$$CH_3-CH_2-\underset{\underset{OH}{|}}{CH}-CH_2-CH_3 \qquad \text{3-pentanol}$$

$$HO-CH_2-\underset{\underset{CH_3}{|}}{CH}-CH_2-CH_3 \qquad \text{2-methyl-1-butanol}$$

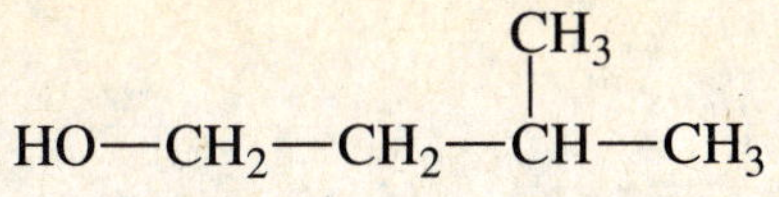

$$\begin{array}{c} \quad\quad\quad\quad CH_3 \\ \quad\quad\quad\quad | \\ HO-CH_2-CH_2-CH-CH_3 \end{array}$$ 3-methyl-1-butanol

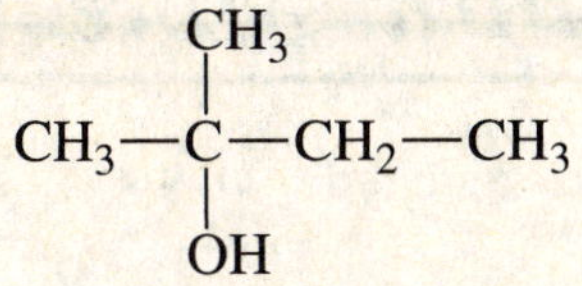

$$\begin{array}{c} \quad\quad CH_3 \\ \quad\quad | \\ CH_3-C-CH_2-CH_3 \\ \quad\quad | \\ \quad\quad OH \end{array}$$ 2-methyl-2-butanol

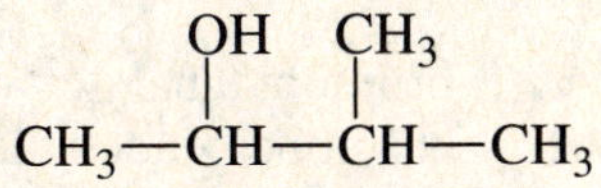

$$\begin{array}{c} \quad\quad OH \quad CH_3 \\ \quad\quad | \quad\quad | \\ CH_3-CH-CH-CH_3 \end{array}$$ 3-methyl-2-butanol

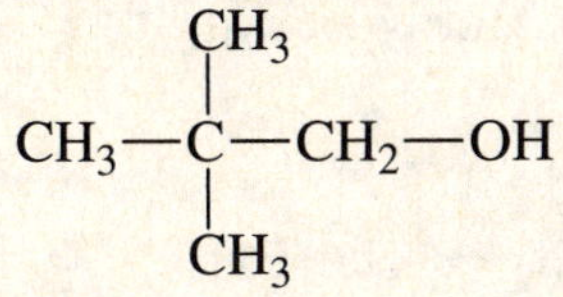

$$\begin{array}{c} \quad\quad CH_3 \\ \quad\quad | \\ CH_3-C-CH_2-OH \\ \quad\quad | \\ \quad\quad CH_3 \end{array}$$ 2,2-dimethyl-1-propanol

14

Aldehydes, Ketones, and Chiral Molecules

14.1 **a.** ketone **b.** aldehyde **c.** ketone **d.** aldehyde

14.3 **a.** (1) isomers of C_3H_6O **b.** (1) isomers of $C_5H_{10}O$ **c.** (2) same compound

14.5 **a.** propanal **b.** 2-methyl-3-pentanone **c.** 3-bromobutanal
d. 2-pentanone **e.** 3-methylcyclohexanone **f.** 4-chlorobenzaldehyde

14.7 **a.** acetaldehyde **b.** methyl propyl ketone **c.** formaldehyde

14.9 **a.** $CH_3\overset{\displaystyle O}{\overset{\|}{-}}C-H$ **b.** $CH_3-\overset{\displaystyle O}{\overset{\|}{C}}-CH_2-\overset{\displaystyle CH_3}{\overset{|}{C}H}-CH_3$

c. $CH_3-\overset{Br}{\overset{|}{C}H}-\overset{Br}{\overset{|}{C}H}-\overset{\displaystyle O}{\overset{\|}{C}}-H$ **d.** $CH_3-\overset{\displaystyle O}{\overset{\|}{C}}-CH_2-CH_2-CH_2-CH_3$

e. $CH_3-CH_2-\overset{\displaystyle CH_3}{\overset{|}{C}H}-CH_2-\overset{\displaystyle O}{\overset{\|}{C}}-H$

14.11

14.13 **a.** $CH_3-\overset{\displaystyle O}{\overset{\|}{C}}-H$ has a polar carbonyl group.
b. Pentanal has more carbons and thus a higher molar mass.
c. 1-butanol hydrogen bonds with other 1-butanol molecules.

14.15 **a.** $CH_3-\overset{\displaystyle O}{\overset{\|}{C}}-\overset{\displaystyle O}{\overset{\|}{C}}-CH_3$; more hydrogen bonding
b. acetaldehyde; acetaldehyde can hydrogen bond.
c. acetone; lower number of carbon atoms

14.17 No. The long, carbon chain diminishes the effect of the carbonyl group.

14.19 **a.** An aldehyde is the product of the oxidation of a primary alcohol: CH_3OH.
b. A ketone is the product of the oxidation of a secondary alcohol: OH

c. A ketone is the product of the oxidation of a secondary alcohol:

$CH_3-\overset{\displaystyle OH}{\overset{|}{C}H}-CH_2-CH_3$

d. An aldehyde is the product of the oxidation of a primary alcohol:

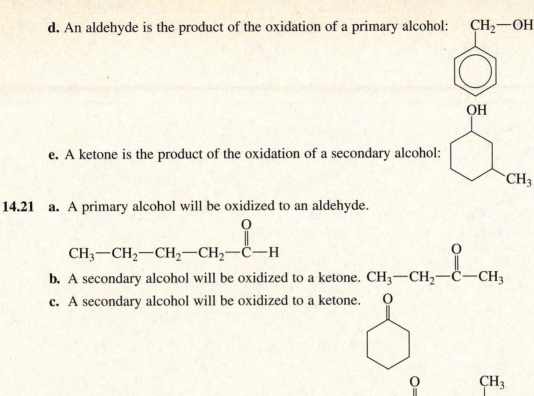

e. A ketone is the product of the oxidation of a secondary alcohol:

14.21 **a.** A primary alcohol will be oxidized to an aldehyde.

$$CH_3-CH_2-CH_2-CH_2-\overset{\overset{\displaystyle O}{\|}}{C}-H$$

b. A secondary alcohol will be oxidized to a ketone. $CH_3-CH_2-\overset{\overset{\displaystyle O}{\|}}{C}-CH_3$

c. A secondary alcohol will be oxidized to a ketone.

d. A secondary alcohol will be oxidized to a ketone. $CH_3-\overset{\overset{\displaystyle O}{\|}}{C}-CH_2-\overset{\overset{\displaystyle CH_3}{|}}{CH}-CH_3$

e. A primary alcohol will be oxidized to an aldehyde. $CH_3-\overset{\overset{\displaystyle CH_3}{|}}{CH}-CH_2-\overset{\overset{\displaystyle O}{\|}}{C}-H$

14.23 In reduction, an aldehyde will give a primary alcohol and a ketone will give a secondary alcohol.
a. Butyraldehyde is the four-carbon aldehyde; it will be reduced to a four-carbon, primary alcohol.
$$CH_3-CH_2-CH_2-CH_2-OH$$
b. Acetone is a three-carbon ketone; it will be reduced to a three-carbon, secondary alcohol.

$$CH_3-\overset{\overset{\displaystyle OH}{|}}{CH}-CH_3$$

c. 3-bromohexanal is a six-carbon aldehyde with bromine attached to carbon 3. It reduces to a six-carbon, primary alcohol with a bromine atom on carbon 3.

$$CH_3-CH_2-CH_2-\overset{\overset{\displaystyle Br}{|}}{CH}-CH_2-CH_2-OH$$

d. 2-methyl-3-pentanone is a five-carbon ketone with a methyl group attached to carbon 2. It will be reduced to a five-carbon, secondary alcohol with a methyl group attached to carbon 2.

$$CH_3-\overset{\overset{\displaystyle CH_3}{|}}{CH}-\overset{\overset{\displaystyle OH}{|}}{CH}-CH_2-CH_3$$

14.25 **a.** $CH_3-\overset{\overset{\displaystyle OH}{|}}{\underset{\underset{\displaystyle OH}{|}}{C}}-H$ **b.** $H-\overset{\overset{\displaystyle OH}{|}}{\underset{\underset{\displaystyle OH}{|}}{C}}-H$

14.27 **a.** hemiacetal (ethanol and formaldehyde) **b.** hemiacetal **c.** acetal
d. hemiacetal **e.** acetal

14.29 A hemiacetal forms when an alcohol is added to the carbonyl of an aldehyde or ketone.

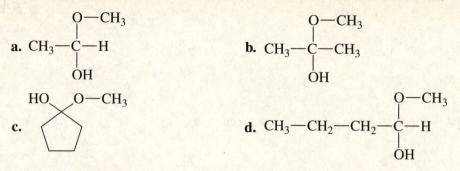

14.31 An acetal forms when a second molecule of alcohol reacts with a hemiacetal.

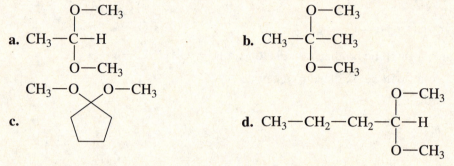

14.33 **a.** Achiral; there are no carbon atoms attached to four different groups.

$$\overset{\text{Br}}{\underset{}{|}}\,\textit{chiral carbon}$$

  b. Chiral CH₃—CH—CH₂—CH₃
  c. Achiral
  d. Achiral; there are no carbon atoms attached to four different groups.

14.35 **a.**
$$\overset{\text{CH}_3}{\underset{}{|}}\qquad\qquad\overset{\text{CH}_3\,\textit{chiral carbon}}{\underset{}{|}}$$
CH₃—C=CH—CH₂—CH₂—CH—CH₂—CH₂—OH

  b.
CH₃ O
| ‖
H₂N—CH—C—OH
chiral carbon

14.37 **a.**
H
|
HO——Br
|
CH₃

  b.
CH₃
|
Cl——Br
|
OH

  c.
CHO
|
HO——H
|
CH₂CH₃

14.39 **a.** identical **b.** enantiomers **c.** enantiomers **d.** enantiomers

14.41 **a.**, **b.**, and **f.** will give positive Tollen's tests, because they are aldehydes.

14.43 **a.** aromatic, aldehyde **b.** aromatic, aldehyde, ether, phenol
  c. aromatic, aldehyde, alkene **d.** cycloalkane, ketone **e.** ketone
  a. 2 **b.** 5 **c.** 4 **d.** 3 **e.** 1

14.45
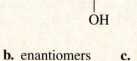
CH₃—CH₂—CH₂—C—H   CH₃—CH—C—H   CH₃—CH₂—C—CH₃
                   (with O and CH₃)   (with O)

14.47 **a.** 2-bromo-4-chlorocyclopentanone   **b.** 4-chloro-3-hydroxybenzaldehyde
c. 3-chloropropanal; 3-chloropropionaldehyde   **d.** 5-chloro-3-hexanone
e. 2-chloro-3-pentanone

14.49 **a.** 3-methylcyclopentanone is a five-carbon cyclic structure with a methyl group located two carbons from the carbonyl group.

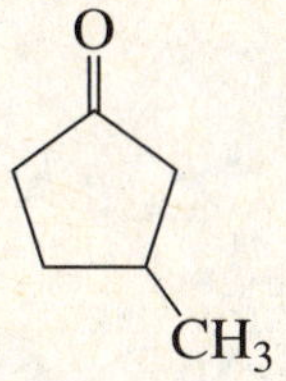

b. 4-chlorobenzaldehyde is a benzene with an aldehyde group and a chlorine atom on carbon 4.

c. 3-chloropropionaldehyde is a three-carbon aldehyde with a chlorine located two carbons from the carbonyl group.

$$Cl-CH_2-CH_2-\overset{\overset{\displaystyle O}{\|}}{C}-H$$

d. Ethyl methyl ketone (butanone) is a four-carbon ketone.

$$CH_3-\overset{\overset{\displaystyle O}{\|}}{C}-CH_2-CH_3$$

e. This is a six-carbon aldehyde with a methyl group on carbon 3.

$$CH_3-CH_2-CH_2-\overset{\overset{\displaystyle CH_3}{|}}{CH}-CH_2-\overset{\overset{\displaystyle O}{\|}}{C}-H$$

14.51 Compounds **b.**, **c.**, and **d.** are soluble in water because they have polar groups with oxygen atoms that hydrogen bond with water and fewer than five carbon atoms.

14.53 **a.** CH_3-CH_2-OH; polar $-OH$ group can hydrogen bond.

b. $CH_3-CH_2-\overset{\overset{\displaystyle O}{\|}}{C}-H$; has a polar carbonyl group.

c. $CH_3-CH_2-CH_2-OH$; polar $-OH$ group can hydrogen bond.

14.55 A chiral carbon is bonded to four different groups.

a.

$$H-\overset{\overset{\displaystyle Cl}{|}}{\underset{\underset{\displaystyle Cl}{|}}{C}}-\overset{\overset{\displaystyle Cl}{|}}{\underset{\underset{\displaystyle H}{|}}{Ⓒ}}-O-H$$

b. none   **c.** none

d. $CH_3-\overset{\overset{\displaystyle NH_2}{|}}{Ⓒ}H-\overset{\overset{\displaystyle O}{\|}}{C}-H$

e. $CH_3-CH_2-\overset{\overset{\displaystyle Br}{|}}{Ⓒ}H-CH_2-CH_2-CH_3$

f. none

14.57 Enantiomers are nonsuperimposable mirror images.
  a. enantiomers   **b.** identical
  c. identical   **d.** identical

14.59 Primary alcohols oxidize to aldehydes and then to carboxylic acids. Secondary alcohols oxidize to ketones.

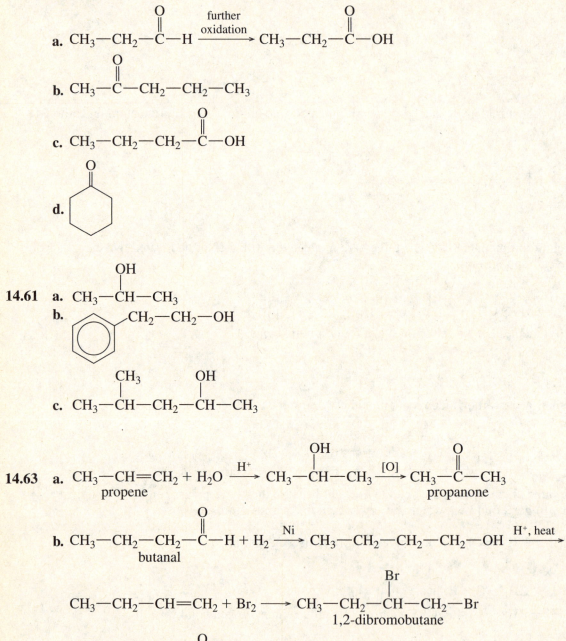

14.67 **a.** acetal; propanal and methanol
b. hemiacetal; butanone and ethanol
c. acetal; cyclohexanone and ethanol

14.69 2-methylpropanal; CH_3 O
                                      | ||
                        $CH_3-CH-C-H$

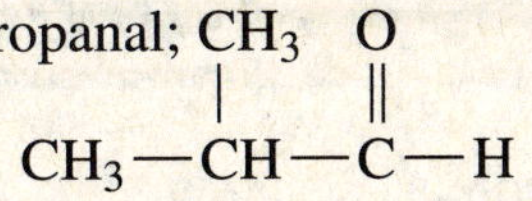

14.71 **1.** true   **2.** false   **3.** true   **4.** true   **5.** false   **6.** true   **7.** true

14.73 $CH_3-CH_2-CH_2-OH$ A 1-propanol

$CH_3-CH=CH_2$ B propene

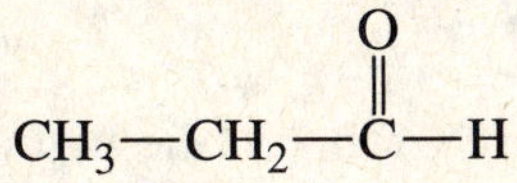

                O
                ||
CH_3-CH_2-C-H C propanal

15.1 Photosynthesis requires CO_2, H_2O, and the energy from the Sun. Respiration requires O_2 from the air and glucose from our foods.

15.3 Monosaccharides can be a chain of three to eight carbon atoms, one in a carbonyl group as an aldehyde or ketone, and the rest attached to hydroxyl groups. A monosaccharide cannot be split into smaller carbohydrates. A disaccharide is composed of two monosaccharide units joined together that can be split.

15.5 Hydroxyl groups are found in all monosaccharides along with a carbonyl group on the first or second carbon.

15.7 The name *ketopentose* tells us that the compound contains a ketone functional group and has five carbon atoms. In addition, all monosaccharides contain hydroxyl groups.

15.9 **a.** This monosaccharide is a ketose; it has a carbonyl on carbon 2.
b. This monosaccharide is an aldose; it has a —CHO, an aldehyde group.
c. This monosaccharide is a ketose; it has a carbonyl on carbon 2.
d. This monosaccharide is an aldose; it has a —CHO, an aldehyde group.
e. This monosaccharide is an aldose; it has a —CHO, an aldehyde group.

15.11 A Fischer projection is a two-dimensional representation of the three-dimensional structure of a molecule. In the D isomer, the —OH on the chiral carbon atom at the bottom of the chain is on the right side, whereas in the L isomer the —OH appears on the left side.

15.13 **a.** This structure is a D isomer since the hydroxyl group on the chiral carbon farthest from the carbonyl is on the right.
b. This structure is a D isomer since the hydroxyl group on the chiral carbon farthest from the carbonyl is on the right.
c. This structure is an L isomer since the hydroxyl group on the chiral carbon farthest from the carbonyl is on the left.
d. This structure is a D isomer since the hydroxyl group on the chiral carbon farthest from the carbonyl is on the right.

15.15

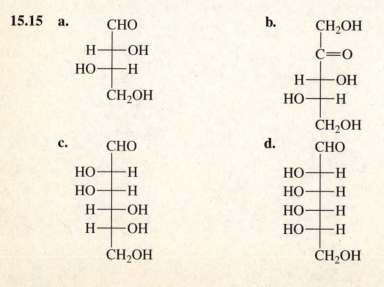

15.17   L-glucose is the mirror image of D-glucose.

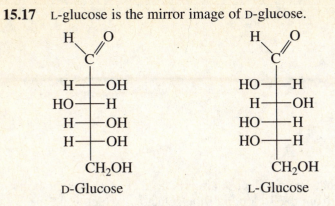

D-Glucose   L-Glucose

15.19   In D-galactose, the hydroxyl on carbon four extends to the left; in glucose, this hydroxyl group goes to the right.

15.21   **a.** Glucose is also called blood sugar.
b. Galactose is not metabolized in the condition called galactosemia.
c. Another name for fructose is fruit sugar.

15.23   In the cyclic structure of glucose, the six-atom ring is a result of the formation of the hemiacetal when the hydroxyl group on carbon 5 reacts with the aldehyde group on carbon 1.

→look up?
—when a chain coils and turns into cyclic hemiacetal

15.25   In the α-form, the hydroxyl (—OH) on carbon 1 is down; in the β-form, the hydroxyl (—OH) on carbon 1 is up.

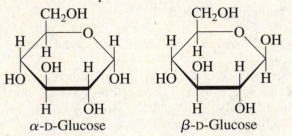

α-D-Glucose   β-D-Glucose

15.27   **a.** This is the α-form because the —OH on carbon 2 is down.
b. This is the α-form because the —OH on carbon 1 is down.

15.29

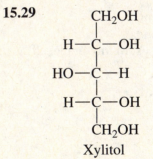

Xylitol

15.31   Oxidation product:

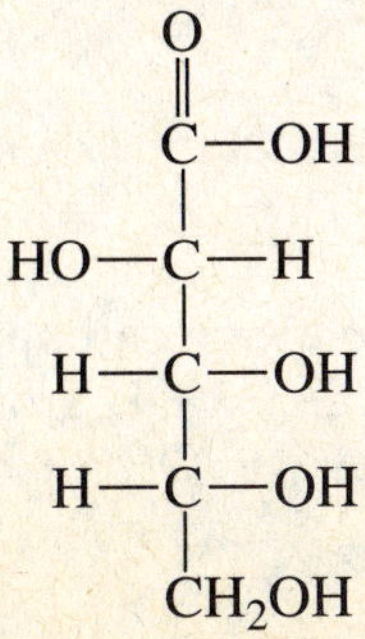

$$\begin{array}{c}
\text{O} \\
\parallel \\
\text{C—OH} \\
| \\
\text{HO—C—H} \\
| \\
\text{H—C—OH} \\
| \\
\text{H—C—OH} \\
| \\
\text{CH}_2\text{OH}
\end{array}$$

Reduction product (sugar alcohol):

$$
\begin{array}{c}
CH_2OH \\
| \\
HO-C-H \\
| \\
H-C-OH \qquad \text{D-Arabitol} \\
| \\
H-C-OH \\
| \\
CH_2OH
\end{array}
$$

15.33 **a.** When this disaccharide is hydrolyzed, galactose and glucose are produced. The glycosidic bond is a β-1,4 bond since the ether bond is up from the 1 carbon of the galactose, which is on the left in the drawing to the 4 carbon of the glucose on the right. β-lactose is the name of this disaccharide since the hydroxyl on the hemiacetal (carbon 1 of glucose) is up.

b. When this disaccharide is hydrolyzed, two molecules of glucose are produced. The glycosidic bond is an α-1,4 bond since the ether bond is down from the 1 carbon of the glucose on the left to the 4 carbon of the glucose on the right. α-maltose is the name of this disaccharide since the hydroxyl on the hemiacetal is down.

15.35 **a.** Lactose can be oxidized; it is a reducing sugar.
b. Maltose can be oxidized; it is a reducing sugar.

15.37 **a.** Another name for table sugar is sucrose.
b. Lactose is the disaccharide found in milk and milk products.
c. Maltose is also called malt sugar.
d. When lactose is hydrolyzed, the products are the monosaccharides galactose and glucose.

15.39 **a.** Amylose is an unbranched polymer of glucose units joined by α-1,4-glycosidic bonds; amylopectin is a branched polymer of glucose joined by α-1,4 and α-1,6-glycosidic bonds.
b. Amylopectin, produced by plants, is a branched polymer of glucose joined by α-1,4-glycosidic and α-1,6-glycosidic bonds. Glycogen, which is made by animals, is a highly branched polymer of glucose joined by α-1,4- and α-1,6-glycosidic bonds.

15.41 **a.** Cellulose is not digestible by humans since we do not have the enzymes necessary to break the β-1,4-glycosidic bonds in cellulose.
b. Amylose and amylopectin are the storage forms of carbohydrates in plants.
c. Amylose is the polysaccharide, which contains only α-1,4-glycosidic bonds.
d. Glycogen contains many α-1,4- and α-1,6-glycosidic bonds and is the most highly branched.

15.43 **a.** Isomaltose is a disaccharide.
b. Isomaltose consists of two α-D-glucose molecules.
c. The glycosidic link in isomaltose is an α-1,6-glycosidic bond.
d. The structure shown is α-isomaltose.
e. Yes, isomaltose is a reducing sugar.

15.45 **a.** Melezitose is a trisaccharide.
b. Melezitose contains two glucose molecules and a fructose molecule.

15.47 D-Fructose is a ketohexose, whereas D-galactose is an aldohexose. In galactose, the —OH on carbon 4 is on the left; in fructose the —OH is on the right.

15.49 D-Galactose is the mirror image of L-galactose. In D-galactose, the —OH groups on carbon 2 and 5 are on the right side, but on the left for carbon 3 and 4. In L-galactose, the —OH groups are reversed; carbons 2 and 5 have —OH on the left, and carbons 3 and 4 have —OH on the right.

15.51 **a.**

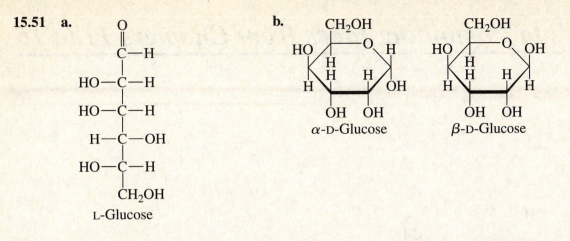

L-Glucose

α-D-Glucose β-D-Glucose

15.53 Since sorbitol can be oxidized to D-glucose, it must contain the same number of carbons with the same groups attached as glucose. The difference is that sorbitol has only hydroxyls while glucose has an aldehyde group. In sorbitol, the aldehyde group is changed to a hydroxyl.

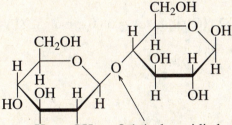

← This hydroxyl is an aldehyde in glucose.

15.55 When the α-galactose forms an open chain structure, and it can close to form either α- or β-galactose.

15.57

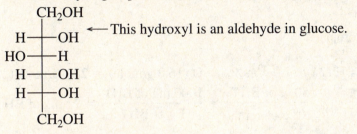

β-1,4-glycosidic bond. The bond from the glucose on the left is up (β).

15.59 **a.**

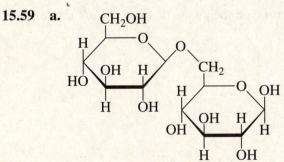

b. Yes. Gentiobiose is a reducing sugar. The ring with the hemiacetal with the —OH group can open up to form an aldehyde that can be oxidized.

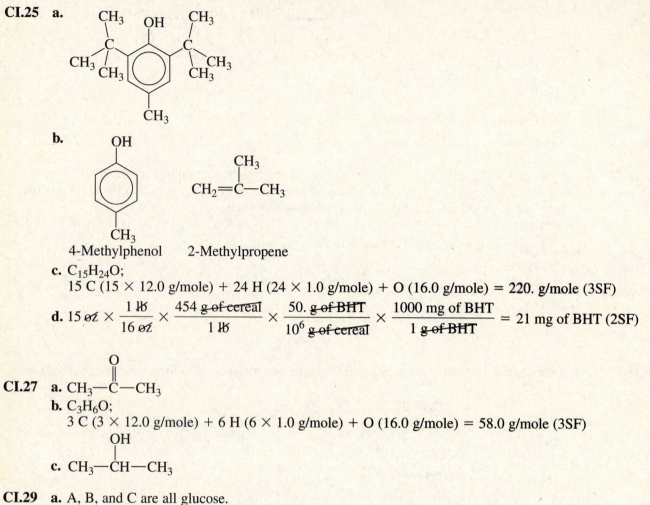

CI.25 **a.**

b. 4-Methylphenol   2-Methylpropene

c. $C_{15}H_{24}O$;
15 C (15 × 12.0 g/mole) + 24 H (24 × 1.0 g/mole) + O (16.0 g/mole) = 220. g/mole (3SF)

d. $15 \; \cancel{oz} \times \dfrac{1 \; \cancel{lb}}{16 \; \cancel{oz}} \times \dfrac{454 \; \cancel{\text{g of cereal}}}{1 \; \cancel{lb}} \times \dfrac{50. \; \cancel{\text{g of BHT}}}{10^6 \; \cancel{\text{g of cereal}}} \times \dfrac{1000 \; \text{mg of BHT}}{1 \; \cancel{\text{g of BHT}}} = 21 \; \text{mg of BHT (2SF)}$

CI.27 **a.** $CH_3-\overset{\overset{\displaystyle O}{\|}}{C}-CH_3$

b. C_3H_6O;
3 C (3 × 12.0 g/mole) + 6 H (6 × 1.0 g/mole) + O (16.0 g/mole) = 58.0 g/mole (3SF)

c. $CH_3-\overset{\overset{\displaystyle OH}{|}}{CH}-CH_3$

CI.29 **a.** A, B, and C are all glucose.
b. An α-1,6-glycosidic bond links A and B.
c. An α-1,4-glycosidic bond links B and C.
d. The structure is drawn as β-panose.
e. Panose is a reducing sugar because the hydroxyl group on the anomeric carbon 1 of structure C allows glucose (structure C) to form the aldehyde.

Carboxylic Acids and Esters

16.1   Methanoic acid (formic acid) is the carboxylic acid that is responsible for the pain associated with ant stings.

16.3   Each compound contains three carbon atoms. They differ because propanal, an aldehyde, contains a carbonyl group bonded to a hydrogen. In propanoic acid, the carbonyl group connects to a hydroxyl group.

16.5   **a.** Ethanoic acid (acetic acid) is the carboxylic acid with two carbons.
   b. Butanoic acid (butyric acid) is the carboxylic acid with four carbons.
   c. 2-chloropropanoic acid (α-chloropropionic acid) is a three-carbon carboxylic acid with a —Cl atom on the carbon next to the carbonyl.
   d. 3-methylhexanoic acid is a six-carbon carboxylic acid with a methyl group on carbon 3.
   e. 3,4-dihydroxybenzoic acid has a carboxylic acid group on benzene and two hydroxyl groups on carbons 3 and 4.
   f. 4-bromopentanoic acid is a five-carbon carboxylic acid with a —Br atom on carbon 4.

16.7   **a.** CH_3—CH_2—$\overset{\displaystyle O}{\overset{\|}{C}}$—OH   Propionic acid has three carbons.

   b. $\overset{\displaystyle O}{\overset{\|}{C}}$—OH on benzene ring   Benzoic acid is the carboxylic acid of benzene.

   c.   Cl—CH_2—$\overset{\displaystyle O}{\overset{\|}{C}}$—OH   2-chloroethanoic acid is a carboxylic acid that has a two-carbon chain with a chlorine atom on carbon 2.

   d.   HO—CH_2—CH_2—$\overset{\displaystyle O}{\overset{\|}{C}}$—OH   3-hydroxypropanoic acid is a carboxylic acid that has a three-carbon chain with a hydroxyl on carbon 3.

   e. CH_3—CH_2—$\overset{\displaystyle CH_3}{\overset{|}{CH}}$—$\overset{\displaystyle O}{\overset{\|}{C}}$—OH α-methylbutyric acid is a carboxylic acid that has a four-carbon chain with a methyl on the second (α) carbon.

   f. CH_3—CH_2—$\overset{\displaystyle Br}{\overset{|}{CH}}$—$CH_2$—$\overset{\displaystyle Br}{\overset{|}{CH}}$—$CH_2$—$\overset{\displaystyle O}{\overset{\|}{C}}$—OH   3,5-dibromoheptanoic acid is a carboxylic acid that has a seven-carbon chain with two bromine atoms, one on carbon 3 and the other on carbon 5.

16.9   Aldehydes and primary alcohols oxidize to produce the corresponding carboxylic acid.

   a. H—$\overset{\displaystyle O}{\overset{\|}{C}}$—OH

   b. CH_3—$\overset{\displaystyle O}{\overset{\|}{C}}$—OH

   c. CH_3—$\overset{\displaystyle CH_3}{\overset{|}{CH}}$—$CH_2$—$\overset{\displaystyle O}{\overset{\|}{C}}$—OH

   d. cyclopentyl—CH_2—$\overset{\displaystyle O}{\overset{\|}{C}}$—OH

16.11 **a.** Butanoic acid has a higher molar mass and would have a higher boiling point.

b. Propanoic acid can form more hydrogen bonds and form dimers, and would have a higher boiling point.

c. Butanoic acid can form more hydrogen bonds and form dimers, and would have a higher boiling point.

16.13 **a.** Propanoic acid is the most soluble because it has the smallest alkyl group.

b. Propanoic acid is the most soluble since carboxylic acids can form more hydrogen bonds.

16.15 **a.** $H-\overset{\overset{\displaystyle O}{\|}}{C}-OH + H_2O \rightleftharpoons H-\overset{\overset{\displaystyle O}{\|}}{C}-O^- + H_3O^+$

b. $CH_3-CH_2-\overset{\overset{\displaystyle O}{\|}}{C}-OH + H_2O \rightleftharpoons CH_3-CH_2-\overset{\overset{\displaystyle O}{\|}}{C}-O^- + H_3O^+$

c. $CH_3-\overset{\overset{\displaystyle O}{\|}}{C}-OH + H_2O \rightleftharpoons CH_3-\overset{\overset{\displaystyle O}{\|}}{C}-O^- + H_3O^+$

16.17 **a.** $H-\overset{\overset{\displaystyle O}{\|}}{C}-OH + NaOH \longrightarrow H-\overset{\overset{\displaystyle O}{\|}}{C}-O^-Na^+ + H_2O$

b. $CH_3-CH_2-\overset{\overset{\displaystyle O}{\|}}{C}-OH + NaOH \longrightarrow CH_3-CH_2-\overset{\overset{\displaystyle O}{\|}}{C}-O^-Na^+ + H_2O$

c. $\overset{\overset{\displaystyle O}{\|}}{C}-OH + NaOH$ (benzene ring) $\overset{\overset{\displaystyle O}{\|}}{C}-O^-Na^+$ (benzene ring) $\longrightarrow$ $+ H_2O$

16.19 A carboxylic acid salt is named by replacing the *–ic* ending of the acid name with *ate*.

a. The acid is methanoic acid (formic acid). The carboxylic acid salt is sodium methanoate (sodium formate).

b. The acid is propanoic acid (propionic acid). The carboxylic acid salt is sodium propanoate (sodium propionate).

c. The acid is benzoic acid. The carboxylic acid salt is sodium benzoate.

16.21 **a.** This is an *aldehyde* since it has a carbonyl bonded to carbon and hydrogen.

b. This is an *ester* since it has a carbonyl bonded to oxygen that is also bonded to a carbon.

c. This is a *ketone* since it has a carbonyl bonded to two carbon atoms.

d. This is a *carboxylic acid* since it has a carboxyl group, a carbonyl bonded to a hydroxyl.

16.23 **a.** $CH_3-\overset{\overset{\displaystyle O}{\|}}{C}-O-CH_3$ Replace the hydrogen atom on the carboxylic acid group with a methyl group.

b. $CH_3-CH_2-CH_2-\overset{\overset{\displaystyle O}{\|}}{C}-O-CH_3$ The carbonyl portion of the ester is a four-carbon chain bonded to a one-carbon methyl group.

c. (benzene ring)$-\overset{\overset{\displaystyle O}{\|}}{C}-O-CH_3$ The carbonyl portion of the ester is a benzene ring with an extra carbon with a methyl group bonded through an oxygen to the carbonyl carbon on the benzene ring.

16.25 A carboxylic acid and an alcohol react to give an ester with the elimination of water.

a. $CH_3-CH_2-\overset{\overset{\displaystyle O}{\|}}{C}-O-CH_2-CH_2-CH_3$

b. $CH_3-CH_2-CH_2-CH_2-\overset{\overset{\displaystyle O}{\|}}{C}-O-\overset{\overset{\displaystyle CH_3}{|}}{CH}-CH_3$

16.27 **a.** The carbonyl portion of the ester is derived from methanoic acid (formic acid). The alcohol is methanol (methyl alcohol).
  b. The carbonyl portion of the ester is derived from ethanoic acid (acetic acid). The alcohol is methanol (methyl alcohol).
  c. The carbonyl portion of the ester is derived from butanoic acid (butyric acid). The alcohol is methanol (methyl alcohol).
  d. The carbonyl portion of the ester is derived from 3-methylbutanoic acid (β-methylbutyric acid). The alcohol is ethanol (ethyl alcohol).

16.29 **a.** The name of this ester is methyl methanoate (methyl formate). The carbonyl portion of the ester contains one carbon; the name is derived from methanoic (formic) acid. The alkyl portion has one carbon; it is methyl.
  b. The name of this ester is methyl ethanoate (methyl acetate). The carbonyl portion of the ester contains two carbons. The name is derived from ethanoic (acetic) acid. The alkyl portion has one carbon, which is methyl.
  c. The name of this ester is methyl butanoate (methyl butyrate). The carbonyl portion of the ester contains four carbons; the name is derived from butanoic (butyric) acid. The alkyl portion has one carbon, which is methyl.
  d. The name of this ester is ethyl 3-methylbutanoate (ethyl β-methylbutyrate). The carbonyl portion of the ester has a four-carbon chain with a methyl group attached to the third (β) carbon, counting the carboxyl carbon as 1. The alkyl portion with two carbons is an ethyl.

16.31 **a.** $CH_3-\overset{\overset{\displaystyle O}{\|}}{C}-O-CH_3$ Acetic acid is the two-carbon carboxylic acid. Methanol gives a one-carbon alkyl group.

  b. $H-\overset{\overset{\displaystyle O}{\|}}{C}-O-CH_2-CH_2-CH_2-CH_3$ Formic acid is the one-carbon carboxylic acid bonded to the four-carbon 1-butanol.

  c. $CH_3-CH_2-CH_2-CH_2-\overset{\overset{\displaystyle O}{\|}}{C}-O-CH_2-CH_3$ Pentanoic acid is the five-carbon carboxylic acid bonded to the two-carbon ethanol.

  d. $CH_3-CH_2-\overset{\overset{\displaystyle O}{\|}}{C}-O-CH_2-\overset{\overset{\displaystyle Br}{|}}{CH}-CH_3$ Propanoic acid is the three-carbon carboxylic acid bonded to the three-carbon 2-bromo-1-propanol.

16.33 **a.** The flavor and odor of bananas is pentyl ethanoate (pentyl acetate).
  b. The flavor and odor of oranges is octyl ethanoate (octyl acetate).
  c. The flavor and odor of apricots is pentyl butanoate (pentyl butyrate) or pentyl propanoate or pentyl ethanoate).

16.35 **a.** $CH_3-\overset{\overset{\displaystyle O}{\|}}{C}-OH$; hydrogen bonds
  b. $CH_3-CH_2-CH_2-CH_2-OH$; hydrogen bonds

  c. $CH_3-O-\overset{\overset{\displaystyle O}{\|}}{C}-CH_3$; dipole–dipole attractions

16.37 Acid hydrolysis of an ester adds water in the presence of acid and gives a carboxylic acid and an alcohol.

16.39 Acid hydrolysis of an ester gives the carboxylic acid and the alcohol, which were combined to form the ester; basic hydrolysis of an ester gives the salt of carboxylic acid and the alcohol, which combine to form the ester.

a. $CH_3-CH_2-\overset{\displaystyle O}{\overset{\|}{C}}-O^-$ Na^+ and CH_3-OH

b. $CH_3-\overset{\displaystyle O}{\overset{\|}{C}}-OH$ and $CH_3-CH_2-CH_2-OH$

c. $CH_3-CH_2-CH_2-\overset{\displaystyle O}{\overset{\|}{C}}-OH$ and CH_3-CH_2-OH

d. ⬡—COOH and CH_3CH_2OH

e. ⬡—COO^-Na^+ and CH_3CH_2OH

16.41 **a.** $CH_3-\overset{\displaystyle O}{\overset{\|}{C}}-O-CH_2-CH_2-CH_3$

b. $CH_3-\overset{\displaystyle O}{\overset{\|}{C}}-OH + HO-CH_2-CH_2-CH_3 \underset{}{\overset{H^+}{\rightleftharpoons}} CH_3-\overset{\displaystyle O}{\overset{\|}{C}}-O-CH_2-CH_2-CH_3$

c. $CH_3-\overset{\displaystyle O}{\overset{\|}{C}}-O-CH_2-CH_2-CH_3 + H_2O \underset{}{\overset{H^+}{\rightleftharpoons}} CH_3-\overset{\displaystyle O}{\overset{\|}{C}}-OH + HO-CH_2-CH_2-CH_3$

d. $CH_3-\overset{\displaystyle O}{\overset{\|}{C}}-O-CH_2-CH_2-CH_3 + NaOH \longrightarrow CH_3-\overset{\displaystyle O}{\overset{\|}{C}}-O^-Na^+ + HO-CH_2-CH_2-CH_3$

e. $1.58 \ \cancel{g} \times \dfrac{1 \ \cancel{mole}}{102.0 \ \cancel{g}} \times \dfrac{1000 \ mL}{0.208 \ \cancel{mole}} = 74.5 \ mL$ (3SF)

16.43 **a.** 3-methylbutanoic acid; β-methylbutyric acid
b. ethyl benzoate
c. ethyl propanoate; ethyl propionate
d. 2-chlorobenzoic acid; *ortho*-chlorobenzoic acid
e. 4-hydroxypentanoic acid
f. 2-propyl ethanoate; isopropyl acetate

16.45 $CH_3-CH_2-CH_2-CH_2-\overset{\displaystyle O}{\overset{\|}{C}}-OH$ $CH_3-CH_2-\overset{\displaystyle CH_3}{\overset{|}{C}}H-\overset{\displaystyle O}{\overset{\|}{C}}-OH$

$CH_3-\overset{\displaystyle CH_3}{\overset{|}{C}}H-CH_2-\overset{\displaystyle O}{\overset{\|}{C}}-OH$ $CH_3-\overset{\displaystyle CH_3}{\underset{\displaystyle CH_3}{\overset{|}{\underset{|}{C}}}}-\overset{\displaystyle O}{\overset{\|}{C}}-OH$

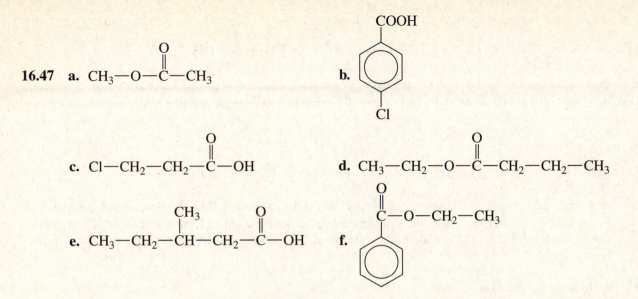

16.47 **a.** CH₃—O—C(=O)—CH₃   **b.** [benzene ring with COOH at top and Cl at bottom]

c. Cl—CH₂—CH₂—C(=O)—OH   **d.** CH₃—CH₂—O—C(=O)—CH₂—CH₂—CH₃

e. CH₃—CH₂—CH(CH₃)—CH₂—C(=O)—OH   **f.** [benzene ring with C(=O)—O—CH₂—CH₃]

16.49 **a.** CH₃—C(=O)—OH; ethanoic acid has a higher boiling point than 1-propanol because two molecules of ethanoic acid hydrogen bond to form a dimer, which effectively doubles the mass and requires a higher temperature to reach the boiling point.

b. CH₃—CH₂—C(=O)—OH; hydrogen bonds and forms dimers

c. CH₃—CH₂—CH₂—C(=O)—OH; butanoic acid has a higher molar mass than ethanoic acid and requires a higher temperature to reach the boiling point.

16.51 The presence of two polar groups in the carboxyl group allows hydrogen bonding, including the formation of a dimer that doubles the effective molar mass and requires a higher temperature to form gas.

16.53 Compounds **b.**, **c.**, **d.**, and **e.** are soluble in water.

16.55 **a.** CH₃—CH₂—C(=O)—O⁻ + H₃O⁺   **b.** CH₃—CH₂—C(=O)—O⁻K⁺ + H₂O

c. CH₃—CH₂—C(=O)—O—CH₃ + H₂O   **d.** [benzene ring with C(=O)—O—CH₂—CH₃] + H₂O

16.57 **a.** 3-methylbutanoic acid is needed to react with methanol (CH₃—OH).
b. 3-chlorobenzoic acid is needed to react with ethanol (CH₃—CH₂—OH).
c. Hexanoic acid is needed to react with methanol (CH₃—OH).

16.59 **a.** CH₃—CH₂—C(=O)—OH and HO—CH(CH₃)—CH₃
b. CH₃—CH(CH₃)—C(=O)—O⁻Na⁺ and HO—CH₂—CH₂—CH₃

123

16.61 a. $CH_2{=}CH_2 + H_2O \xrightarrow{H^+} CH_3{-}CH_2{-}OH \xrightarrow{[O]} CH_3{-}\overset{\displaystyle O}{\underset{\displaystyle \|}{C}}{-}OH$

b. $CH_3{-}CH_2{-}CH_2{-}CH_2{-}OH \xrightarrow{[O]} CH_3{-}CH_2{-}CH_2{-}\overset{\displaystyle O}{\underset{\displaystyle \|}{C}}{-}OH$

16.63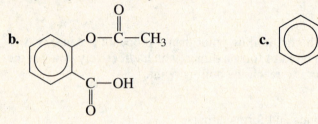

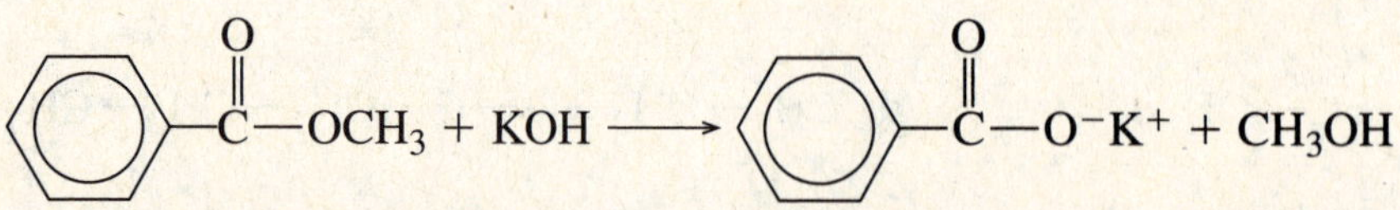

A soluble salt, potassium benzoate, is formed. When acid is added, the salt is converted to insoluble benzoic acid. In KOH solution, the ester undergoes saponification to form the soluble salt of potassium benzoate. When acid is added to a solution of potassium benzoate, it is converted to insoluble benzoic acid.

16.65 a. hydroxyl and carboxyl acid

b.

c.

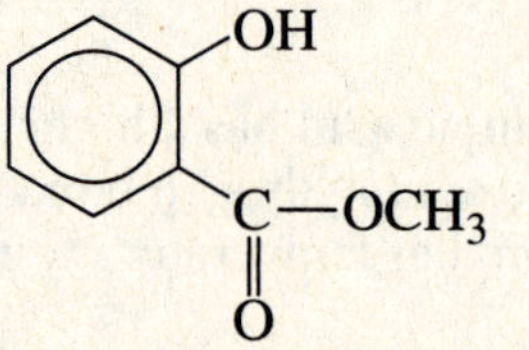

17.1 Lipids provide energy, protection, and insulation for the organs in the body. Lipids are also an important component of cell membranes.

17.3 Since lipids are not soluble in water, a polar solvent, they are nonpolar molecules.

17.5 All fatty acids contain a long chain of carbon atoms with a carboxylic acid group. Saturated fatty acids contain only carbon–carbon single bonds; unsaturated fatty acids contain one or more double bonds.

17.7 **a.** Palmitic acid  COOH

     b. Oleic acid

17.9 **a.** Lauric acid has only carbon–carbon single bonds; it is saturated.
     b. Linolenic acid has three carbon–carbon double bonds; it is unsaturated.
     c. Palmitoleic acid has one carbon–carbon double bond; it is unsaturated.
     d. Stearic acid has only carbon–carbon single bonds; it is saturated.

17.11 In a cis fatty acid, the hydrogen atoms are on the same side of the double bond, which produces a bend in the carbon chain. In a trans fatty acid, the hydrogen atoms are on opposite sides of the double bond, which gives a carbon chain without any bend.

17.13 In an omega-3 fatty acid, the first double bond occurs at carbon 3 counting from the methyl group. In an omega-6 fatty acid, the first double bond occurs at carbon 6 counting from the methyl group.

17.15 Arachidonic acid contains four double bonds and no side groups. In PGE_1, a part of the chain forms cyclopentane, and there are hydroxyl and ketone functional groups.

17.17 Prostaglandins raise or lower blood pressure and stimulate contraction and relaxation of smooth muscle, and may cause inflammation and pain.

17.19 Palmitic acid is the 16-carbon saturated fatty acid and myricyl alcohol has a 30-carbon chain:

$$CH_3-(CH_2)_{14}-\overset{\displaystyle O}{\overset{\|}{C}}-O-(CH_2)_{29}-CH_3$$

17.21 Fats are composed of fatty acids and glycerol. In this case, the fatty acid is stearic acid, an 18-carbon saturated fatty acid.

$$CH_2-O-\overset{\displaystyle O}{\overset{\|}{C}}-(CH_2)_{16}-CH_3$$
$$CH-O-\overset{\displaystyle O}{\overset{\|}{C}}-(CH_2)_{16}-CH_3$$
$$CH_2-O-\overset{\displaystyle O}{\overset{\|}{C}}-(CH_2)_{16}-CH_3$$

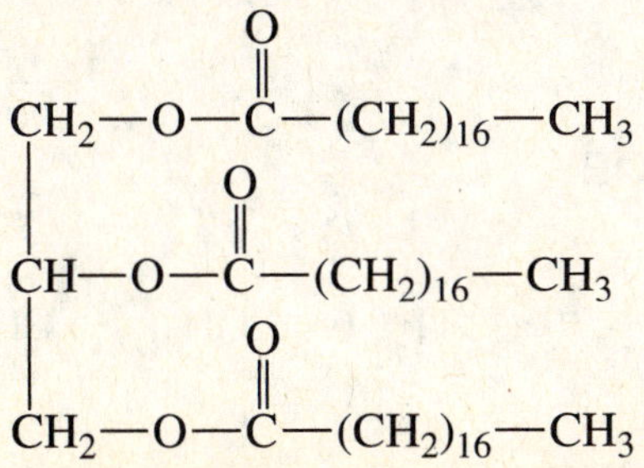

17.23 Glyceryl tripalmitate (tripalmitin) has three palmitic acids (16-carbon saturated fatty acid) forming ester bonds with glycerol.

$$CH_2-O-\overset{\overset{\textstyle O}{\|}}{C}-(CH_2)_{14}-CH_3$$
$$CH-O-\overset{\overset{\textstyle O}{\|}}{C}-(CH_2)_{14}-CH_3$$
$$CH_2-O-\overset{\overset{\textstyle O}{\|}}{C}-(CH_2)_{14}-CH_3$$

17.25 Safflower oil contains fatty acids with two or more double bonds; olive oil contains a large amount of oleic acid, which has a single (monounsaturated) double bond.

17.27 Although coconut oil comes from a vegetable or plant source, it has large amounts of saturated fatty acids and small amounts of unsaturated fatty acids. Since coconut oil contains the same kinds of fatty acids as animal fat, coconut oil has a melting point similar to the melting point of animal fats.

17.29

$$CH_2-O-\overset{\overset{\textstyle O}{\|}}{C}-(CH_2)_7-CH=CH-(CH_2)_7-CH_3$$
$$CH-O-\overset{\overset{\textstyle O}{\|}}{C}-(CH_2)_7-CH=CH-(CH_2)_7-CH_3 + 3H_2 \xrightarrow{\text{Ni}}$$
$$CH_2-O-\overset{\overset{\textstyle O}{\|}}{C}-(CH_2)_7-CH=CH-(CH_2)_7-CH_3$$

$$CH_2-O-\overset{\overset{\textstyle O}{\|}}{C}-(CH_2)_{16}-CH_3$$
$$CH-O-\overset{\overset{\textstyle O}{\|}}{C}-(CH_2)_{16}-CH_3$$
$$CH_2-O-\overset{\overset{\textstyle O}{\|}}{C}-(CH_2)_{16}-CH_3$$

17.31 **a.** Partial hydrogenation means that some of the double bonds in the unsaturated fatty acids have been converted to single bonds.
b. Since the margarine has more saturated fatty acids than the original vegetable oil, the fatty acids interact more strongly and remain solid at higher temperatures.

17.33 Acid hydrolysis of a fat gives glycerol and the fatty acids. Basic hydrolysis (saponification) of fat gives glycerol and the salts of the fatty acids.
a.

$$CH_2-O-\overset{\overset{\textstyle O}{\|}}{C}-(CH_2)_{12}-CH_3$$
$$CH-O-\overset{\overset{\textstyle O}{\|}}{C}-(CH_2)_{12}-CH_3 + 3H_2O \xrightarrow{H^+}$$
$$CH_2-O-\overset{\overset{\textstyle O}{\|}}{C}-(CH_2)_{12}-CH_3$$

$$CH_2-OH$$
$$CH-OH + 3HO-\overset{\overset{\textstyle O}{\|}}{C}-(CH_2)_{12}-CH_3$$
$$CH_2-OH$$

b.

$$CH_2-O-\overset{\overset{\textstyle O}{\|}}{C}-(CH_2)_{12}-CH_3$$
$$CH-O-\overset{\overset{\textstyle O}{\|}}{C}-(CH_2)_{12}-CH_3 + 3NaOH \longrightarrow$$
$$CH_2-O-\overset{\overset{\textstyle O}{\|}}{C}-(CH_2)_{12}-CH_3$$

$$CH_2-OH$$
$$CHOH + 3Na^{+\,-}O-\overset{\overset{\textstyle O}{\|}}{C}-(CH_2)_{12}-CH_3$$
$$CH_2-OH$$

17.35 A triacylglycerol is composed of glycerol with three hydroxyl groups that form ester links with three long-chain fatty acids. In olestra, six to eight long-chain fatty acids form ester links with the hydroxyl groups on sucrose, a sugar. The olestra cannot be digested because our enzymes cannot break down the large olestra molecule.

17.37

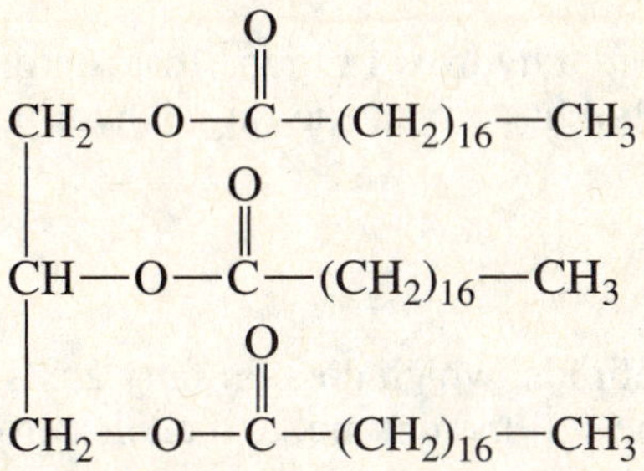

$$
\begin{array}{l}
CH_2-O-\overset{\displaystyle O}{\overset{\|}{C}}-(CH_2)_{16}-CH_3 \\[4pt]
CH-O-\overset{\displaystyle O}{\overset{\|}{C}}-(CH_2)_{16}-CH_3 \\[4pt]
CH_2-O-\overset{\displaystyle O}{\overset{\|}{C}}-(CH_2)_{16}-CH_3
\end{array}
$$

17.39 A triacylglycerol consists of glycerol and three fatty acids. A glycerophospholipid consists of glycerol, two fatty acids, a phosphate group, and an amino alcohol.

17.41

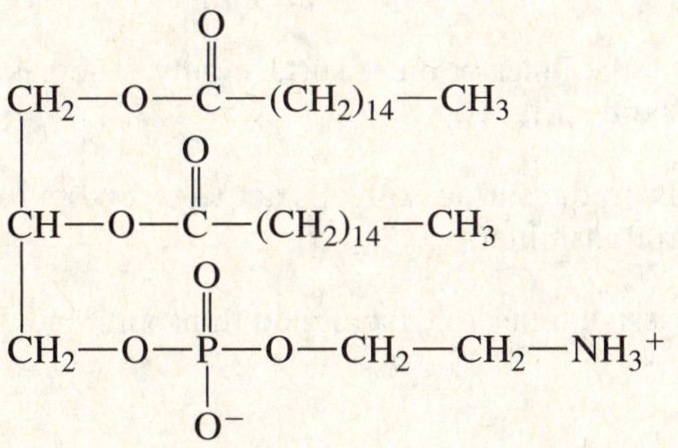

$$
\begin{array}{l}
CH_2-O-\overset{\displaystyle O}{\overset{\|}{C}}-(CH_2)_{14}-CH_3 \\[4pt]
CH-O-\overset{\displaystyle O}{\overset{\|}{C}}-(CH_2)_{14}-CH_3 \\[4pt]
CH_2-O-\overset{\displaystyle O}{\overset{\|}{P}}-O-CH_2-CH_2-NH_3^+ \\[4pt]
\underset{O^-}{}
\end{array}
$$

This is a cephalin.

17.43 This glycerophospholipid is a cephalin. It contains glycerol, oleic acid, stearic acid, phosphate, and ethanolamine.

17.45 A ceramide contains the amino alcohol sphingosine (instead of glycerol) and one fatty acid. A glycerophospholipid consists of glycerol, two fatty acids, a phosphate group, and an amino alcohol.

17.47

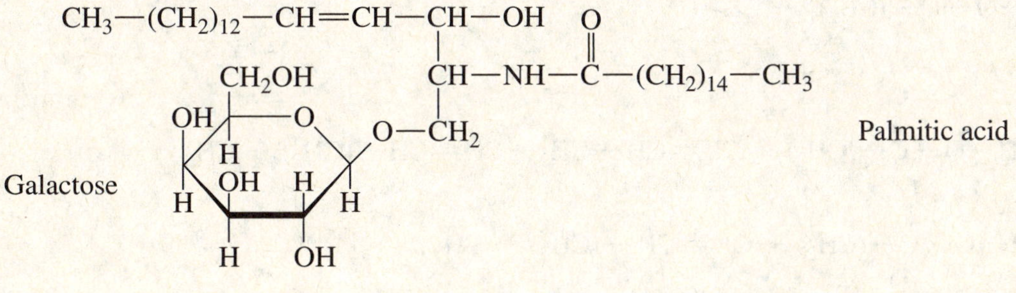

$CH_3-(CH_2)_{12}-CH=CH-CH-OH$

$CH-NH-\overset{\displaystyle O}{\overset{\|}{C}}-(CH_2)_{14}-CH_3$

Palmitic acid

Galactose

17.49

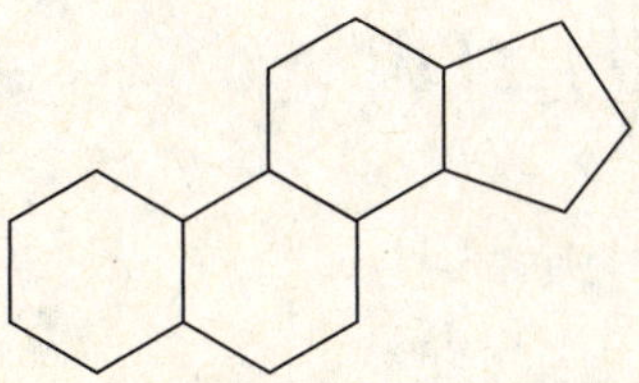

17.51 Bile salts emulsify fat globules, which makes the fat easier to digest by lipases.

17.53 Lipoproteins are large, spherically shaped molecules that transport lipids in the bloodstream. They consist of an outer layer of glycerophospholipids and proteins surrounding an inner core of hundreds of nonpolar lipids and cholesteryl esters.

127

17.55 Chylomicrons have a lower density than VLDLs. They pick up triacylglycerols from the intestine, whereas VLDLs transport triacylglycerols synthesized in the liver.

17.57 "Bad" cholesterol is the cholesterol carried by LDLs to the tissues where it can form deposits called plaque, which can narrow the arteries.

17.59 Both estradiol and testosterone contain the steroid nucleus and a hydroxyl group. Testosterone has a ketone group, a double bond, and two methyl groups. Estradiol has a benzene ring, a hydroxyl group in place of the ketone, and a methyl group.

17.61 **d.** Testosterone is a male sex hormone.

17.63 Cell membranes contain a number of lipids: glycerophospholipids, which contain fatty acids with cis double bonds; glycolipids, which are on the outside of the cell membrane; and cholesterol, which is in animal membranes.

17.65 The function of the lipid bilayer in the plasma cell membrane is to keep the cell contents separated from the outside environment and to allow the cell to regulate the movement of substances into and out of the cell.

17.67 The peripheral proteins in the membrane emerge on the inner or outer surface only, whereas the integral proteins extend through the membrane to both surfaces.

17.69 The carbohydrates in glycoproteins and glycolipids on the surface of cells act as receptors for cell recognition and chemical messengers such as neurotransmitters.

17.71 Substances move through the cell membrane by passive transport, facilitated transport, and active transport.

17.73

$$
\begin{array}{l}
CH_2-O-\overset{\overset{\displaystyle O}{\|}}{C}-(CH_2)_{14}-CH_3 \\
| \qquad\qquad\quad O \\
CH-O-\overset{\overset{\displaystyle O}{\|}}{C}-(CH_2)_{14}-CH_3 \qquad \text{Glyceryl tripalmitate (tripalmitin)} \\
| \qquad\qquad\quad O \\
CH_2-O-\overset{\overset{\displaystyle O}{\|}}{C}-(CH_2)_{14}-CH_3
\end{array}
$$

17.75 a.

$$
\begin{array}{l}
CH_2-O-\overset{\overset{\displaystyle O}{\|}}{C}-(CH_2)_7-CH=CH-CH_2-CH=CH-(CH_2)_4-CH_3 \\
| \qquad\qquad\quad O \\
CH-O-\overset{\overset{\displaystyle O}{\|}}{C}-(CH_2)_7-CH=CH-(CH_2)_7-CH_3 \\
| \qquad\qquad\quad O \\
CH_2-O-\overset{\overset{\displaystyle O}{\|}}{C}-(CH_2)_7-CH=CH-CH_2-CH=CH-(CH_2)_4-CH_3 \\
\qquad\qquad\qquad\quad O \\
CH_2-O-\overset{\overset{\displaystyle O}{\|}}{C}-(CH_2)_7-CH=CH-CH_2-CH=CH-(CH_2)_4-CH_3 \\
| \qquad\qquad\quad O \\
CH-O-\overset{\overset{\displaystyle O}{\|}}{C}-(CH_2)_7-CH=CH-CH_2-CH=CH-(CH_2)_4-CH_3 \\
| \qquad\qquad\quad O \\
CH_2-O-\overset{\overset{\displaystyle O}{\|}}{C}-(CH_2)_7-CH=CH-(CH_2)_7-CH_3
\end{array}
$$

b.

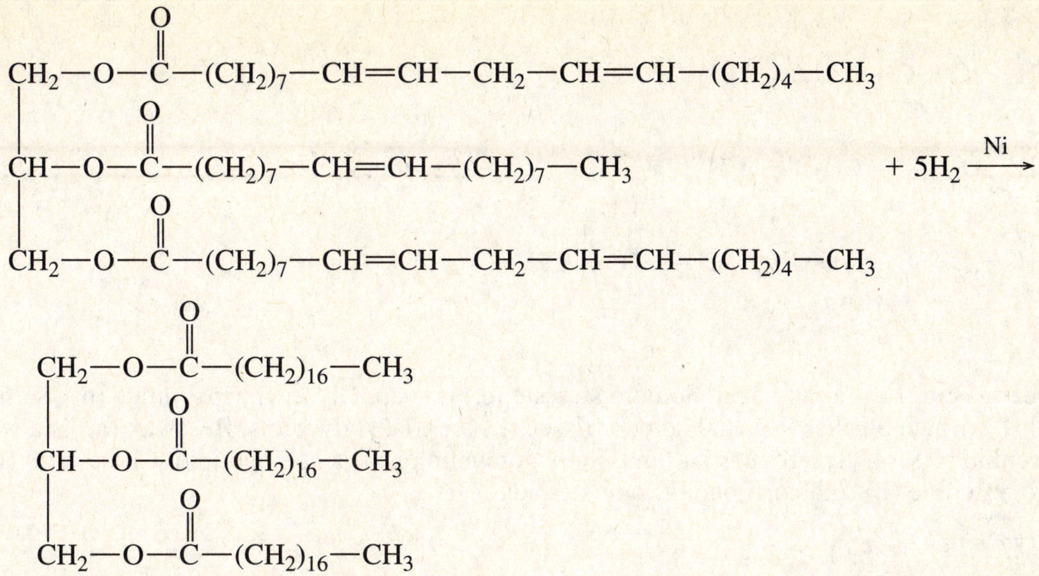

$$CH_2-O-\overset{\overset{O}{\|}}{C}-(CH_2)_7-CH=CH-CH_2-CH=CH-(CH_2)_4-CH_3$$

$$CH-O-\overset{\overset{O}{\|}}{C}-(CH_2)_7-CH=CH-(CH_2)_7-CH_3 \qquad +\ 5H_2 \xrightarrow{\text{Ni}}$$

$$CH_2-O-\overset{\overset{O}{\|}}{C}-(CH_2)_7-CH=CH-CH_2-CH=CH-(CH_2)_4-CH_3$$

$$CH_2-O-\overset{\overset{O}{\|}}{C}-(CH_2)_{16}-CH_3$$

$$CH-O-\overset{\overset{O}{\|}}{C}-(CH_2)_{16}-CH_3$$

$$CH_2-O-\overset{\overset{O}{\|}}{C}-(CH_2)_{16}-CH_3$$

17.77 Beeswax and carnauba wax are waxes. Vegetable oil and glyceryl tricaprate (tricaprin) are triacylglycerols.

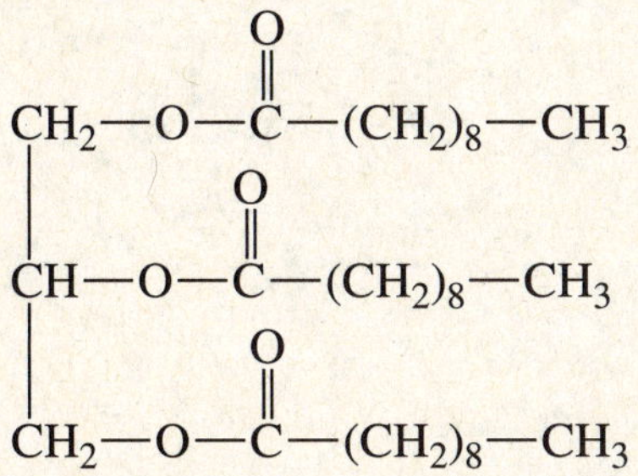

$$CH_2-O-\overset{\overset{O}{\|}}{C}-(CH_2)_8-CH_3$$

$$CH-O-\overset{\overset{O}{\|}}{C}-(CH_2)_8-CH_3 \qquad \text{Glycerol tricaprate (tricaprin)}$$

$$CH_2-O-\overset{\overset{O}{\|}}{C}-(CH_2)_8-CH_3$$

17.79 **a.** A typical unsaturated fatty acid has a cis double bond.
b. A trans fatty acid has a trans double bond with the alkyl groups on opposite sides of the double bond. A cis fatty acid has a cis double bond with the alkyl groups on the same side of the double bond.
c.

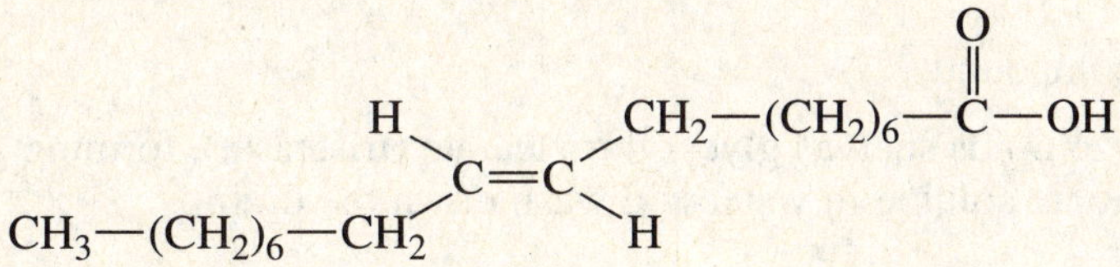

$$CH_3-(CH_2)_6-CH_2 \overset{H}{\underset{}{}}C=C\overset{CH_2-(CH_2)_6-\overset{\overset{O}{\|}}{C}-OH}{\underset{H}{}}$$

17.81

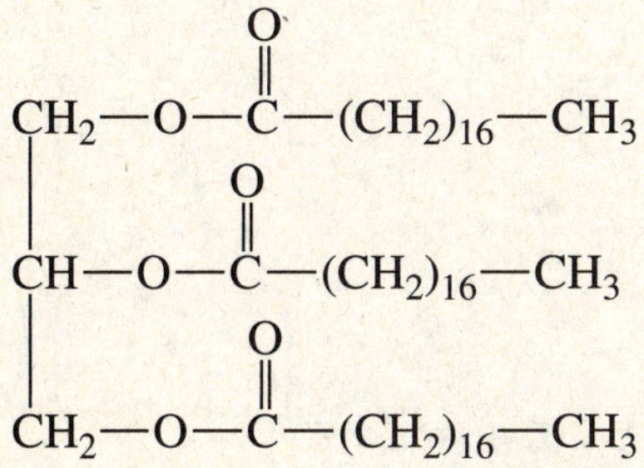

$$CH_2-O-\overset{\overset{O}{\|}}{C}-(CH_2)_{16}-CH_3$$

$$CH-O-\overset{\overset{O}{\|}}{C}-(CH_2)_{16}-CH_3 \qquad \text{Glyceryl tristerate (tristearin)}$$

$$CH_2-O-\overset{\overset{O}{\|}}{C}-(CH_2)_{16}-CH_3$$

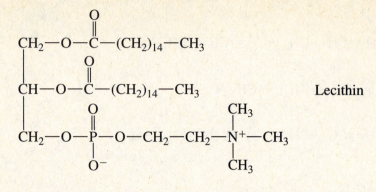

Lecithin

17.83 Stearic acid (**l.**) is a fatty acid. Sodium stearate (**e.**) is soap. Glyceryl tripalmitate (**d.**), safflower oil (**f.**), whale blubber (**h.**), and adipose tissue (**i.**) are triacylglycerols. Beeswax (**a.**) is a wax. Lecithin (**c.**) is a glycerophospholipid. Sphingomyelin (**g.**) is a sphingolipid. Cholesterol (**b.**), progesterone (**j.**), and cortisone (**k.**) are steroids.

17.85   **a.** 5   **b.** 1, 2, 3, 4
       c. 2   **d.** 1, 2
       e. 1, 2, 3, 4   **f.** 2, 3, 4, 6

17.87   **a.** 4   **b.** 3
       c. 1   **d.** 4
       e. 4   **f.** 3
       g. 2   **h.** 1

17.89

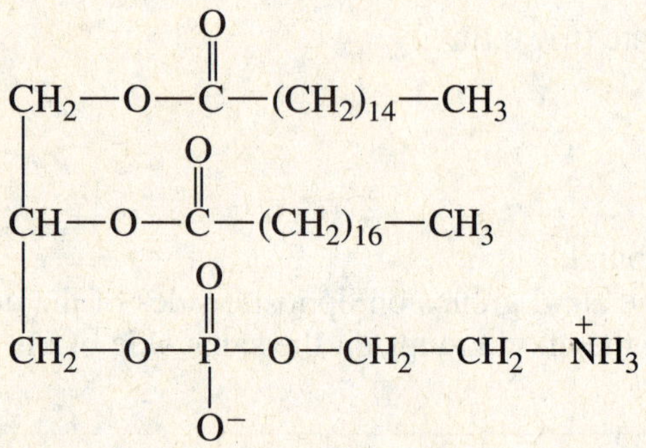

$$CH_2-O-\overset{\overset{\displaystyle O}{\|}}{C}-(CH_2)_{14}-CH_3$$

$$CH-O-\overset{\overset{\displaystyle O}{\|}}{C}-(CH_2)_{16}-CH_3$$

$$CH_2-O-\overset{\overset{\displaystyle O}{\|}}{\underset{\underset{\displaystyle O^-}{|}}{P}}-O-CH_2-CH_2-\overset{+}{N}H_3$$

There are other isomers of this compound.

17.91   **a.** Adding NaOH would hydrolyze lipids such as glyceryl tristearate (tristearin), forming glycerol and salts of the fatty acids that are soluble in water and wash down the drain.

      b.

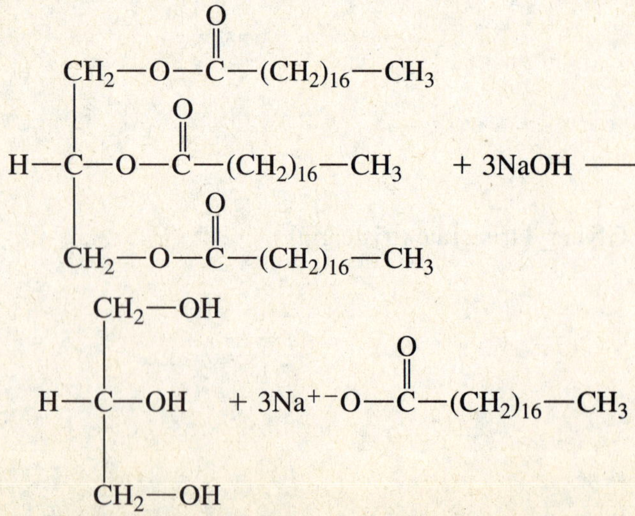

$$CH_2-O-\overset{\overset{\displaystyle O}{\|}}{C}-(CH_2)_{16}-CH_3$$

$$H-\overset{}{C}-O-\overset{\overset{\displaystyle O}{\|}}{C}-(CH_2)_{16}-CH_3 \quad + \; 3NaOH \longrightarrow$$

$$CH_2-O-\overset{\overset{\displaystyle O}{\|}}{C}-(CH_2)_{16}-CH_3$$

$$\begin{array}{c}CH_2-OH\\ |\\ H-C-OH \quad + \; 3Na^+\;{}^-O-\overset{\overset{\displaystyle O}{\|}}{C}-(CH_2)_{16}-CH_3\\ |\\ CH_2-OH\end{array}$$

    Glycerol   Salts of stearic acid

amines C—N—H
amides —C(=O)—N—H

18.1 In a primary amine, there is one alkyl group (and two hydrogen atoms) attached to a nitrogen atom.

18.3   **a.** This is a primary (1°) amine; there is only one alkyl group attached to the nitrogen atom.
   b. This is a secondary (2°) amine; there are two alkyl groups attached to the nitrogen atom.
   c. This is a primary (1°) amine; there is only one alkyl group attached to the nitrogen atom.
   d. This is a tertiary (3°) amine; there are three alkyl groups attached to the nitrogen atom.
   e. This is a tertiary (3°) amine; there are three alkyl groups attached to the nitrogen atom.

18.5 The common name of an amine consists of naming the alkyl groups bonding to the nitrogen atom in alphabetical order. In the IUPAC name, the *e* in the alkane chain is replaced with *amine.*
   a. An ethyl group attached to $-NH_2$ is ethylamine. In the IUPAC name, the *e* in ethane is replaced by *amine*: ethanamine.
   b. Two alkyl groups attach to nitrogen as methyl and propyl for methylpropylamine. The IUPAC name based on the longer chain of propane with a methyl group attached to the nitrogen atom is *N*-methyl-1-propanamine.
   c. Diethylmethylamine; *N*-methyl-*N*-ethylethanamine
   d. Isopropylamine; 2-propanamine

18.7 The amine of benzene is called aniline. In amines where a more oxidized functional group takes priority, the $-NH_2$ group is named as an *amino* group and numbered.
   a. 2-butanamine   **b.** 2-chloroaniline, *ortho*-chloroaniline
   c. 3-aminopropanal   **d.** *N*-ethylaniline

18.9   **a.** $CH_3-CH_2-NH_2$ **b.**

$$\underset{\text{phenyl ring}}{\begin{array}{c} H \\ | \\ N-CH_3 \end{array}}$$

   c. $CH_3-CH_2-CH_2-CH_2-\overset{\overset{\displaystyle H}{|}}{N}-CH_2-CH_2-CH_3$ **d.** $CH_3-\overset{\overset{\displaystyle NH_2}{|}}{CH}-CH_2-CH_2-CH_3$

18.11 Amines have higher boiling points than hydrocarbons but lower boiling points than alcohols of similar mass. Boiling point increases with molecular mass. Branching of alkyl groups reduces their boiling points.
   a. CH_3-CH_2-OH has a higher boiling point because the $-OH$ forms stronger hydrogen bonds than the $-NH_2$.
   b. $CH_3-CH_2-CH_2-NH_2$ has a higher boiling point because it has a higher molar mass.
   c. $CH_3-CH_2-CH_2-NH_2$ has a higher boiling point because it is a primary amine that forms hydrogen bonds. A tertiary amine cannot form hydrogen bonds with other tertiary amines.

18.13 Propylamine is a primary amine and forms two hydrogen bonds, which gives it the highest boiling point. Ethylmethylamine, a secondary amine, forms one hydrogen bond, and butane cannot form hydrogen bonds. Thus, butane has the lowest boiling point of the three compounds.

18.15 Amines with one to five carbon atoms are soluble. The solubility in water of amines with longer carbon chains decreases.
   a. yes; soluble since it has only 2 carbon atoms   **b.** yes; soluble since it has only 2 carbon atoms
   c. no; insoluble since it has 9 carbon atoms   **d.** yes; soluble since it has only 4 carbon atoms

18.17 Amines, which are weak bases, bond with a proton from water to give a hydroxide ion and an ammonium ion.

a. $CH_3-NH_2 + H_2O \rightleftharpoons CH_3-NH_3^+ + OH^-$

b. $CH_3-\overset{\overset{\displaystyle CH_3}{|}}{N}H + H_2O \rightleftharpoons CH_3-\overset{\overset{\displaystyle CH_3}{|}}{N}H_2^+ + OH^-$

c.

$\text{(}C_6H_5NH_2\text{)} + H_2O \rightleftharpoons \text{(}C_6H_5NH_3^+\text{)} + OH^-$

18.19 Amines, which are weak bases, combine with the proton from HCl to yield the ammonium chloride salt.

a. $CH_3-NH_2 + HCl \rightarrow CH_3-NH_3^+Cl^-$

b. $CH_3-\overset{\overset{\displaystyle CH_3}{|}}{N}H + HCl \rightarrow CH_3-\overset{\overset{\displaystyle CH_3}{|}}{N}H_2^+ + Cl^-$

c.

$\text{(}C_6H_5NH_2\text{)} + HCl \rightarrow \text{(}C_6H_5NH_3^+Cl^-\text{)}$

18.21 a.

$H_2N-\bigcirc-\overset{\overset{\displaystyle O}{||}}{C}-O-CH_2-CH_2-\overset{\overset{\displaystyle CH_2-CH_3}{|+}}{\underset{\underset{\displaystyle CH_2-CH_3}{|}}{N}}-H\ Cl^-$

b. The amine salt is more soluble in water and body fluids than the amine.

18.23 a. Aniline is an amine.
b. A compound with three alkyl groups attached to the nitrogen atom is an amine.
c. A nitrogen atom in a ring is a heterocyclic amine.
d. A nitrogen atom in a ring is a heterocyclic amine.

18.25 The heterocyclic amines contain one or more nitrogen atom(s) in a ring. Compounds **a.** and **b.** are amines, not heterocyclic amines.
c. Pyrimidine has two nitrogen atoms in a ring of six atoms.
d. Pyrrole has one nitrogen atom in a ring of five atoms.

18.27 The five-atom ring with one nitrogen atom and two double bonds is pyrrole.

18.29 Carboxylic acids react with amines to eliminate water and form amides.

a. $CH_3-\overset{\overset{\displaystyle O}{||}}{C}-NH_2$

b. $CH_3-\overset{\overset{\displaystyle O}{||}}{C}-NH-CH_2-CH_3$

c.

$\bigcirc-\overset{\overset{\displaystyle O}{||}}{C}-\overset{\overset{\displaystyle H}{|}}{N}-CH_2-CH_2-CH_3$

18.31 **a.** *N*-methylethanamide (*N*-methylacetamide). The *N*-methyl means that there is a one-carbon alkyl group attached to the nitrogen. Ethanamide tells us that the carbonyl portion has two carbon atoms.
 b. Butanamide (butyramide) is a chain of four carbon atoms bonded to an amino group.
 c. Methanamide (formamide) has only the carbonyl carbon bonded to the amino group.
 d. *N*-methylbenzamide; the *N*-methyl means that there is a one-carbon alkyl group attached to the nitrogen. Benzamide tells us that this is the amide of benzoic acid.

18.33 **a.** This is an amide of propionic acid, which has three carbon atoms.

$$CH_3-CH_2-\overset{\overset{\displaystyle O}{\|}}{C}-NH_2$$

 b. This is an amide of pentanoic acid, which has five carbon atoms.

$$CH_3-CH_2-CH_2-CH_2-\overset{\overset{\displaystyle O}{\|}}{C}-NH_2$$

 c. This is the simplest of the amides with only one carbon atom.

$$H-\overset{\overset{\displaystyle O}{\|}}{C}-NH_2$$

 d. The nitrogen atom in *N*-ethylbenzamide is bonded to an ethyl group. Benzamide tells us that this is the amide of benzoic acid.

$$\text{(benzene ring)}-\overset{\overset{\displaystyle O}{\|}}{C}-\overset{\overset{\displaystyle H}{|}}{N}-CH_2-CH_3$$

 e. The nitrogen atom is bonded to an ethyl group in *N*-ethylbutyramide.

$$CH_3-CH_2-CH_2-\overset{\overset{\displaystyle O}{\|}}{C}-\overset{\overset{\displaystyle H}{|}}{N}-CH_2-CH_3$$

18.35 **a.** Acetamide has the higher melting point because it forms more hydrogen bonds as a primary amide than *N*-methylpropanamide, which is a secondary amide.
 b. Propionamide has the higher melting point because it forms hydrogen bonds, but butane does not.
 c. *N*-methylpropanamide has the higher melting point because it forms hydrogen bonds as a secondary amide, but *N,N*–dimethylpropanamide cannot form hydrogen bonds as a tertiary amide.

18.37 Acid hydrolysis of amides gives the carboxylic acid and the amine salt.
 a. $CH_3-COOH + NH_4{}^+Cl^-$ **b.** $CH_3-CH_2-COOH + NH_4{}^+Cl^-$

 c. $CH_3-CH_2-CH_2-COOH + CH_3-NH_3{}^+Cl^-$ **d.** $\text{(benzene ring)}-COOH + NH_4{}^+\ Cl^-$

 e. $CH_3-CH_2-CH_2-CH_2-COOH + CH_3-CH_2-NH_3{}^+Cl^-$

18.39 carboxylic acid, aromatic, amine, amide, ester

18.41

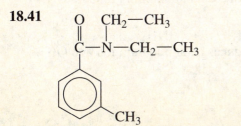

18.43 $CH_3-CH_2-CH_2-NH_2$ $CH_3-CH_2-NH-CH_3$ $\underset{\displaystyle CH_3-\overset{\displaystyle |}{N}-CH_3}{CH_3}$

          Propylamine 1°   Ethylmethylamine 2°   Trimethylamine 3°

        $\underset{\displaystyle CH_3-\overset{\displaystyle |}{C}H-NH_2}{CH_3}$ Isopropylamine 1°

18.45 **a.** diethylmethylamine; *N*-ethyl-*N*-methylethanamine; tertiary (3°)
        b. butylamine; 1-butanamine; primary (1°)
        c. ethylpropylamine; *N*-ethyl-1-propanamine; secondary (2°)

18.47 **a.** $\underset{\displaystyle CH_3-CH_2-\overset{\displaystyle |}{C}H-CH_2-CH_3}{NH_2}$
        b.   NH₂ (cyclohexanamine structure)

        c. This is an ammonium salt with two methyl groups bonded to the nitrogen atom.

          $\underset{\displaystyle CH_3-\overset{\displaystyle |}{N}H_2^+Cl^-}{CH_3}$
        d. Three ethyl groups are bonded to a nitrogen atom.

          $\underset{\displaystyle CH_3-\overset{\displaystyle |}{N}-CH_3}{CH_3}$

18.49 **a.** An alcohol with an —OH group such as 1-butanol forms stronger hydrogen bonds than an amine and has a higher boiling point than an amine.
        b. Propylamine, a primary amine, forms hydrogen bonds and has a higher boiling point than trimethylamine, a tertiary amine that does not form hydrogen bonds.

18.51 The smaller amines are more soluble in water.
        a. Ethylamine is a small amine that is soluble because it forms hydrogen bonds with water. Dibutylamine has two large nonpolar alkyl groups that decrease the solubility in water.
        b. Trimethylamine is a small tertiary amine that is soluble because it hydrogen bonds with water.

18.53 **a.** methanamide   **b.** propanamide   **c.** *N*-methylethanamide

18.55 **a.** Quinine obtained from the bark of the cinchona tree is used in the treatment of malaria.
        b. Nicotine is a stimulant found in cigarettes and cigars.
        c. Caffeine is an alkaloid in coffee, tea, soft drinks, and chocolate.
        d. Morphine and codeine are painkillers obtained from the oriental poppy plant.

18.57 **a.** An amine in water accepts a proton from water, which produces an ammonium ion and OH⁻.
          $CH_3-CH_2-NH_3^+ + OH^-$
        b. The amine accepts a proton to give an ammonium salt: $CH_3-CH_2-NH_3^+Cl^-$
        c. An amine in water accepts a proton from water, which produces an ammonium ion and OH⁻.
          $CH_3-CH_2-\overset{+}{N}H_2-CH_3 + OH^-$

18.59 carboxylic acid salt, aromatic, amine, haloaromatic

18.61 **a.** aromatic, amine, amide, carboxylic acid, cycloalkene
b. aromatic, ether, alcohol, amine
c. aromatic, carboxylic acid
d. phenol, amine, carboxylic acid
e. aromatic, ether, alcohol, amine, ketone
f. aromatic, amine

18.63 $CH_3-NH_2 + H_2O \rightleftarrows CH_3-NH_3^+ + OH^-$

$c = [OH^-] = [CH_3-NH_3^+]$

$K = 4.4 \times 10^{-4} = \dfrac{[CH_3-NH_3^+][OH^-]}{[CH_3-NH_2]} = \dfrac{c^2}{1.0\ M};$ $c = 2.1 \times 10^{-2}\ M = [OH^-]$

$[H_3O^+] = \dfrac{1.0 \times 10^{-14}}{[OH^-]} = 4.8 \times 10^{-13}\ M$ (2SF) pH $= 12.32$ (2 places after decimal point)

19.1 **a.** Hemoglobin, which carries oxygen in the blood, is a transport protein.
b. Collagen, which is a major component of tendon and cartilage, is a structural protein.
c. Keratin, which is found in hair, is a structural protein.
d. Amylases, which catalyze the breakdown of starch, are enzymes.

19.3 All amino acids contain a carboxylate group and an ammonium group on the alpha carbon.

19.5

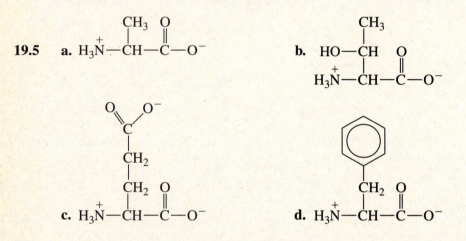

19.7 **a.** Alanine, which has a methyl (hydrocarbon) R group, is hydrophobic (nonpolar).
b. Threonine has an R group that contains the polar —OH. Threonine is hydrophilic (polar, neutral).
c. Glutamic acid has an R group containing a polar carboxylic acid. Glutamic acid is hydrophilic (acidic).
d. Phenylalanine has an R group with a nonpolar benzene ring. Phenylalanine is hydrophobic (nonpolar).

19.9 The abbreviations of most amino acids are derived from the first three letters in the name.
a. alanine   **b.** valine   **c.** lysine   **d.** cysteine

19.11 In the L isomer, the —NH_3^+ is on the left side of the horizontal line of the Fischer projection; in D isomer, the —NH_3^+ group is on the right.

19.13 A zwitterion is formed when the H^+ from the acid part of the amino acid is transferred to the amine portion of the amino acid. The resulting dipolar ion has an overall zero charge.

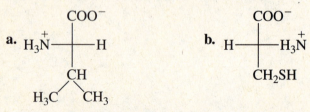

c.

$$\begin{array}{c} CH_3 \\ | \\ HCOH \quad O \\ | \qquad \| \\ H_3\overset{+}{N}-CH-C-O^- \end{array}$$

d.

$$\begin{array}{c} CH_3 \quad O \\ | \qquad \| \\ H_3\overset{+}{N}-CH-C-O^- \end{array}$$

19.15 At low pH (highly acidic), the $-COO^-$ of the zwitterion accepts H^+ and the amino acid has a positive charge overall.

a.

$$\begin{array}{c} H \quad O \\ | \qquad \| \\ H_3\overset{+}{N}-CH-C-OH \end{array}$$

b.

$$\begin{array}{c} SH \\ | \\ CH_2 \quad O \\ | \qquad \| \\ H_3\overset{+}{N}-CH-C-OH \end{array}$$

c.

$$\begin{array}{c} CH_3 \\ | \\ HCOH \quad O \\ | \qquad \| \\ H_3\overset{+}{N}-CH-C-OH \end{array}$$

d.

$$\begin{array}{c} CH_3 \quad O \\ | \qquad \| \\ H_3\overset{+}{N}-CH-C-OH \end{array}$$

19.17 **a.** A negative charge means the zwitterion donated H^+ from $-NH_3^+$, which occurs at pH levels above the isoelectric point.
b. A positive charge means the zwitterion accepted H^+ from an acidic solution, which occurs at a pH level below the isoelectric point.
c. A zwitterion with a net charge of zero means that the pH level is equal to the isoelectric point.

19.19 In a peptide, the amino acids are joined by peptide bonds (amide bonds). The first amino acid has a free amine group, and the last one has a free carboxyl group.

a.

$$\begin{array}{c} \qquad\qquad SH \\ \qquad\qquad | \\ CH_3 \quad O \quad CH_2 \quad O \\ | \qquad \| \qquad | \qquad \| \\ H_3\overset{+}{N}-CH-C-NH-CH-C-O^- \end{array}$$
Ala-Cys

b.

$$\begin{array}{c} OH \\ | \\ CH_2 \quad O \qquad CH_2 \quad O \\ | \qquad \| \qquad\quad | \qquad \| \\ H_3\overset{+}{N}-CH-C-NH-CH-C-O^- \end{array}$$
Ser-Phe

c.

$$\begin{array}{c} \qquad\qquad\qquad\qquad\qquad CH_3 \\ \qquad\qquad\qquad\qquad\qquad | \\ O \qquad CH_3 \quad O \quad H_3C-CH \quad O \\ \| \qquad | \qquad \| \qquad\qquad | \qquad \| \\ H_3\overset{+}{N}-CH_2-C-NH-CH-C-NH-CH-C-O^- \end{array}$$
Gly-Ala-Val

d.

$$\begin{array}{c} \qquad\qquad\qquad CH_3 \\ \qquad\qquad\qquad | \\ CH_3 \qquad\quad CH_2 \\ | \qquad\qquad | \\ H_3C-CH \quad O \quad H_3C-CH \quad O \qquad CH_2 \quad O \\ | \qquad \| \qquad\quad | \qquad \| \qquad | \qquad \| \\ H_3\overset{+}{N}-CH-C-NH-CH-C-NH-CH-C-O^- \end{array}$$
Val-Ile-Trp

19.21 The primary structure of a protein is the order of amino acids; the bonds that hold the amino acids together in a protein are amide or peptide bonds.

19.23 The possible primary structure of a tripeptide of one valine and two serines are Val-Ser-Ser, Ser-Val-Ser, and Ser-Ser-Val.

19.25 The primary structure remains unchanged and intact as hydrogen bonds form between carbonyl oxygen atoms and amino hydrogen atoms in the secondary structure. The common secondary structures are the α helix, the β-pleated sheet, and the triple helix.

19.27 In the α helix, hydrogen bonds form between the carbonyl oxygen atom and the amino hydrogen atom of the fourth amino acid in the next turn of the helix of the polypeptide chain. In the β-pleated sheet, hydrogen bonds occur between parallel peptides or across sections of a long polypeptide chain.

19.29 **a.** The two cysteine residues have —SH groups, which react to form a disulfide bond.
b. Glutamic acid is acidic and lysine is basic; the two groups form an ionic bond, or salt bridge.
c. Serine has a polar —OH group that can form a hydrogen bond with the carboxyl group of aspartic acid.
d. Two leucine residues are hydrocarbons and nonpolar. They would have a hydrophobic interaction.

19.31 **a.** The R group of cysteine with the —SH group can form disulfide cross-links.
b. Leucine and valine are found on the inside of the protein since they have nonpolar R groups and are hydrophobic.
c. The cysteine and aspartic acid are on the outside of the protein since they are polar.
d. The order of the amino acids (the primary structure) provides the R groups, whose interactions determine the tertiary structure of the protein.

19.33 **a.** Disulfide bonds join different sections of the protein chain to give a three-dimensional shape. Disulfide bonds are important in the tertiary and quaternary structures.
b. Peptide bonds join the amino acid building blocks in the primary structure.
c. Hydrogen bonds that hold protein chains together are found in the secondary structures of β-pleated sheets of fibrous proteins and in the triple helices of collagen.
d. In the secondary structure of α helices, hydrogen bonding occurs between the carbonyl oxygen and nitrogen atom in the amide bonds.

19.35 The complete hydrolysis of the tripeptide Gly-Ala-Ser will give the amino acids glycine (Gly), alanine (Ala), and serine (Ser).

19.37 Partial hydrolysis of the tetrapeptide His-Met-Gly-Val could give the following dipeptides: Met-Gly, His-Met, and Gly-Val.

19.39 The primary level, the sequence of amino acids in the protein, is affected by hydrolysis.

19.41 **a.** Placing an egg in boiling water coagulates the proteins of the egg by breaking the hydrogen bonds and disrupting the hydrophobic interactions.
b. Using an alcohol swab coagulates the proteins of any bacteria present by forming new hydrogen bonds and disrupting hydrophobic interactions.
c. The heat from an autoclave will coagulate the proteins of any bacteria on the surgical instruments by breaking the hydrogen bonds and disrupting the hydrophobic interactions.
d. Cauterization (heating) of a wound leads to coagulation of the proteins and helps to close the wound by breaking hydrogen bonds and disrupting hydrophobic interactions.

19.43 **a.** yes   **b.** no   **c.** no

19.45 **a.** (1)   **b.** (3)   **c.** (2)

19.47 **a.** asparagine and serine; hydrogen bond
b. aspartic acid and lysine; salt bridge
c. two cysteines; disulfide bond
d. leucine and alanine; hydrophobic interaction

19.49   **a.** α-Keratins are fibrous proteins that provide structure to hair, wool, skin, and nails.
b. α-Keratins have a high content of cysteine.

19.51   **a.**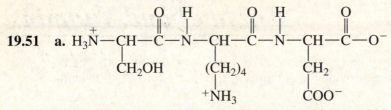

b. This segment contains polar R groups, which would be found on the surface of a globular protein, where they can hydrogen bond with water.

19.53   **a.** The β-pleated sheet is a secondary structure that contains high amounts of Val, Pro, and Ser, which have small R groups.
b. His, Met, and Leu are found predominantly in an α helix secondary structure.

19.55   Serine is a polar amino acid, whereas valine is nonpolar. Initially valine would be in the center of the tertiary structure. The replacement of valine with serine would pull that part of the chain to the outside surface of the protein, where serine forms hydrogen bonds with water.

19.57   **a.** $H_3\overset{+}{N}$—CH—$\overset{\overset{\textstyle O}{\|}}{C}$—OH   **b.** $H_3\overset{+}{N}$—CH—$\overset{\overset{\textstyle O}{\|}}{C}$—OH   **c.** $H_3\overset{+}{N}$—CH—$\overset{\overset{\textstyle O}{\|}}{C}$—OH
$\qquad\qquad$ | $\qquad\qquad\qquad\qquad$ | $\qquad\qquad\qquad\qquad$ |
$\qquad$ CH$_2$OH $\qquad\qquad\qquad\quad$ CH$_3$ $\qquad\qquad\qquad$ (CH$_2$)$_4$
$\qquad\qquad\qquad\qquad\qquad\qquad\qquad\qquad\qquad\qquad\qquad\qquad\qquad$ $\overset{+}{|}$
$\qquad\qquad\qquad\qquad\qquad\qquad\qquad\qquad\qquad\qquad\qquad\qquad\qquad$ NH$_3$

19.59   **a.** 0   **b.** 1+   **c.** 1−   **d.** 1+   **e.** 1−

19.61   **a.** Aspartic acid, which is negative (1−), since the buffer pH is above the isoelectric point (pI).
b. Histidine; since the buffer pH is below the isoelectric pH of histidine, the amino acid will have a positive charge (1+).
c. Cysteine has a net charge of 0, since the isoelectric pH is the same as the buffer pH. Cysteine will not move from where it is placed.

19.63   **a.** The secondary structure of a protein depends on hydrogen bonds to form a helix or a pleated sheet. The tertiary structure is determined by the interactions of R groups such as disulfide bonds and salt bridges, and determines the three-dimensional structure of the protein.
b. Nonessential amino acids are synthesized by the body, but essential amino acids must be supplied by the diet.
c. Polar amino acids have hydrophilic R groups, while nonpolar amino acids have hydrophobic R groups.
d. Dipeptides contain two amino acids, whereas tripeptides contain three amino acids.

19.65   The tartaric acid and the mechanical whipping (agitation) of the egg white denatures the proteins, which turn into solids as meringue.

20.1 These chemical reactions can occur without enzymes, but the rates are too slow. Catalyzed reactions, which are many times faster, provide the amounts of products needed by the cell at a particular time.

20.3 **a.** Oxidoreductases catalyze oxidation and reduction.
b. Transferases move (or transfer) groups, such as amino or phosphate groups, from one substance to another.
c. Hydrolases use water to split bonds in molecules such as carbohydrates, peptides, and lipids.

20.5 **a.** A hydrolase enzyme would catalyze the hydrolysis of sucrose.
b. An oxidoreductase enzyme would catalyze the addition of oxygen (oxidation).
c. An isomerase enzyme would catalyze converting glucose to fructose.
d. A transferase enzyme would catalyze moving an amino group.

20.7 **a.** A lyase such as a decarboxylase removes CO_2 from a molecule.
b. The transfer of an amino group to another molecule would be catalyzed by a transferase.

20.9 **a.** Succinate oxidase catalyzes the oxidation of succinate.
b. Fumarate hydrase catalyzes the addition of water to fumarate.
c. Alcohol dehydrogenase removes 2H from an alcohol.

20.11 **a.** An enzyme (2) has a tertiary structure that recognizes the substrate.
b. The combination of the enzyme and substrate is the enzyme–substrate complex (1).
c. The substrate (3) has a structure that complements the structure of the enzyme's active site.

20.13 **a.** The equation for an enzyme–catalyzed reaction is:
$$E + S \rightleftharpoons ES \rightarrow E + P$$
E = enzyme, S = substrate, ES = enzyme–substrate complex, P = products
b. The active site is a region or pocket within the tertiary structure of an enzyme that accepts the substrate, aligns the substrate for reaction, and catalyzes the reaction.

20.15 Isoenzymes are slightly different forms of an enzyme that catalyze the same reaction in different organs and tissues of the body.

20.17 A doctor might run tests for the enzymes CK, LDH, and AST to determine if the patient had a heart attack.

20.19 **a.** Decreasing the substrate concentration decreases the rate of reaction.
b. Running the reaction at a pH below optimum pH will decrease the rate of reaction.
c. Temperatures above 37 °C (optimum temperature) will denature the enzymes and decrease the rate of reaction.
d. Increasing the enzyme concentration would increase the rate of reaction, as long as there are still free polypeptides to react ($[S] < [E]$).

20.21 pepsin, pH 2; sucrase, pH 6; trypsin, pH 8

20.23 **a.** (1) If the inhibitor has a structure similar to the structure of the substrate, the inhibitor is competitive. (2) This type of inhibition is reversible.
b. (1) If adding more substrate cannot reverse the effect of the inhibitor, the inhibitor is noncompetitive. (2) This type of inhibition is irreversible (reversible if inhibitor is removed).

c. (1) If the inhibitor competes with the substrate for the active site, it is a competitive inhibitor. (2) This type of inhibition is reversible.

d. (1) If the structure of the inhibitor is not similar to the structure of the substrate, the inhibitor is noncompetitive. (2) This type of inhibition may be either reversible or irreversible.

e. (1) If adding more substrate reverses inhibition, the inhibitor is competitive. (2) This type of inhibition is reversible.

20.25 **a.** Methanol has the structural formula $CH_3 — OH$, whereas ethanol is $CH_3 — CH_2 — OH$.
b. Ethanol has a structure similar to methanol and could compete for the active site.
c. Ethanol is a competitive inhibitor of methanol oxidation.

20.27 Enzymes that act on proteins are proteases and would digest the proteins of the organ where they are produced if they were active immediately upon synthesis.

20.29 In feedback control, the product binds to the first enzyme in a series, changing the shape of the active site. If the active site can no longer bind the substrate effectively, the reaction stops.

20.31 When a regulator molecule binds to an allosteric site, the shape of the enzyme is altered, which makes the active site more or less reactive and thereby increases or decreases the rate of the reaction.

20.33 **a.** (3) A negative regulator binds to the allosteric site and slows down the reaction.
b. (4) Typically the first enzyme in a reaction sequence is an allosteric enzyme, which regulates the flow of substrates through the sequence to yield end product.
c. (1) A zymogen is an inactive form of an enzyme.

20.35 **a.** The active form of this enzyme requires a cofactor.
b. The active form of this enzyme requires a cofactor.
c. A simple enzyme is active as a protein.

20.37 **a.** THF   **b.** NAD^+.

20.39 **a.** Pantothenic acid (vitamin B_5) is part of coenzyme A.
b. Tetrahydrofolate (THF) is a reduced form of folic acid.
c. Niacin (vitamin B_3) is a component of NAD^+.

20.41 **a.** A deficiency of vitamin D or cholecalciferol can lead to rickets.
b. A deficiency of ascorbic acid or vitamin C can lead to scurvy.
c. A deficiency of niacin or vitamin B_3 can lead to pellagra.

20.43 Vitamin B_6 is a water–soluble vitamin, which means that each day any excess of vitamin B_6 is eliminated from the body.

20.45 The side chain $—CH_2OH$ on the ring is oxidized to $—CHO$, and the other $—CH_2OH$ forms a phosphate ester.

20.47 **a.** The oxidation of glycol to an aldehyde and carboxylic acid is catalyzed by an oxidoreductase.
b. Ethanol would act as a competitive inhibitor of ethylene glycol, saturate the enzyme, and allow ethylene glycol to be removed from the body without producing oxalic acid.

20.49 **a.** Fresh pineapple contains an enzyme that breaks down protein, which means that a gelatin dessert would not turn solid. The high temperatures used to prepare canned pineapple will denature the enzyme so it no longer can break down protein.
b. The enzyme in fresh pineapple juice can be used to tenderize tough meat because the enzyme breaks down proteins.

20.51 The many different reactions that take place in cells require different enzymes because enzymes react with only a certain type of substrate.

20.53 Enzymes are catalysts that are proteins and typically function only at mild temperature and pH. Catalysts used in chemistry laboratories are usually inorganic materials that can function at high temperatures and in strongly acidic or basic conditions.

20.55 **a.** The disaccharide lactose is a substrate (S).
b. The *–ase* in lactase indicates that it is an enzyme (E).
c. The *–ase* in urease indicates that it is an enzyme (E).
d. Trypsin is an enzyme which hydrolyzes polypeptides (E).
e. Pyruvate is a substrate (S).
f. The *–ase* in transaminase indicates that it is an enzyme (E).

20.57 **a.** Urea is the substrate of urease.
b. Lactose is the substrate of lactase.
c. Aspartate is the substrate of aspartate transaminase.
d. Phenylalanine is the substrate of phenylalanine hydroxylase.

20.59 **a.** The transfer of an acyl group is catalyzed by a transferase.
b. Oxidases are classified as oxidoreductases.
c. A lipase, which splits esters bonds in lipids with water, is a hydrolase.
d. A decarboxylase is classified as a lyase.

20.61 Sucrose fits the shape of the active site in sucrase, but lactose does not.

20.63 A heart attack may be the cause. Normally the enzymes LDH and CK are present only in low levels in the blood.

20.65 **a.** An enzyme is saturated if adding more substrate does not increase the rate.
b. An enzyme is unsaturated when increasing the substrate increases the rate.

20.67 In a reversible inhibition, the inhibitor can dissociate from the enzyme, whereas in irreversible inhibition, the inhibitor forms a strong covalent bond with the enzyme and does not dissociate. Irreversible inhibitors act as poisons to enzymes.

20.69 **a.** Antibiotics, such as amoxicillin, are irreversible inhibitors.
b. Antibiotics, such as amoxicillin, inhibit enzymes needed to form cell walls in bacteria, not humans.

20.71 **a.** When pepsinogen enters the stomach, the low pH cleaves a peptide from its protein chain to form pepsin.
b. An active protease would digest the proteins of the stomach rather than the proteins in the foods.

20.73 An allosteric enzyme contains sites for regulators that alter the enzyme and speed up or slow down the rate of the catalyzed reaction.

20.75 In feedback control, the end product of the reaction pathway binds to the enzyme to decrease or stop the first reaction in the reaction pathway.

20.77 **a.** The Mg^{2+} is a cofactor, which is required by this enzyme.
b. A protein that is catalytically active is a simple enzyme.
c. Folic acid is a coenzyme, which is required by this enzyme.

20.79 **a.** Coenzyme A (3) requires pantothenic acid (B_5).
b. NAD^+ (1) requires niacin (B_3).
c. TPP (2) needs thiamine (B_1).

20.81 A vitamin combines with an enzyme only when the enzyme and coenzyme are needed to catalyze a reaction. When the enzyme is not needed, the vitamin dissociates for use by other enzymes in the cell.

20.83 **a.** A deficiency of niacin can lead to pellagra (3).
b. A deficiency of vitamin A can lead to night blindness (1).
c. A deficiency of vitamin D can weaken bone structure (2).

20.85 **a.** The reactant is lactose and the products are glucose and galactose.

b.

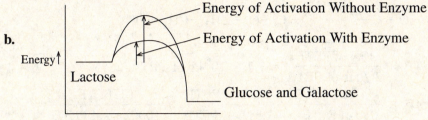

c. By lowering the energy of activation, the enzyme furnishes a lower energy pathway by which the reaction can take place.

20.87 **a.** In this reaction, oxygen is added to an aldehyde. The enzyme that catalyzes this reaction would be an oxidoreductase.
b. In this reaction, a dipeptide is hydrolyzed. The enzyme that catalyzes this reaction would be a hydrolase.
c. In this reaction, water is added to a double bond. The enzyme that catalyzes this reaction would be a lyase.

CI.31 **a.**

b.

c. 1.7×10^9 lb of PETE $\times \dfrac{1 \text{ kg of PETE}}{2.20 \text{ lb of PETE}} = 7.7 \times 10^8$ kg of PETE (2SF)

d. 1.7×10^9 lb of PETE $\times \dfrac{454 \text{ g of PETE}}{1 \text{ lb of PETE}} \times \dfrac{1 \text{ mL of PETE}}{1.38 \text{ g of PETE}} \times \dfrac{1 \text{ L PETE}}{1000 \text{ mL of PETE}} =$

   5.6×10^8 L of PETE (2SF)

e. 5.6×10^8 L of PETE $\times \dfrac{1 \text{ landfill}}{2.7 \times 10^7 \text{ L of PETE}} = 21$ landfills (2SF)

CI.33 **a.**

b. The molecular formulas of 3-methylbenzoic acid, diethylamine, and DEET are $C_8H_8O_2$, $C_4H_{11}N$, and $C_{12}H_{17}NO$, respectively.

c. $C_8H_8O_2$: 8 C (8 $\times$ 12.0 g/mole) + 8 H (8 $\times$ 1.0 g/mole) + 2 O (2 $\times$ 16.0 g/mole) = 136 g/mole
   $C_4H_{11}N$: 4 C (4 $\times$ 12.0 g/mole) + 11 H (11 $\times$ 1.0 g/mole) + N (14.0 g/mole) = 73.0 g/mole
   $C_{12}H_{17}NO$: 12 C (12 $\times$ 12.0 g/mole) + 17 H (17 $\times$ 1.0 g/mole) + 1 $\times$ N (14.0 g/mole) +
   O (16.0 g/mole) = 191 g/mole

d. 6.0 fl oz $\times \dfrac{1 \text{ qt}}{32 \text{ fl oz}} \times \dfrac{1000 \text{ mL}}{1.06 \text{ qt}} \times \dfrac{1.0 \text{ g of solution}}{1 \text{ mL}} \times \dfrac{25.0 \text{ g of DEET}}{100 \text{ g of solution}} =$

   44 g of DEET (2SF)

e. 6.0 fl oz $\times \dfrac{1 \text{ qt}}{32 \text{ fl oz}} \times \dfrac{1000 \text{ mL}}{1.06 \text{ qt}} \times \dfrac{1.0 \text{ g of solution}}{1 \text{ mL}} \times \dfrac{25.0 \text{ g of DEET}}{100 \text{ g of solution}} \times \dfrac{1 \text{ mole of DEET}}{191 \text{ g of DEET}} \times$

   $\dfrac{6.02 \times 10^{23} \text{ molecules of DEET}}{1 \text{ mole of DEET}} = 1.4 \times 10^{23}$ molecules of DEET (2SF)

f. From 10.0 g of benzoic acid

   10.0 g of $C_8H_8O_2$ $\times \dfrac{1 \text{ mole of } C_8H_8O_2}{136 \text{ g of } C_8H_8O_2} \times \dfrac{1 \text{ mole of DEET}}{1 \text{ mole of } C_8H_8O_2} = 0.0735$ mole of DEET

   From 10.0 g of diethylamine

   10.0 g of $C_4H_{11}N$ $\times \dfrac{1 \text{ mole of } C_4H_{11}N}{73.0 \text{ g of } C_4H_{11}N} \times \dfrac{1 \text{ mole of DEET}}{1 \text{ mole of } C_4H_{11}N} = 0.137$ moles of DEET

   Using 0.0735 moles as the smaller number of moles of DEET

   0.0735 mole of DEET $\times \dfrac{191 \text{ g of DEET}}{1 \text{ mole of DEET}} =$

14.0 g of DEET theoretical yield

$$\% \text{ Yield} = \frac{12.5 \text{ g of DEET (actual)}}{14.0 \text{ g of DEET (theoretical)}} \times 100\% = 89.3\% \text{ yield (3SF)}$$

CI.35 a.
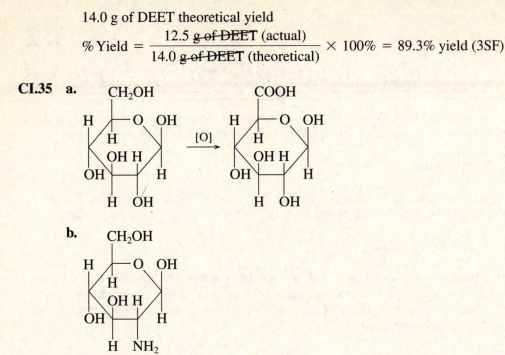

b.
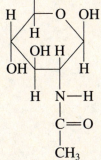

c.

d. They are β-1,4- and β-1,3-glycosidic bonds.

e.
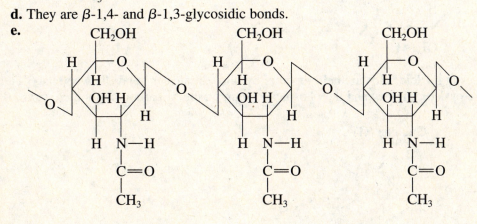

21

Nucleic Acids and Protein Synthesis

21.1 DNA contains two purines, adenine (A) and guanine (G), and two pyrimidines, cytosine (C) and thymine (T). RNA contains the same bases, except thymine (T) is replaced by the pyrimidine uracil (U).
a. pyrimidine   **b.** pyrimidine

21.3 DNA contains two purines, adenine (A) and guanine (G), and two pyrimidines, cytosine (C) and thymine (T). RNA contains the same bases, except thymine (T) is replaced by the pyrimidine uracil (U).
a. DNA   **b.** both DNA and RNA

21.5 Nucleotides contain a base, a sugar, and a phosphate group. The nucleotides found in DNA would all contain the sugar deoxyribose. The four nucleotides are deoxyadenosine 5′-monophosphate (dAMP), deoxythymidine 5′-monophosphate (dTMP), deoxycytidine 5′-monophosphate (dCMP), and deoxyguanosine 5′-monophosphate (dGMP).

21.7 **a.** Adenosine is a nucleoside found in RNA.
b. Deoxycytidine is a nucleoside found in DNA.
c. Uridine is a nucleoside found in RNA.
d. Cytidine 5′-monophosphate is a nucleotide found in RNA.

21.9

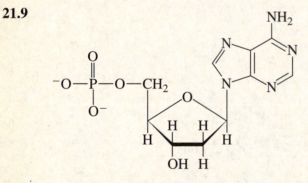

21.11 The nucleotides in nucleic acids are held together by phosphodiester bonds between the 3′–OH of a sugar (ribose or deoxyribose) and the phosphate group on the 5′-carbon of another sugar.

21.13

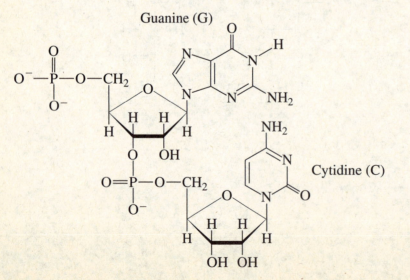

146

21.15   The two DNA strands are held together by hydrogen bonds between the bases in each strand.

21.17   **a.** Since T pairs with A, if one strand of DNA has the sequence
$5'$—A—A—A—A—A—A—$3'$, the second strand would be
$3'$—T—T—T—T—T—T—$5'$.
b. Since C pairs with G, if one strand of DNA has the sequence
$5'$—G—G—G—G—G—G—$3'$, the second strand would be
$3'$—C—C—C—C—C—C—$5'$.
c. Since T pairs with A, and C pairs with G, if one strand of DNA has the sequence
$5'$—A—G—T—C—C—A—G—G—T—$3'$, the second strand would be
$3'$—T—C—A—G—G—T—C—C—A—$5'$.
d. Since T pairs with A, and C pairs with G, if one strand of DNA has the sequence
$5'$—C—T—G—T—A—T—A—C—G—T—T—A—$3'$, the second strand would be
$3'$—G—A—C—A—T—A—T—G—C—A—A—T—$5'$.

21.19   The enzyme helicase unwinds the DNA helix to prepare the parent DNA strand for the synthesis of daughter DNA strands.

21.21   First, the two DNA strands separate in a way that is similar to the unzipping of a zipper. Then the enzyme DNA polymerase begins to copy each strand by pairing each of the bases in the strands with its complementary base: A pairs with T and C with G. Finally, a phosphodiester bond joins the base to the new, growing strand. This process produces two exact copies of the original DNA.

21.23   The three types of RNA are messenger RNA (mRNA), ribosomal RNA (rRNA), and transfer RNA (tRNA).

21.25   A ribosome, which is about 65% rRNA and 35% protein, consists of a small subunit and a large subunit.

21.27   In transcription, the sequence of nucleotides on a DNA template (one strand) is used to produce the base sequences of a messenger RNA. The DNA unwinds, and one strand is copied as complementary bases are placed in the mRNA molecule. In RNA, U (uracil) is paired with A in DNA.

21.29   In mRNA, C, G, and A pair with G, C, and T in DNA. However, in mRNA, U will pair with A in DNA. The strand of mRNA would have the following sequence:
$5'$—G—G—C—U—U—C—C—A—A—G—U—G—$3'$.

21.31   In eukaryotic cells, genes contain sections called exons that code for proteins and sections called introns that do not code for protein.

21.33   An operon is a section of DNA that regulates the synthesis of one or more proteins.

21.35   When the lactose level is low in *E. coli*, a repressor produced by the mRNA from the regulatory gene binds to the operator blocking the synthesis of mRNA from the genes and preventing the synthesis of protein.

21.37   A codon is the three-base sequence (triplet) in mRNA that codes for a specific amino acid in a protein.

21.39   **a.** The codon CUU in mRNA codes for the amino acid leucine (Leu).
b. The codon UCA in mRNA codes for the amino acid serine (Ser).
c. The codon GGU in mRNA codes for the amino acid glycine (Gly).
d. The codon AGG in mRNA codes for the amino acid arginine (Arg).

21.41   When AUG is the first codon, it signals the start of protein synthesis and incorporates methionine as the first amino acid in the peptide. Eventually, the initial methionine is removed as the protein forms its secondary and tertiary protein structure. In the middle of an mRNA sequence, AUG codes for methionine.

21.43 A codon is a base triplet in the mRNA template. An anticodon is the complementary triplet on a tRNA for a specific amino acid.

21.45 The three steps in translation are initiation, translocation, and termination.

21.47 The mRNA must be divided into triplets and the amino acid coded for by each triplet read from the table.
    a. The codon AAA in mRNA codes for lysine: —Lys—Lys—Lys—.
    b. The codon UUU codes for phenylalanine and CCC for proline: —Phe—Pro—Phe—Pro—.
    c. The codon UAC codes for tyrosine, GGG for glycine, AGA for arginine, and UGU for cysteine: —Tyr—Gly—Arg—Cys—.

21.49 The new amino acid is joined by a peptide bond to the growing peptide chain. The ribosome moves to the next codon, which attaches to a tRNA carrying the next amino acid.

21.51   **a.** The mRNA sequence would be: 5'—CGA—AAA—GUU—UUU—3'.
    b. The tRNA triplet anticodons would be: GCU, UUU, CAA, and AAA.
    c. From the table of mRNA codons, the amino acids would be: Arg—Lys—Val—Phe.

21.53 In a substitution mutation, an incorrect base replaces a base in DNA.

21.55 If the resulting codon still codes for the same amino acid, there is no effect. If the new codon codes for a different amino acid, there is a change in the order of amino acids in the polypeptide. Every amino acid from this point forward could be changed, depending on how the new codons code for amino acids.

21.57 The normal triplet TTT in DNA transcribes to AAA in mRNA. AAA codes for lysine.
The mutation TTC in DNA transcribes to AAG in mRNA, which also codes for lysine.
Thus, there is no effect on the amino acid sequence.

21.59   **a.** —Thr—Ser—Arg—Val— is the amino acid sequence produced by normal DNA.
    b. —Thr—Thr—Arg—Val— is the amino acid sequence produced by a mutation.
    c. —Thr—Ser—Gly—Val— is the amino acid sequence produced by a mutation.
    d. —Thr—STOP; protein synthesis would terminate early. If this mutation occurs early in the formation of the polypeptide, the resulting protein will probably be nonfunctional.
    e. The new protein will contain the sequence —Asp—Ile—Thr—Gly—.
    f. The new protein will contain the sequence —His—His—Gly—.

21.61   **a.** Both codons GCC and GCA code for alanine.
    b. A vital ionic cross-link in the tertiary structure of hemoglobin cannot be formed when the polar glutamic acid is replaced by valine, which is nonpolar. The resulting hemoglobin is malformed and less capable of carrying oxygen.

21.63 *E. coli* bacterial cells contain several small circular plasmids of DNA that can be isolated easily. After the recombinant DNA is formed, *E. coli* multiply rapidly, producing many copies of the recombinant DNA in a relatively short time.

21.65 The cells of the *E. coli* are soaked in a detergent solution, which dissolves the plasma membrane and frees the plasmids, which can then be collected.

21.67 When a gene has been obtained using restriction enzymes, it is mixed with the plasmids that have been opened by the same enzymes. When mixed together in a fresh *E. coli* culture, the sticky ends of the DNA fragments bond with the sticky ends of the plasmid DNA to form a recombinant DNA.

21.69 In DNA fingerprinting, restriction enzymes cut a sample DNA into fragments, which are sorted by size by gel electrophoresis. After tagging the DNA fragments with a radioactive isotope, a piece of X-ray film placed over the gel is exposed by the radioactivity to give a pattern of dark and light bands known as a DNA fingerprint.

21.71   A virus contains either DNA or RNA, but not both, inside a protein coating.

21.73   **a.** An RNA-containing virus must make viral DNA from the RNA to produce a protein coat, allowing the virus to replicate and leave the cell to infect new cells.
b. A virus that uses reverse transcription is a retrovirus.

21.75   Nucleoside analogs such as AZT and ddI are similar to the nucleosides required to make viral DNA in reverse transcription. However, they interfere with the ability of the DNA to form and thereby disrupt the life cycle of the HIV-1 virus.

21.77   **a.**

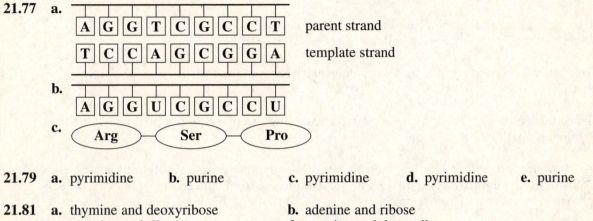

21.79   **a.** pyrimidine   **b.** purine   **c.** pyrimidine   **d.** pyrimidine   **e.** purine

21.81   **a.** thymine and deoxyribose   **b.** adenine and ribose
c. cytosine and ribose   **d.** guanine and deoxyribose

21.83   They are both pyrimidines, but thymine has a methyl group.

21.85

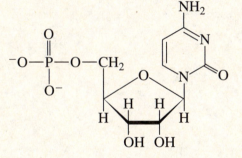

21.87   They are both polymers of nucleotides connected through phosphodiester bonds between alternating sugar and phosphate groups with bases extending out from each sugar.

21.89   A DNA with 28% adenine also has 28% thymine, which means that cytosine and guanine are each 22%.

21.91   **a.** There are two hydrogen bonds between A and T in DNA.
b. There are three hydrogen bonds between G and C in DNA.

21.93   **a.** 3′—C—T—G—A—A—T—C—C—G—5′
b. 5′—A—C—G—T—T—T—G—A—T—C—G—A—3′
c. 3′—T—A—G—C—T—A—G—C—T—A—G—C—5′

21.95   DNA polymerase synthesizes the leading strand continuously in the 5′ to 3′ direction. The lagging strand is synthesized in small segments called Okazaki fragments because it must grow in the 3′ to 5′ direction.

21.97 One strand of the parent DNA is found in each of the two copies of the daughter DNA molecule.

21.99 **a.** transfer RNA (tRNA) **b.** ribosomal RNA (rRNA)
c. messenger RNA (mRNA)

21.101 **a.** ACU, ACC, ACA, and ACG **b.** UCU, UCC, UCA, UCG, AGU, and AGC
c. UGU and UGC

21.103 **a.** AAG codes for lysine. **b.** AUU codes for isoleucine.
c. CGG codes for arginine.

21.105 Using the genetic code, the codons indicate the following:
Met (start) — Tyr — Gly — Gly — Phe — Leu — STOP

21.107 The anticodon consists of the three complementary bases to the codon.
a. UCG **b.** AUA **c.** GGU

21.109 Three nucleotides are needed for each amino acid, plus a start and stop triplet, which makes a minimum total of 33 nucleotides.

21.111 A DNA virus attaches to a cell and injects viral DNA that uses the host cell to produce copies of DNA to make viral RNA. A retrovirus injects viral RNA, from which complementary DNA is produced by reverse transcription.

22

Metabolic Pathways for Carbohydrates

22.1 The digestion of polysaccharides takes place in Stage 1.

22.3 A catabolic reaction breaks down larger molecules to smaller molecules, accompanied by the release of energy.

22.5 **a.** (3) Smooth endoplasmic reticulum is the site for the synthesis of fats and steroids.
b. (1) Lysosomes contain hydrolytic enzymes.
c. (2) The Golgi complex modifies products from the rough endoplasmic reticulum.

22.7 The phosphodiester bonds (P — O — P) cleave to free a phosphate group from ATP; the release of energy is sufficient for energy-requiring processes in the cell.

22.9 **a.** PEP + H_2O → pyruvate + P_i + 14.8 kcal/mole
b. ADP + P_i + 7.3 kcal/mole → ATP + H_2O
c. Combined: PEP + ADP → ATP + pyruvate + 7.5 kcal/mole

22.11 **a.** Pantothenic acid is usually a component of coenzyme A.
b. Niacin is the vitamin component of NAD^+.
c. Ribitol is the alcohol sugar that is a component of riboflavin in FAD.

22.13 In biochemical systems, oxidation is usually accompanied by gain of oxygen or loss of hydrogen. Loss of oxygen or gain of hydrogen usually accompanies reduction.
a. The reduced form of NAD^+ is abbreviated NADH.
b. The oxidized form of $FADH_2$ is abbreviated FAD.

22.15 The coenzyme FAD accepts hydrogen when a dehydrogenase forms a carbon–carbon double bond.

22.17 Digestion breaks down the large molecules in food into smaller compounds that can be absorbed by the body. Hydrolysis is the main reaction involved in the digestion of carbohydrates.

22.19 **a.** The disaccharide lactose is digested in the small intestine to yield galactose and glucose.
b. The disaccharide sucrose is digested in the small intestine to yield glucose and fructose.
c. The disaccharide maltose is digested in the small intestine to yield two glucose molecules.

22.21 Glucose is the starting reactant for glycolysis.

22.23 In the initial reactions of glycolysis, ATP molecules are required to add phosphate groups to glucose (phosphorylation reactions).

22.25 When fructose-1,6-bisphosphate splits, glyceraldehyde-3-phosphate and dihydroxyacetone phosphate are formed. The dihydroxyacetone phosphate is converted to glyceraldehyde-3-phosphate for subsequent reactions.

22.27 ATP is produced directly in glycolysis in two places. In reaction 7, phosphate from 1,3-bisphosphoglycerate is transferred to ADP and yields ATP. In reaction 10, phosphate from phosphoenolpyruvate is transferred directly to ADP.

22.29 **a.** In glycolysis, phosphorylation is catalyzed by the enzyme hexokinase in reaction 1, and by phosphofructokinase in reaction 3.
b. In glycolysis, direct transfer of a phosphate group is catalyzed by the enzyme phosphoglycerate kinase in reaction 7, and pyruvate kinase in reaction 10.

22.31 **a.** In the phosphorylation of glucose to glucose-6-phosphate, one ATP is required.
    b. One NADH is produced in the conversion of glyceraldehyde-3-phosphate to 1,3-bisphosphoglycerate.
    c. When glucose is converted to pyruvate, two ATP and two NADH are produced.

22.33 **a.** The first ATP is hydrolyzed in the first reaction in glycolysis, the phosphorylation of glucose to glucose-6-phosphate.
    b. Direct substrate phosphorylation occurs in reaction 7 of glycolysis when the transfer of phosphate from 1,3-bisphosphoglycerate to ADP generates ATP. In reaction 10 of glycolysis, phosphate is transferred from phosphoenolpyruvate directly to ADP.
    c. In reaction 4 of glycolysis, the six-carbon fructose-1,6-bisphosphate is split into two three-carbon molecules, glyceraldehyde-3-phosphate and dihydroxyacetone phosphate.

22.35 Galactose reacts with ATP to yield galactose-1-phosphate, which is converted to glucose-6-phosphate, an intermediate in glycolysis. Fructose reacts with ATP to yield fructose-1-phosphate, which is cleaved to give dihydroxyacetone phosphate and glyceraldehyde. Dihydroxyacetone phosphate isomerizes to glyceraldehyde-3-phosphate, and glyceraldehyde is phosphorylated to glyceraldehyde-3-phosphate, which is an intermediate in glycolysis.

22.37 **a.** Low levels of ATP activate phosphofructokinase to increase the rate (activate) of glycolysis.
    b. When ATP levels are high, ATP inhibits phosphofructokinase and slows or prevents (inhibits) glycolysis.

22.39 A cell converts pyruvate to acetyl CoA only under aerobic conditions; there must be sufficient oxygen available.

22.41 The overall reaction for the conversion of pyruvate to acetyl CoA is:

$$\underset{\text{Pyruvate}}{CH_3-\overset{\overset{\textstyle O}{\|}}{C}-COO^-} + NAD^+ + HS-CoA \rightarrow \underset{\text{Acetyl CoA}}{CH_3-\overset{\overset{\textstyle O}{\|}}{C}-S-CoA} + CO_2 + NADH + H^+$$

22.43 When pyruvate is reduced to lactate, the NAD^+ is used to oxidize glyceraldehyde-3-phosphate, which recycles NADH.

22.45 During fermentation, the three-carbon compound pyruvate is reduced to ethanol while decarboxylation removes one carbon as CO_2.

22.47 In glycogenesis, glycogen is synthesized from glucose molecules.

22.49 Muscle cells break down glycogen to glucose-6-phosphate, which enters glycolysis.

22.51 Glycogen phosphorylase cleaves the glycosidic bonds at the ends of glycogen chains to remove glucose monomers as glucose-1-phosphate.

22.53 When there are no glycogen stores remaining in the liver, gluconeogenesis synthesizes glucose from noncarbohydrate compounds such as pyruvate and lactate.

22.55 The enzymes in glycolysis that are also used in their reverse directions for gluconeogenesis are phosphoglucose isomerase, aldolase, triose phosphate isomerase, glyceraldehyde-3-phosphate dehydrogenase, phosphoglycerate kinase, phosphoglycerate mutase, and enolase.

22.57 **a.** Low glucose levels activate glucose synthesis.
    b. Glucagon produced when glucose levels are low activates gluconeogenesis.
    c. Insulin produced when glucose levels are high inhibits gluconeogenesis.

22.59 $2.5 \; \cancel{h} \times \dfrac{350 \; \cancel{kcal}}{1 \; \cancel{h}} \times \dfrac{1 \text{ mole of ATP}}{7.3 \; \cancel{kcal}} = 120$ moles of ATP (2SF)

22.61 Metabolism includes all the reactions in cells that provide energy and material for cell growth.

22.63 Stage 1 involves the digestion of large molecules, such as polysaccharides.

22.65 A eukaryotic cell has a nucleus, whereas a prokaryotic cell does not.

22.67 ATP is the abbreviation for adenosine triphosphate.

22.69 $ATP + H_2O \rightarrow ADP + P_i + 7.3$ kcal/mole (or 31 kJ/mole)

22.71 FAD is the abbreviation for flavin adenine dinucleotide.

22.73 NAD^+ is the abbreviation for nicotinamide adenine dinucleotide.

22.75 The reduced forms of these coenzymes include hydrogen obtained from an oxidation reaction.
a. $FADH_2$ **b.** $NADH + H^+$

22.77 Lactose undergoes digestion in the mucosal cells of the small intestine to yield galactose and glucose.

22.79 Galactose and fructose are converted in the liver to glucose phosphate compounds that can enter the glycolysis pathway.

22.81 Glucose is the reactant and pyruvate is the product of glycolysis.

22.83 Reactions 1 and 3 involve phosphorylation of hexoses with ATP, and reactions 7 and 10 involve direct substrate phosphorylation that generates ATP.

22.85 Reaction 4, catalyzed by aldolase, converts fructose-1,6-bisphosphate into two three-carbon phosphates.

22.87 Phosphoglucose isomerase converts glucose-6-phosphate to the isomer fructose-6-phosphate.

22.89 Pyruvate is converted to lactate when oxygen is not present in the cell (anaerobic) to regenerate NAD^+ for glycolysis.

22.91 Phosphofructokinase is an allosteric enzyme that is activated by high levels of AMP and ADP because the cell needs to produce more ATP. When ATP levels are high due to a decrease in energy needs, ATP inhibits phosphofructokinase, which reduces its catalysis of fructose-6-phosphate.

22.93 The rate of glycogenolysis increases when blood glucose levels are low and glucagon has been secreted, which accelerate the breakdown of glycogen.

22.95 The breakdown of glycogen in the liver produces glucose.

22.97 **a.** A low blood glucose increases the breakdown of glycogen.
b. Insulin produced when glucose levels are high decreases the rate of glycogenolysis in the liver.
c. Glucagon secreted when glucose levels are low increases the breakdown of glycogen.
d. High levels of ATP decrease the breakdown of glycogen.

22.99 **a.** High glucose levels decrease the synthesis of glucose (gluconeogenesis).
b. Insulin produced when glucose levels are high decreases glucose synthesis.
c. Glucagon secreted when glucose levels are low increases glucose synthesis.
d. High levels of ATP decrease glucose synthesis (gluconeogenesis).

22.101 The cells in the liver, but not skeletal muscle, contain a phosphatase enzyme needed to convert glucose-6-phosphate to free glucose that can diffuse through cell membranes into the blood stream. Glucose-6-phosphate, which is the end product of glycogenolysis in muscle cells, cannot diffuse easily across cell membranes.

22.103 Insulin increases the rate of glycogenesis and glycolysis and decreases the rate of glycogenolysis. Glucagon decreases the rate of glycogenesis and glycolysis and increases the rate of glycogenolysis.

22.105 The Cori cycle is a cyclic process that involves the transfer of lactate from muscle to the liver, where glucose is synthesized, which can be used again by the muscle.

22.107 a. $24 \text{ h} \times \dfrac{3600}{1 \text{ h}} \times \dfrac{3600 \text{ s}}{1 \text{ h}} \times \dfrac{2 \times 10^6 \text{ ATP}}{1 \text{ s cell}} \times 10^{13} \text{ cells} \times \dfrac{1 \text{ mole ATP}}{6.02 \times 10^{23} \text{ ATP}} \times \dfrac{7.3 \text{ kcal}}{1 \text{ mole ATP}}$

   $= 21 \text{ kcal (2SF)}$

   b. $24 \text{ h} \times \dfrac{3600}{1 \text{ h}} \times \dfrac{3600 \text{ s}}{1 \text{ h}} \times \dfrac{2 \times 10^6 \text{ ATP}}{1 \text{ s cell}} \times 10^{13} \text{ cells} \times \dfrac{1 \text{ mole of ATP}}{6.02 \times 10^{23} \text{ ATP}} \times \dfrac{507 \text{ g ATP}}{1 \text{ mole of ATP}}$

   $= 1500 \text{ g of ATP (2SF)}$

23

Metabolism and Energy Production

23.1 Other names for the citric acid cycle are the Krebs cycle and tricarboxylic acid cycle.

23.3 One turn of the citric acid cycle converts 1 acetyl CoA to $2CO_2$, $3NADH + 3H^+$, $FADH_2$, GTP (ATP), and HS—CoA.

23.5 The reactions in steps 3 and 4 involve oxidative decarboxylation, which reduces the length of the carbon chain by one carbon in each reaction.

23.7 NAD^+ is reduced by the oxidation reactions 3, 4, and 8 of the citric acid cycle.

23.9 In reaction 5, GDP undergoes a direct substrate phosphorylation to yield GTP, which converts ADP to ATP and regenerates GDP for the citric acid cycle.

23.11 **a.** The six-carbon compounds in the citric acid cycle are citrate and isocitrate.
b. Decarboxylation reactions remove carbon atoms as CO_2, which reduces the number of carbon atoms in a chain (reactions 3 and 4).
c. The one five-carbon compound is α-ketoglutarate.
d. Several reactions are oxidation reactions: isocitrate $\rightarrow \alpha$-ketoglutarate; α-ketoglutarate $\rightarrow$ succinyl CoA; succinate $\rightarrow$ fumarate; malate $\rightarrow$ oxaloacetate.
e. Secondary alcohols are oxidized in reactions 3 and 8.

23.13 **a.** Citrate synthase combines oxaloacetate with acetyl CoA.
b. Succinate dehydrogenase and aconitase converts a carbon–carbon single bond to a double bond.
c. Fumarase adds water to the double bond in fumarate.

23.15 **a.** NAD^+ accepts 2H from the oxidative decarboxylation of isocitrate.
b. GDP is phosphorylated in the formation of succinate.

23.17 Isocitrate dehydrogenase and α-ketoglutarate dehydrogenase are allosteric enzymes, which increase or decrease the flow of materials through the citric acid cycle.

23.19 High levels of ADP means there are low levels of ATP. To provide more ATP for the cell, the reaction rate of the citric acid cycle increases.

23.21 The Fe^{3+} is the oxidized form of the iron in cytochrome *b*.

23.23 **a.** The loss of $2H^+$ and $2e^-$ is oxidation.
b. The gain of $2H^+ + 2e^-$ is reduction.

23.25 NADH and $FADH_2$ produced in glycolysis, oxidation of pyruvate, and the citric acid cycle provide the electrons for electron transport.

23.27 FAD is reduced to $FADH_2$, which provides $2H^+$ and $2e^-$ for coenzyme Q, then cytochrome *b*, and then cytochrome *c*.

23.29 The mobile carrier coenzyme Q (or Q) transfers electrons from complex I to complex III.

23.31 When NADH transfers electrons to FMN in complex I, NAD^+ is produced.

23.33 **a.** NADH + H$^+$ + <u>FMN</u> → NAD$^+$ + FMNH$_2$
b. QH$_2$ + 2 cyt b (Fe^{3+}) → <u>Q</u> + 2 cyt b (Fe^{2+}) + 2H$^+$

23.35 In oxidative phosphorylation, the energy from the oxidation reactions in electron transport is used to drive ATP synthesis.

23.37 Protons must pass through F$_0$ channel of ATP synthase to return to the matrix. During the process, energy is released to drive the synthesis of ATP in F$_1$.

23.39 The oxidation of the reduced coenzymes NADH and FADH$_2$ by electron transport generates energy to drive the synthesis of ATP.

23.41 ATP synthase consists of two protein complexes known as F$_0$ and F$_1$.

23.43 The loose (L) site in ATP synthase begins the synthesis of ATP by binding ADP and P$_i$.

23.45 Glycolysis takes place in the cytoplasm, not in the mitochondria. Because NADH cannot cross the mitochondrial membrane, one ATP is hydrolyzed to transport the electrons from NADH to FAD. The resulting FADH$_2$ produces only two ATP for each NADH produced in glycolysis.

23.47 **a.** Three ATP are produced by the oxidation of NADH in electron transport.
b. Six ATP are produced in glycolysis when glucose degrades to 2 pyruvate ions.
c. Six ATP are produced when 2 pyruvate are oxidized to 2 acetyl CoA and 2CO$_2$.

23.49 **a.** citric acid cycle   **b.** electron transport   **c.** both
d. electron transport   **e.** electron transport   **f.** both
g. citric acid cycle   **h.** both

23.51 **f.** FMNH$_2$ **e.** QH$_2$ **h.** cyt b **g.** cyt c_1 **d.** cyt c
c. cyt a **a.** cyt a_3 **b.** O$_2$

23.53 **a.** Aconitase uses H$_2$O.
b. Succinate dehydrogenase uses FAD.
c. Fumarase uses H$_2$O.
d. Isocitrate dehydrogenase uses NAD$^+$.
e. Succinyl CoA synthetase uses GDP.
f. Malate dehydrogenase uses NAD$^+$.

23.55 The oxidation reactions of the citric acid cycle produce a source of reduced coenzymes for electron transport and ATP synthesis.

23.57 The oxidized coenzymes NAD$^+$ and FAD needed for the citric acid cycle are regenerated by electron transport.

23.59 **a.** Citrate and isocitrate are six-carbon compounds in the citric acid cycle.
b. α-Ketoglutarate is a five-carbon compound.
c. The compounds α-ketoglutarate, succinyl CoA, and oxaloacetate have keto groups.

23.61 **a.** In reaction 4, α-ketoglutarate, a five-carbon keto acid, is decarboxylated.
b. In reactions 2 and 7, double bonds in aconitate and fumarate are hydrated.
c. NAD$^+$ is reduced in reactions 3, 4, and 8.
d. In reactions 3 and 8, a secondary hydroxyl group in isocitrate and malate is oxidized.

23.63 **a.** NAD$^+$ is the coenzyme for the oxidation of a secondary hydroxyl group in isocitrate to a keto group in α-ketoglutarate.
b. NAD$^+$ and CoA are needed in the oxidative decarboxylation of α-ketoglutarate to succinyl CoA.

23.65 **a.** High levels of NADH inhibit isocitrate dehydrogenase and α-ketoglutarate dehydrogenase to slow the rate of the citric acid cycle.
  b. High levels of ATP inhibit isocitrate dehydrogenase to slow the rate of the citric acid cycle.

23.67 **a.** A heme group is found in all the cytochromes (4).
  b. FMN (1) contains a ribitol group.

23.69 **a.** CoQ is a mobile carrier.
  b. Fe–S clusters are found in complexes I, III, and IV.
  c. Cyt a_3 is part of complex IV.

23.71 **a.** $FADH_2$ is oxidized in complex II: $FADH_2 + Q \rightarrow FAD + QH_2$.
  b. Cyt a (Fe^{2+}) is oxidized in complex IV:
    Cyt a (Fe^{2+}) + cyt a_3 (Fe^{3+}) $\rightarrow$ cyt a (Fe^{3+}) + cyt a_3 (Fe^{2+})

23.73 **a.**

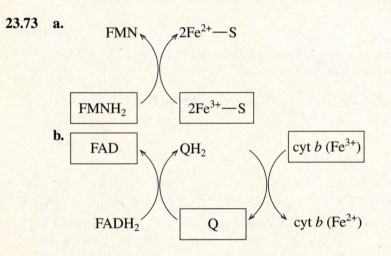

23.75 The transfer of electrons by complexes I, III, and IV generates energy to pump protons out of the matrix into the inter membrane space.

23.77 In the chemiosmotic model, energy released by the flow of protons through the ATP synthase is utilized for the synthesis of ATP.

23.79 In the inter membrane space, there is a higher concentration of protons, which reduces the pH and forms an electrochemical gradient. As a result, protons flow into the matrix, where the proton concentration is lower and the pH is higher.

23.81 Two ATP molecules are produced from the energy generated by the electrons from $FADH_2$ moving through electron transport to oxygen.

23.83 **a.** Amytal® and rotenone inhibit the transfer of electrons in NADH dehydrogenase (complex I).
  b. Antimycin A inhibits electron flow from cyt b to cyt c_1 in complex III.
  c. Cyanide and carbon monoxide inhibit the flow of electrons through cytochrome c oxidase (complex IV).

23.85 The oxidation of glucose to pyruvate by glycolysis produces 6 ATP. Two ATP are formed by direct phosphorylation along with 2 NADH. Because the 2 NADH are produced in the cytosol, the electrons are transferred to form 2 $FADH_2$, which produces an additional 4 ATP. The oxidation of glucose to CO_2 and H_2O produces 36 ATP.

23.87 The ATP synthase extends through the inner mitochondrial membrane with the F_0 part in contact with the proton gradient in the intermembrane space, whereas the F_1 complex is in the matrix.

23.89 As protons from the proton gradient move through the ATP synthase to return to the matrix, energy is released and used to drive ATP synthesis at F_1 ATP synthase.

23.91 A hibernating bear has stored fat as brown fat, which can be used during the winter for heat rather than ATP energy.

23.93 **a.** 6 ~~moles of ATP~~ $\times \dfrac{7.3 \text{ kcal}}{1 \text{ ~~mole of ATP~~}}$ = 44 kcal (2SF)

b. 6 ~~moles of ATP~~ $\times \dfrac{7.3 \text{ kcal}}{1 \text{ ~~mole of ATP~~}}$ = 44 kcal (2SF) (2 pyruvate ions to 2 acetyl CoA)

c. 24 ~~moles of ATP~~ $\times \dfrac{7.3 \text{ kcal}}{1 \text{ ~~mole of ATP~~}}$ = 180 kcal (2SF) (2 acetyl CoA in the citric acid cycle)

d. 36 ~~moles of ATP~~ $\times \dfrac{7.3 \text{ kcal}}{1 \text{ ~~mole of ATP~~}}$ = 260 kcal (2SF) (complete oxidation of glucose to CO_2 and H_2O)

23.95 In a calorimeter, the complete combustion of glucose gives 680 kcal. The efficiency of ATP synthesis is determined by comparing the total kcal in 36 ATP

$\left(36 \text{ ~~moles of ATP~~} \times \dfrac{7.3 \text{ kcal}}{1 \text{ ~~mole of ATP~~}} = 260 \text{ kcal} \right)$ to the energy obtained from glucose in a calorimeter.

$\dfrac{260 \text{ ~~kcal~~}}{680 \text{ ~~kcal~~}} \times 100\% = 38\%$ (2SF)

23.97 1.0 ~~μg of acetyl CoA~~ $\times \dfrac{1 \text{ ~~g of acetyl CoA~~}}{10^6 \text{ ~~μg of acetyl CoA~~}} \times \dfrac{1 \text{ ~~mole of acetyl CoA~~}}{809 \text{ ~~g of acetyl CoA~~}} \times \dfrac{12 \text{ moles of ATP}}{1 \text{ ~~mole of acetyl CoA~~}}$

$= 1.5 \times 10^{-8}$ mole of ATP (2SF)

24

Metabolic Pathways for Lipids and Amino Acids

24.1 The bile salts emulsify fat to give small fat globules for lipase hydrolysis.

24.3 Fats are mobilized when blood glucose and glycogen stores are depleted.

24.5 Glycerol is converted to glycerol-3-phosphate and then to dihydroxyacetone phosphate, which is an intermediate of glycolysis.

24.7 Fatty acids are activated in the cytosol at the outer mitochondrial membrane.

24.9 The coenzymes FAD, NAD^+, and HS–CoA are required for β oxidation.

24.11 The designation β carbon is based on the common names of carboxylic acids where the α carbon and the β carbons are adjacent to the carboxyl group.

a. $CH_3-CH_2-CH_2-CH_2-CH_2-\underset{\beta}{CH_2}-CH_2-\overset{O}{\overset{\|}{C}}-S-CoA$

b. $CH_3-(CH_2)_{14}-\underset{\beta}{CH_2}-CH_2-\overset{O}{\overset{\|}{C}}-S-CoA$

c. $CH_3-CH_2-CH=CH-CH_2-CH_2-CH_2-\underset{\beta}{CH_2}-CH_2-\overset{O}{\overset{\|}{C}}-S-CoA$

24.13 a. and b. $CH_3-(CH_2)_6-\underset{\beta}{CH_2}-\underset{\alpha}{CH_2}-\overset{O}{\overset{\|}{C}}-S-CoA$

c. $CH_3-(CH_2)_8-\overset{O}{\overset{\|}{C}}-S-CoA + NAD^+ + FAD + H_2O + SH-CoA \rightarrow$

$CH_3-(CH_2)_6-\overset{O}{\overset{\|}{C}}-S-CoA + CH_3-\overset{O}{\overset{\|}{C}}-S-CoA + NADH + H^+ + FADH_2$

d. $CH_3-(CH_2)_8-COOH + 4HS-CoA + 4FAD + 4NAD^+ + 4H_2O \rightarrow$
5 acetyl CoA + $4FADH_2$ + 4NADH + $4H^+$

24.15 The hydrolysis of ATP to AMP hydrolyzes ATP to ADP and ADP to AMP, which provides the same amount of energy as the hydrolysis of two ATP to two ADP.

24.17 a. The β oxidation of a chain of 10 carbon atoms produces 5 acetyl CoA molecules.
b. A C_{10} fatty acid will go through four β-oxidation cycles.
c. 60 ATP from 5 acetyl CoA (citric acid cycle) + 12 ATP from 4 NADH + 8 ATP from 4 $FADH_2$ − 2 ATP (activation) = 80 − 2 = 78 ATP

24.19 Ketogenesis is the synthesis of ketone bodies from excess acetyl CoA from fatty acid oxidation, which occurs when glucose is not available for energy. This occurs in starvation, fasting, low-carbohydrate diets, and diabetes.

24.21 Acetoacetate undergoes reduction using NADH + H^+ to yield β-hydroxybutyrate.

24.23 High levels of ketone bodies lead to ketosis, a condition characterized by acidosis (a drop in blood pH values) and by excessive urination and strong thirst.

24.25 Fatty acid synthesis takes place in the cytosol of cells in liver and adipose tissue.

24.27 Fatty acid synthesis starts when acetyl CoA, HCO_3^-, and ATP produce malonyl CoA.

24.29 **a.** (3) Malonyl CoA transacylase converts malonyl CoA to malonyl-ACP.
b. (1) Acetyl CoA carboxylase combines acetyl CoA with bicarbonate to yield malonyl CoA.
c. (2) Acetyl CoA transacylase converts acetyl CoA to acetyl-ACP.

24.31 **a.** A C_{10} fatty acid requires the formation of 4 malonyl-ACP, which uses 4 HCO_3^-.
b. Four ATP are required to produce 4 malonyl CoA.
c. Five acetyl CoA are needed to make 1 acetyl-ACP and 4 malonyl-ACP.
d. A C_{10} fatty acid requires 4 malonyl-ACP and 1 acetyl-ACP.
e. A C_{10} fatty acid chain requires 4 cycles with 2 NADPH/cycle or a total of 8 NADPH.
f. The four cycles remove a total of 4 CO_2.

24.33 The digestion of proteins begins in the stomach and is completed in the small intestine.

24.35 Hormones, heme, purines and pyrimidines for nucleotides, proteins, nonessential amino acids, amino alcohols, and neurotransmitters require nitrogen obtained from amino acids.

24.37 The reactants are an amino acid and an α-keto acid, and the products are a new amino acid and a new α-keto acid.

24.39 In transamination, an amino group replaces a keto group in the corresponding α-keto acid.

$$\text{a. } \underset{}{H-\overset{\overset{\displaystyle O}{\|}}{C}-COO^-} \qquad \text{b. } CH_3-\overset{\overset{\displaystyle O}{\|}}{C}-COO^- \qquad \text{c. } CH_3-\overset{\overset{\displaystyle CH_3}{|}}{CH}-\overset{\overset{\displaystyle O}{\|}}{C}-COO^-$$

24.41 In an oxidative deamination, the amino group in an amino acid such as glutamate is removed as an ammonium ion. The reaction requires NAD^+ or $NADP^+$.

$$^-OOC-\overset{\overset{\displaystyle \overset{+}{NH_3}}{|}}{CH}-CH_2-CH_2-COO^- + H_2O + NAD^+ \, (NADP^+) \xrightarrow{\text{\textit{Glutamate Dehydrogenase}}}$$

Glutamate

$$^-OOC-\overset{\overset{\displaystyle O}{\|}}{C}-CH_2-CH_2-COO^- + NH_4^+ + NADH \, (NADPH) + H^+$$

α-Ketoglutarate

24.43 NH_4^+ is toxic if allowed to accumulate in the liver.

24.45 $H_2N-\overset{\overset{\displaystyle O}{\|}}{C}-NH_2$

24.47 The carbon atom in urea is obtained from the CO_2 produced by the citric acid cycle.

24.49 Glucogenic amino acids can be used to produce intermediates for gluconeogenesis, which is glucose synthesis.

24.51 **a.** The three-carbon atom structure of alanine is converted to pyruvate.
b. The four-carbon structure of aspartate is converted to oxaloacetate.

c. Valine is converted to succinyl CoA.

d. The five-carbon structure from glutamine can be converted to α-ketoglutarate.

24.53 Humans can synthesize only nonessential amino acids.

24.55 Glutamine synthetase catalyzes the addition of an amino group to glutamate using energy from the hydrolysis of ATP.

24.57 **phenylketonuria**

24.59 Lauric acid, $CH_3-(CH_2)_{10}-COOH$, is a C_{12} fatty acid. ($C_{12}H_{24}O_2$)

    a. and b. $CH_3-(CH_2)_8-\underset{\beta}{CH_2}-\underset{\alpha}{CH_2}-\overset{\displaystyle O}{\overset{\|}{C}}-CoA$

    c. Lauryl CoA + 5HS–CoA + 5FAD + $5NAD^+$ + $5H_2O \rightarrow$

      6acetyl CoA + $5FADH_2$ + 5NADH + $5H^+$

    d. Six acetyl CoA units are produced.

    e. Five cycles of β oxidation are needed.

    f.

Activation		$\rightarrow$	-2 ATP
6 Acetyl CoA	$\times$ 12	$\rightarrow$	72 ATP
5 $FADH_2$	$\times$ 2	$\rightarrow$	10 ATP
5 NADH	$\times$ 3	$\rightarrow$	15 ATP
Total			95 ATP

24.61 Triacylglycerols are hydrolyzed to monoacylglycerols and fatty acids in the small intestine, which are reformed into triacylglycerols in the intestinal lining for transport as lipoproteins to the tissues.

24.63 Fats can be stored in unlimited amounts in adipose tissue compared with the limited storage of carbohydrates as glycogen.

24.65 The fatty acids cannot diffuse across the blood–brain barrier.

24.67 **a.** Glycerol is converted to glycerol-3-phosphate and to dihydroxyacetone phosphate, which can enter glycolysis or gluconeogenesis.

    b. Activation of fatty acids occurs on the outer mitochondrial membrane.

    c. The energy cost is equal to 2 ATP.

    d. Only fatty acyl CoA can move into the intermembrane space for transport by carnitine into the matrix.

24.69 **a.** β oxidation   **b.** β oxidation   **c.** fatty acid synthesis

    d. β oxidation   **e.** fatty acid synthesis   **f.** fatty acid synthesis

24.71 **a.** (1) fatty acid oxidation   **b.** (2) the synthesis of fatty acids

24.73 Ammonium ions are toxic if allowed to accumulate in the liver.

24.75 **a.** citrulline   **b.** carbamoyl phosphate

24.77 **a.** The carbon atom structure of serine is converted to pyruvate.

    b. Lysine, a ketogenic amino acid, is converted to acetoacetyl CoA.

    c. The degradation of methionine produces succinyl CoA.

    d. Glutamate can be converted to five-carbon α-ketoglutarate.

24.79 Serine is degraded to pyruvate, which is oxidized to acetyl CoA. The oxidation produces NADH + H^+, which provides 3 ATP. In one turn of the citric acid cycle, the acetyl CoA provides 12 ATP. Thus, serine can provide a total of 15 ATP.

24.81   **a.** 14 ~~kg of fat~~ $\times$ $\dfrac{1000 \text{ g of fat}}{1 \text{ kg of fat}}$ $\times$ $\dfrac{0.491 \text{ moles of ATP}}{1 \text{ g of fat}}$ = 6900 moles of ATP (2SF)

b. 6900 ~~moles of ATP~~ $\times$ $\dfrac{7.3 \text{ kcal}}{1 \text{ mole of ATP}}$ = 5.0×10^4 kcal (2SF)

24.83   **a.**
$$\underset{}{CH_3}{-}\overset{\displaystyle CH_3}{\underset{\displaystyle |}{CH}}{-}\overset{\displaystyle \overset{+}{NH_3}}{\underset{\displaystyle |}{CH}}{-}\overset{\displaystyle O}{\underset{\displaystyle \|}{C}}{-}O^-$$

b.
$$CH_3{-}CH_2{-}\overset{\displaystyle CH_3}{\underset{\displaystyle |}{CH}}{-}\overset{\displaystyle \overset{+}{NH_3}}{\underset{\displaystyle |}{CH}}{-}\overset{\displaystyle O}{\underset{\displaystyle \|}{C}}{-}O^- \quad \text{isoleucine}$$

c.
$$^-O{-}\overset{\displaystyle O}{\underset{\displaystyle \|}{C}}{-}CH_2{-}\overset{\displaystyle \overset{+}{NH_3}}{\underset{\displaystyle |}{CH}}{-}\overset{\displaystyle O}{\underset{\displaystyle \|}{C}}{-}O^- \quad \text{aspartic acid}$$

Answers to Combining Ideas from Chapters 21 to 24

CI.37   **a.** citric acid cycle   **b.** electron transport   **c.** both
        d. electron transport   **e.** citric acid cycle   **f.** electron transport
        g. citric acid cycle   **h.** both

CI.39   **a.** The components of coenzyme A are aminoethanethiol, pantothenic acid (vitamin B_5), diphosphate of adenosine $3'$-phosphate (phosphorylated ADP).
        b. Coenzyme A carries the acetyl group to the citric acid cycle for oxidation.
        c. The acetyl group links to the thiol group ($-S-$) atom in the aminoethanethiol part of CoA.
        d. $C_{23}H_{38}N_7O_{17}P_3S$: 23 C (23 $\times$ 12.0 g/mole) + 38 H (38 $\times$ 1.0 g/mole) + 7 N (7 $\times$ 14.0 g/mole) + 17 O (17 $\times$ 16.0 g/mole) + 3 P (3 $\times$ 31.0 g/mole) + S (32.1 g/mole) = 809 g/mole (3SF)

        e. $1.0 \ \mu\text{g of acetyl CoA} \times \dfrac{1 \ \text{g of acetyl CoA}}{10^6 \ \mu\text{g of acetyl CoA}} \times \dfrac{1 \ \text{mole of acetyl CoA}}{809 \ \text{g of acetyl CoA}} \times$

        $\dfrac{12 \ \text{moles of ATP}}{1 \ \text{mole of acetyl CoA}} = 1.5 \times 10^{-8} \ \text{mole of ATP (2SF)}$

CI.41   **a.**

        b. glyceryl tripalmitate, $C_{51}H_{98}O_6$
           51 C (51 $\times$ 12.0 g/mole) + 98 H (98 $\times$ 1.0 g/mole) + 6 O (6 $\times$ 16.0 g/mole) = 806 g/mole (3SF)
        c. One palmitic acid will yield 8 acetyl CoA, 7 NADH, and 7 $FADH_2$. This will give

           Activation of palmitic acid = -2 ATP
     8 Acetyl CoA $\times$ 12 ATP/acetyl CoA = 96 ATP
           7 NADH $\times$ 3 ATP/NADH = 21 ATP
           7 $FADH_2$ $\times$ 2 ATP/$FADH_2$ = 14 ATP
     Total   129 **ATP**

        d. $0.50 \ \text{oz of butter} \times \dfrac{80. \ \text{oz of tripalmitate}}{100 \ \text{oz of butter}} \times \dfrac{1 \ \text{lb}}{16 \ \text{oz}} \times \dfrac{454 \ \text{g}}{1 \ \text{lb}} \times \dfrac{1 \ \text{mole of tripalmitin}}{806 \ \text{g}} \times$

        $\dfrac{3 \ \text{moles of palmitic acid}}{1 \ \text{mole of tripalmitin}} \times \dfrac{129 \ \text{moles of ATP}}{1 \ \text{mole of palmitic acid}} \times \dfrac{7.3 \ \text{kcal}}{1 \ \text{mole of ATP}} = 40. \ \text{kcal (2SF)}$

        e. $45 \ \text{min} \times \dfrac{750 \ \text{kcal}}{60 \ \text{min}} \times \dfrac{1 \ \text{pat of butter}}{40. \ \text{kcal}} = 14 \ \text{pats of butter (2SF)}$

CI.43   **a.** maltose   **b.** stearic acid   **c.** glucose
        d. caprylic acid   **e.** citrate